Quantitative Methods
in Social Science

Stephen Gorard

 continuum
NEW YORK • LONDON

Continuum

The Tower Building
11 York Road
London SE1 7NX

15 East 26th Street
New York
NY 10010

www.continuumbooks.com

British Library Cataloguing-in-Publication Data
A catalogue record for this book is available from the British Library.

ISBN 0-8264-65870 (hardback)
     0-8264-65862 (paperback)

Typeset by BookEns Ltd., Royston, Herts
Printed and bound in Great Britain by Biddles Ltd, King's Lynn, Norfolk

Quantitative Methods in Social Science

Contents

List of figures

List of tables

Preface

The idea for this book arose from my teaching on research methods courses at the Cardiff University School of Social Sciences and my work as examiner for similar courses in other institutions. Part of my teaching role involves holding 'surgeries' for students and staff on research design and analysis. In these, novice researchers come to me for advice and solutions to problems, particularly relating to quantitative approaches. Year on year, and despite the best efforts of lecturers including myself, the same problems arise again and again. Such problems include collecting data with no clear idea how to analyse it, creation of shoddy questionnaires, attempts to measure the unmeasurable, the over-use of statistical tests, inappropriate use of statistical tests, confusion between levels of measurement, confusion between design error and random variation, missing comparators and several more. I hope that this book deals with all of these problems, and many more, and will therefore reduce their occurrence (please!).

Social science research as a field of endeavour faces several problems. One is to give satisfactory evidence of its quality and its relevance. Another is to provide a specific form of answers such as evidence bases and 'what works?'. There appears to be a growing schism between a minority of social scientists who use measurement (who are prepared to try 'quantitative' techniques and work with numbers) and those who do not and perhaps cannot. There is therefore a danger that quantitative researchers will become a band apart, refereeing each other's work, beholden to no one and divorced from the majority of work in their field. This book attempts to deal with all of these issues, by arguing that all researchers need a working knowledge of the techniques explained herein, if only to enable them to make informed criticism of the work of others. The book does not set out to argue that quantitative techniques are better than the more usual interview, ethnography or case study approaches. In fact, I hope to make quite clear that all approaches should be seen as complementary and that a researcher who does only numbers is as dangerous as a researcher who can't do numbers.

My own work is relevant to the areas of education, sociology, psychology and criminology, and it is these areas that naturally provide many of the examples used in this book. However, the ideas and principles herein are just as relevant to other areas of social science including social policy, geography, business studies and economics. In addition to descriptions of standard techniques for research design and analysis and discussion of wider issues relating to social science research, this book also contains real examples of research which I believe contain simple mistakes in the design, analysis or reporting of results. Where this research has been published in peer-reviewed journals I have identified the authors. However, it should be noted that the examples are not selected because they are extreme but often simply because they relate to the fields in which I do the most reading. From the reports of others and my own wider reading I have no reason to believe that the areas in which I work are any 'worse' in terms of analytical errors than any other areas of social or even natural sciences. In fact, I have collected equivalent examples from medicine, dentistry, housing, astronomy and many others. Where I have used examples of problems from the work of students I make no individual identification. All of us make mistakes. They are a valuable component of learning. In fact, my rather tired aphorism on this is that someone who claims not to make any mistakes is probably not doing enough work. I hope that the reader will learn from the mistakes, mine and others, illustrated in this book.

I am engaged professionally in capability-building within the research community (see, for example, www.cf.ac.uk/socsi/capacity). I see this new book as an important part of that process. There is a mystique about statistics that can often create a climate of fear for some and sometimes a climate of complacency and even arrogance for others. I hope to show that, for the most part, quantitative methods in social science research are easy – common sense with arithmetic perhaps. Did you know that 'statistics' as you probably envisage it now (probabilities and significance testing and so on) is actually redundant in most quantitative research designs? Its sole purpose is to separate out the random error in your results due to the nature of your sample. If you do not use a sample (which is what I recommend in this book) or do not use a probability sample (like most social scientists) or if your design error dwarfs the variation due to your sample (as it does in most social science research designs), then statistics of that kind cannot help you. People might still use null hypothesis significance tests out of habit or ignorance, for a rhetorical flourish or to exclude you from criticizing their work. But you should be able to see through these ruses. Therefore, this is not a traditional textbook, nor a book on statistics, nor a technical cookbook. It is, in essence, a plea to use your common sense with simple arithmetic. Numbers are easy.

THE STRUCTURE OF THIS BOOK

This book can be envisaged in several ways. It can be referenced as five main sections. Chapters Two and Three describe sources and uses of existing numeric data, Chapter Four deals with general issues of sampling, Chapters Five and Six deal with questionnaire design and analysis, and Chapters Seven, Eight and Nine consider the rationale for and conduct and analysis of experiments. Chapters Ten and Eleven provide a brief introduction to more complex issues, such as multivariate analysis and combining data from different sources.

On the other hand, the book can also be divided into one section on the design of research (Chapters Four, Seven and Eleven), another on the collection of data (Chapters Two, Five and Eight) and a third on the analysis of results (Chapters Three, Six, Nine and Ten). The first part of the book tends to deal with what are traditionally termed 'non-parametric' approaches (using data in categories) and passive approaches (such as surveys), while the second part deals with parametric approaches (using real numbers) and active approaches (such as intervention studies). However, the connecting passages in each chapter have been written for someone wishing to read the book in its entirety from beginning to end.

Chapter One suggests a variety of reasons why all of us should have some awareness of the role of numbers in social science research, including the need to read and criticize the work of others.

Chapters Two and Three concern the growing use of data already collected for another purpose, such as official statistics. This is discussed from the point of view of: a researcher wanting to provide some context for a small-scale study; a researcher wanting to judge the quality of an achieved sample; and a researcher intending to use only secondary data. A variety of techniques for the analysis and presentation of numeric data are presented.

Chapter Four illustrates, through real life examples, the importance of having a large sample, offers simple techniques for estimating the sample size needed and describes common methods of selecting cases for the sample.

Chapters Five and Six present guidelines for designing and conducting a survey, with illustrations of both good and poor techniques. The illustrations continue with elementary analyses of categorical data, introducing the chi-square test of significance.

Chapter Seven looks in more detail at the process of modelling social processes using numbers and the difficulties of searching for causal models.

Chapters Eight and Nine present guidelines for conducting laboratory experiments and field trials. The illustrations continue with elementary analyses using real numbers, by introducing t-tests and analysis of variance.

Chapter Ten introduces measures of correlation and the associated techniques of linear and logistic regression, and hierarchical and multi-level modelling. Again, these techniques are illustrated with real examples.

Chapter Eleven moves beyond 'quantitative' methods in isolation, and outlines ways in which datasets involving numbers and 'qualitative' evidence can be combined.

Abbreviations

BERA British Educational Research Association – the main professional organization of educational researchers in the UK

BERJ *British Educational Research Journal* – the research journal of BERA

BPS British Psychological Society – the main professional organization of psychologists in the UK

BSA British Sociological Association – the main professional organization of sociologists in the UK

CERI Centre for Educational Research and Innovation – a dedicated research centre of OECD

DfEE Department for Education and Employment (now DfES, Department for Education and Skills) – the main UK government department for education, with chief responsibility for schools and colleges in England (rather than Scotland, Northern Ireland or Wales)

ESRC Economic and Social Research Council – major public funding body for social science research in the UK

ETAG Education and Training Action Group – a temporary body formed in Wales after devolution to create an education and training policy for the new National Assembly

FSM Free school meals (eligibility for) – an indicator of a child from a family in poverty, counted on the annual census return by schools in the UK

GCSE General Certificate of Secondary Education – the main academic qualification taken in England and Wales at age 16, which is the end of compulsory schooling

ICT Information and Communications Technology

KS   Key Stage – one of four periods of statutory assessment in schools in the UK, from KS1 at age 7 in primary school to KS4 at age 16 in secondary school

LEA   Local Education Authority (or Unitary Authority) – local government-appointed body responsible for running most schools and colleges in its area

LFS   Labour Force Survey – quarterly survey of the employment and training of a rolling sample of 150,000 people in the UK

MIMAS   Manchester Information and Associated Services – reservoir with associated website of useful datasets (especially spatial)

NACETT   National Council for Education and Training Targets – a body created to set up and monitor targets for participation and achievement in lifelong learning in the UK. Replaced in 2001 by the Learning Skills Council

NAfW   National Assembly for Wales – 'Parliament' of elected representatives responsible for devolved budget in Wales

NERPP   National Educational Research Policy and Priorities Board, of the USA

NHS   National Health Service – the health service in the UK that is free to all at point of delivery

NHST   Null Hypothesis Significance Testing – calculating the probability that two or more sets of scores are actually from the same population

NOMIS   National On-line Manpower Information System – reservoir with associated website of useful datasets (especially labour markets)

NRC   National Research Council, of the USA

NS   Office for National Statistics UK – reservoir and publisher of a large number of useful datasets

OECD   Organisation for Economic and Commercial Development; Organisation for Economic Cooperation and Development

OFSTED   Office for Standards in Education – the name of the school inspection system in England

ONS   *see* NS

RCT   Randomized controlled trial

SEN   Special Educational Needs (or Additional Educational Needs)

SPSS   Statistical Package for Social Sciences — a set of related
            computer programs for storing, analysing and reporting
            on statistical results
TTA   Teacher Training Agency — government-appointed
            body in UK responsible for teacher training recruitment,
            curriculum and qualification

Introduction: the role of numbers in research

WHY WE ALL NEED NUMBERS

A local paper recently ran a front-page story claiming that Cardiff was the worst area in Wales for unpaid television licences – it had 'topped the league of shame for the second year running'. The evidence for this proposition was that there were more people in Cardiff (4,400) caught using TV without a licence than in any other 'area' of Wales (and it is important for readers to know that Cardiff is the largest city in Wales). Not surprisingly, the next worst area in the league of shame was Swansea (the second city of Wales), followed by Newport, then Wrexham, and so on. Everyone to whom I have told this story laughs at the absurdity of the claim and points out that the claim would have to be proportionate to the population of each area. Cardiff may then still be the worst, but at present we would have to assume that, as the most populous unitary authority in Wales, Cardiff would tend to have the most of *any* raw-score indicator (including, presumably, the number of people using TV *with* a licence). Why does this matter? It matters because very similar propositions are made routinely in social science research, and rather than being sifted out in peer review, they are publicized and often feted (see Chapter Three for some examples). This is indicative of the rather poor state of research involving very basic numbers – not that work like this gets done but rather that no one seems to care about the inconsistencies between the evidence and the conclusions drawn from it.

I have encountered books on all forms of social science research, some on statistical analysis and some on specialist topics such as survey design or sampling. There is not, to my knowledge, another practical book of advice for students on carrying out a research project using quantitative techniques that links the three main methods of data derivation (secondary, survey and interventions) with their common methods of analysis. This is an important point, since the somewhat artificial separation of design and analysis leads to many of the common problems actually faced by students and those who deal with them (such as 'I have collected all this data, now please tell me what to do with it'). These issues are becoming more important as the climate in publicly funded research changes in favour of evidence-based policy and practice, with a growing interest in large-scale experimental trials and in the more general use of official data already collected for another purpose. This use of secondary data allows all students, perhaps for the first time, to carry out significant projects within a realistic timescale.

Above all, there is no book that steers a middle path of suggesting that *all* researchers should use numbers routinely in their research (even if only as 'consumers' of the quantitative research of others), while also cautioning against the potential artificiality of quantitative approaches and other associated perils. As well as laying out specific designs for both large- and small-scale social science research involving numbers, the book therefore also seeks to combat two idealized 'villains' – the student who does not 'do numbers' and is therefore forced to ignore all numeric results, and the student who is prepared only to 'do numbers' and tends to accept all numeric results at face value. Both extremes are common, in my experience, and dangerous. The emphasis throughout this book is therefore on selecting and using appropriate techniques, while considering the limitations inherent in any one approach. My underlying assumption is that there is no best method for social science research. There is simply differential fitness for purpose dependent upon the research question(s).

Some people have suggested that there should be more statistical ('quantitative') studies in social science research because this form of evidence is intrinsically preferable and of higher quality than other forms. I feel that this is completely the wrong way of looking at it. On the contrary, one reason to encourage a greater awareness of statistical techniques among all researchers is that quantitative work is currently often very poor, but largely unchecked. There are many other reasons why all researchers should learn something about techniques for research involving numbers. These reasons are outlined here and then presented in more detail throughout the book.

• So we won't get fooled again
The first and most obvious point is that the process of research involves some consideration of previous work in the same field. All researchers read and use the research of others. Therefore they need to develop what Brown and Dowling (1998) refer to as a 'mode of interrogation' for reading and using research results. If they do not have any understanding of research techniques involving numbers then they must either accept all such results without question, a very dangerous decision, or ignore all such results, a very foolish decision. In practice, many commentators attempt to create a middle way of accepting some results and rejecting others, even though they do not understand how the results were derived. This usually means that results are accepted on the basis of ideology or of whether they agree with what the commentator wants to believe. This is both dangerous *and* foolish. Whatever the people who do this like to call themselves, this is not a social scientific approach to research.

• Context is everything
Whatever your choice of primary method, there is a good chance that your research should involve numbers, at least at the outset. You may wish, for example, to document the experiences of the growing number of homeless people from ethnic minority backgrounds. Whatever approach you intend to use (participant observation, focus groups, anthropology, and so on) you should start from a quantitative basis. In order to direct your search you would use as much information as is available to you from the outset. You need to establish not only how many homeless people there are, but also where they are, how the socio-economic and ethnic patterns of these groups change over time and space, and so on. Such figures, termed 'secondary data', already exist, and therefore a preliminary analysis of them is the best place to start any study. Only then can you sensibly select a smaller group (a sample) for more detailed study. Existing figures, whatever their limitations, provide a context for any new study that is as important as the 'literature review' and the 'theoretical background'.

• Some techniques are common to all research
The use of a sample, for example, is a common phenomenon in all kinds of research using many different approaches to data collection and analysis. This book describes the process of sampling as it applies to all research involving samples, and is not specific to what have traditionally been considered as quantitative designs.

• We need an ideal
It is made clear in this book that experimental approaches have severe limitations in social science research. Nevertheless the ideal experiment, by isolating cause and effect, can provide us with a universal template for the perfect piece of research that leads to safe knowledge. We can then judge our more limited studies against that ideal, and so understand and explain the ways in which our own findings are less than secure (for sadly such is the fate of all real world research). True experiments may be rare in much social science research, but for the above reasons all researchers should still be able to design one (at least as a thought experiment). Even where an experiment is not used, we can adapt the formal logic of this scientific approach to deal with essentially passive approaches like observation (Boudon 1974). Once a discipline or field, like social science, is mature enough then some of its arguments can be converted into formal structures involving numbers. This helps to reduce ambiguity, clarify reasoning and reveal errors (see Chapter Seven).

• Because it is easy
Above all, it is important to realize that what is termed 'quantitative' research is generally very easy. Much analysis in social science involves nothing more complex than addition or multiplication – primary-school arithmetic in fact. Even this, along with any more complex calculations, is conducted for you by a computer. You have no need for paper and pencil. There is no need to practise any sums or memorize anything. Not only does this book *not* generally explain how to derive the formulae we use, generally it does not even state what those formulae are. These formulae are finished and complete. Therefore, no mathematics is involved in basic quantitative work. You can use statistics perfectly safely, just as you would drive a car without knowing or even caring how it works. There are always other books, software and expert advisers available to help if you 'break down'. The purpose of this book is to help explain when and how to use numeric techniques and how to report their results. The difficult bit lies in explaining your results and transforming them into practical reports for the users of research. This stage is, of course, common to all forms of research.

THE PENDULUM SWINGS

In 1988 *The Guardian* newspaper published an article called 'Who needs sociologists?', which described the near demise of the discipline, and called for higher quality, less politically biased, and more relevant research. This led Marshall (1990) to comment that 'sociology ... is widely ridiculed by the ignorant ... and is regularly caricatured as left-wing rhetoric masquerading as scholarship'. To some extent, the latter position reflected the findings of the Rothschild (1982) report into the future of funding for UK social science research, which expressed 'disappointment' at progress in the field, and it also reflected the 'crisis of confidence' in all social sciences caused by the concurrent attacks of Sir Keith Joseph (then minister for Education and Science). These were linked to significant cuts in public funding for social science and even the threat of no funding at all, and were matched in other developed countries (Flather 1987). It was at this point that the Social Science Funding Council became the Economic and Social Research Council – removing the word 'science' from the title, perhaps as a sign of the political disdain for the soft methodologies of sociology in particular. Sociology is still not held in high general esteem, but perhaps the feeling is that little needs to be done about it because, unlike other fields, it seems to have little practical value. 'It is one thing having junk departments turning out junk sociologists, but quite another to be turning out junk engineers. If you think this is a point of no importance, imagine the next time you enter a lift...' (Brignell 2000, p. 12).

Over the last decade, the value and effectiveness of many other areas of social science research have been increasingly called into question (e.g. Lewis 2001, Hargreaves 1997, Tooley and Darby 1998). Educational research, for example, has been accused of being both 'second rate' and irrelevant to the needs and interests of practitioners. The Chief Executive of the Teacher Training Agency argued that 'despite the expenditure of over £65 million of public funding on educational research each year, there are surprisingly few studies which, individually or collectively, contribute systematically to the development of a comprehensive body of high quality evidence about pedagogy' (Millett 1997, p. 2). Research has been accused of being both 'second rate' and irrelevant to the needs and interests of practitioners. Her Majesty's Chief Inspector for Schools claimed to have given up reading research as 'life is too short. There is too much to do in the real world with real teachers in real schools to worry about methodological quarrels or to waste time decoding unintelligible, jargon-ridden prose to reach (if one is lucky) a conclusion that is often so transparently partisan as to be worthless' (Woodhead 1998, p. 51). This crisis of confidence is not confined to the UK, having been pre-dated in the USA for example (Berliner and Biddle 1995, NRC 1999, NERPP 2000, Resnick 2000), nor to public policy research alone (Pirrie 2001, see also the fierce debates in anthropology, Tierney 2000). Indeed, it is currently characteristic of the relationship between the majority of professions and research, and there have been similar comments about the conduct of research in many public services (Dean 2000). Put simply, it seems that 'too many ... researchers produce second-rate work, and there are, for the most part, too few checks against this occurring' (Evans 2002, p. 44).

Of course, despite their public appeal, the evidence base for these criticisms is often weak, and this is part of what Marshall (1990) was writing about. However, these criticisms are general and strident enough for us to have to examine the quality of social science research. Part of the problem is an apparent system-wide shortage in expertise in large-scale studies, especially field trials derived from laboratory experimental designs. Over the last twenty years, there has undoubtedly been a move towards much greater use of 'qualitative' approaches (Hayes 1992), even in traditionally numerate areas of research (Ellmore and Woehilke 1998). In addition, acceptance rates for 'qualitative' publications are higher than for 'quantitative' pieces, by a ratio of around two to one in one US journal (Taylor 2001). There is a danger therefore of applying different standards of rigour to studies depending on their method and, presumably, on their referees. In some fields, the 1990s were dominated by generally small-scale funding leading to predominantly qualitative thinking (McIntyre and McIntyre 2000), entailing a considerable potential for bias (Dyson and Desforges 2002).

However, quantitative work has not stood still, and in the same period techniques for multivariate analysis, especially of data based on categories, have become considerably more sophisticated. While welcome, these twin developments may have increased the tendency towards a methodological schism, because individual researchers tend to specialize in one approach or the other. It is not unusual for one researcher never to have conducted any form of textual analysis and for another to admit to not having the least idea what 'multi-level modelling' is about, for example. Funders, such as the Economic and Social Research Council, of which Marshall is (at the time of writing) Chief Executive, want to see the pendulum swing back towards a more balanced portfolio of skills (e.g. Sooben 2002), and the ESRC currently has no fewer than fourteen initiatives in place to increase the use of quantitative approaches among social scientists. Similar sentiments have been expressed in other developed countries (e.g. Diamond 2002). Part of the purpose of this book is to assist that swing.

INTRODUCING TWO VILLAINS

I have written this book as a general introduction to research design and statistical analysis for all students of social sciences. However, in doing so I have been particularly concerned to hinder the creation of two 'villainous' identities, both of which I meet regularly among students and even among more established researchers. They represent, if you like, two extreme viewpoints about numeric data – 'numbers are fab' and 'numbers are rubbish'.

Numbers are fab
This villain is perhaps most common in relatively established disciplines such as psychology, where there has been a tradition that only numeric data is of relevance. Students are therefore, perhaps unwittingly, encouraged to count or measure everything, even where this is not necessarily appropriate (as with some attitude scales, for example). One outcome is that statistical analysis is done badly and so gets a bad press. Allied to this approach is a cultural phenomenon I have observed, particularly with some international students and their sponsors, which again approves only research involving numbers. A corollary for both groups appears to be that forms of evidence not based on numbers are despised, while evidence based on numbers is accepted somewhat uncritically.

This last is clearly a problem, as I quite regularly come across findings that when reanalysed show the opposite to what is being claimed (e.g. Gorard 1997a, 2000a). In fact, I suspect that social science journals, books and edited chapters are full of quite basic arithmetic errors (and some of these are used for illustration throughout this book). Part of the problem here may be the 'cronyism' among reviewers that in-depth knowledge of advanced statistical procedures tends to generate, which leads to poorly explained and over-technical reports (where incomprehensible software-generated variable names are used routinely in descriptions of the analysis, for example).

As you will see throughout this book, I am a great fan of using computer software packages for statistical analysis, but the increasing quality and availability of these has exacerbated the problems outlined above in two ways. Software allows more and more complex statistical models to be built and used, so that in the end most consumers of research simply cannot, or would not wish to, comprehend them. Even those who work on such high-level models have trouble transforming their findings into a format that does their analysis justice but also makes any sense to practitioners and policy-makers (see Goldstein et al. 2000 on the difficulties of this). This means that the 'average' consumer of research has either to implicitly accept the findings or to reject them as incomprehensible. Linked to the greater use of computers is the shotgun or dredging approach to analysis in which multiple exploratory analyses are run with the same set of data (see Chapter Nine). As well as liberating us from the drudgery of multiple calculations the computer has therefore increased the frequency of the 'blind or mindless application of methods without regard to their suitability for the solution of the problem at hand, or even in the complete absence of a clearly formulated problem' (Pedhazur 1982, p. 3).

Normal statistical textbooks describe ideal procedures to follow, but several studies of actual behaviour have observed different common practices among researchers. 'Producing a statistic is a social enterprise' (Gephart 1988 p. 15), and the stages of selecting variables, making observations and coding the results take place in everyday settings where practical influences arise. The divergence between the ideal and the actual is probably growing because of the increased accessibility to statistical software packages and a tendency to see these as 'expert systems' rather than convenient calculators. Statistical packages are making decisions for us that we may not even be aware of (through default settings). The possible dangers of this are increased because statistics have an under-stated rhetoric of their own, able to persuade specific audiences of their objectivity (Firestone 1987). The average researcher may be easily fooled by large numbers, confused by probabilities, prone to the fallacy *of post hoc ergo propter hoc*, and, without expertise of their own, led (and perhaps misled) by authorities (Brighton 2000). Perhaps this helps to explain why so few academic disputes over figures and subsequent corrections by authors appear in the literature.

Numbers are rubbish
The other villain is perhaps more common in the sociological tradition. Having realized that numbers can be used erroneously, sometimes even unscrupulously, some researchers simply reject all numeric evidence and its use (displaying what Mortimore and

Sammons [1997] call 'crude anti-quantitative attitudes', p. 185). This is as ludicrous a position as its opposite. As Clegg (1992) points out, we know that people sometimes lie to us but we do not therefore reject all future conversation. Why should lying with numbers be any different? I suspect, through my contact with students, that the key issue with numbers is a kind of fear or lack of confidence. But lack of confidence *can* be seen as a reasonably helpful characteristic for a researcher. It is surely better than the unjustifiable over-certainty represented by the 'numbers are fab' villain.

If we reject numeric evidence and its associated concerns about validity, generalizability and so on as the basis for research, then we are left with primarily subjective judgements. The danger therefore for 'qualitative' research conducted in isolation from numeric approaches is that it could be used simply as a rhetorical basis for retaining an existing prejudice. Without a combination of approaches we are often left with no clear way of deciding between competing conclusions. My argument is therefore not just that numeric evidence forms the basis of good qualitative studies and can be used to test its findings (the middle way, see Gorard 1998a). I am not even convinced that the very distinction between the two forms of evidence is a useful one (see the next section).

COMMON PROBLEMS IN RESEARCH

In each section of the book I illustrate some of the points being made through a consideration of problems I have encountered in my own research, the research of others and my work with novice researchers. To start with, here are three classic situations that you may find yourself in once you start to research.

- Being imprisoned by a 'paradigm'
- Deciding on a method before a topic
- Now ... how do I analyse all this?

Being imprisoned by a 'paradigm'
The term 'paradigm' is often applied to approaches to social science research. To my mind, this is never justified. Whatever its original value as a description of the 'chauvinism' that tends to appear in 'normal science' and the resistance to change in light of new ideas

(Kuhn 1970), the term has now done more harm than good to several generations of novice researchers. Instead of using 'paradigm' to refer to a topic or field of research (such as traditional physics) that might undergo a radical shift (to quantum physics, for example), people now use it to refer to a whole approach to research including philosophy, values and method. Moreover, and ironically of course, people tend to use the term to defend themselves against the need to change. Students, quite wrongly, can quickly become imprisoned in a 'paradigm' or feel they have to engage in pointless paradigm wars. They learn (because they are taught) that if they use any numbers in their research then they must be positivist or realist in philosophy, and they must be hypothetico-deductive or traditional in style. No one ever explains why these things are associated (apart from contingently). Texts making these bold claims apparently have no idea what terms like 'positivist' actually mean – Comte, the archetypal positivist, was against the use of statistical information in his 'social physics', for example (see also Steele 2002). If, on the other hand, students disavow the use of numbers in research then they must be interpretivist, holistic and alternative, believing in multiple perspectives rather than truth, and so on (e.g. Clarke 1999). This is such a common misunderstanding of the difference between the nature of numeric and non-numeric evidence and of the nature of truth, that it would require another whole book to discuss (but see Chapter Eleven). The important thing for the present is to consider that numbers can be used quite properly by *all* researchers whatever other methods they use. 'Qualitative and quantitative evidence' refers to a false dualism (Frazer 1995) and one that as researchers we would be better off without. One practical reason would be that we could cease wasting time and energy in pointless debates about the virtues of one approach over the other. Let's not be imprisoned by other peoples' ideas, at least until we have learnt a lot more about research in general.

The supposed distinction between qualitative and quantitative evidence is essentially a distinction between the traditional methods for their analysis rather than between underlying philosophies, paradigms or methods of data collection. As Heraclitus has written, 'logic is universal even if most people behave differently' (for if logic were not universal we could not debate with each other, so making research pointless). To some extent all methods of social science research deal with qualities, even when the observed qualities are counted. Similarly, all methods of analysis use some form of number, such as 'tend, most, some, all, none, few', and so on. This is what the patterns in qualitative analysis are based on (even where the claim is made that a case is 'unique' since *uni*queness is, of course, a numeric description). Words can be counted and numbers can be descriptive. Patterns are, by definition, numbers, and the things that are numbered are qualities (Popkewitz 1984). In fact, I sometimes wonder how many writers use qualitative analysis precisely to avoid the criticism that would be aimed at a more formal and transparent analysis. Examples of numeric analyses disguised as qualitative research appear later in this book.

Deciding on a method before a topic
Students have been heard to exclaim before deciding on a topic and research questions that they intend to use 'qualitative' methods of data collection or analysis, or that they are committed to the idea of a questionnaire. Perhaps 'it comes as no particular surprise to discover that a scientist formulates problems in a way which requires for their solution just those techniques in which he himself is especially skilled' (Pedhazur 1982, p. 28), but to understand this temptation is not to condone it. You must decide on your research topic and the questions you are curious about first, and only then consider how best to answer them. Don't fit your proposed study to your favourite approach (a case of the cart pulling the horse), and then try to disguise this as a philosophical, rather than a methodological decision (see above). This is another reason why all researchers need some knowledge of all methods.

Now ... how do I analyse all this?
Anyone who has dealt with student/novice researchers will have encountered this problem. In my institution this is not as frequent as it was, but I still see a reasonable number of people per year (perhaps sent by their supervisors for advice) who say, 'I have conducted a survey. Now can you tell me what to do with the answers?'. This is usually clear evidence of poor design. The reason that this book has alternate chapters on design and analysis is to try and help you see the two phases of research as concurrent. You cannot possibly design a sensible research instrument without considering in some detail how you will analyse the data you set out to collect. Otherwise you will not know if you have asked the right questions or collected data in the right format. The apparently separate phases of reading, formulating research questions, design, collection of data, analysis and reporting are really concurrent and iterative.

As outlined above, this book combines a consideration of the design and analysis of social science research involving numeric data. There is very little epistemology here. For those interested, my principles of research, such as they are, are very similar to the five norms described by Hammersley (1995, p. 76). I particularly like the first, which is that 'the overriding concern of researchers is the truth of claims, not their political implications or practical consequences'. For more on the philosophy of social science see Chapter Seven. For more on the ethical issues involved in research see Chapter Eight. For more about research 'paradigms' see Chapter Eleven. For a simple, sometimes amusing discussion of issues to put you in the 'right' frame of mind to grapple with research, see Fairbairn and Winch (1996), Huff (1991) and Thouless (1974). For a more serious approach to the abuse of statistics read Reichmann (1961). If you feel the need for some reminders about simple calculations see Solomon and Winch (1994). For a good introduction to social science research read Gilbert (1997), to formal statistics Clegg (1992) or Fielding and Gilbert (2000), and for help on writing a dissertation see Preece (1994) and many many others.

Finding secondary data: the 'idle' researcher

SUMMARY: USING SECONDARY DATA

As mentioned in Chapter One, one of the main reasons why all researchers are likely to need numbers, irrespective of their primary method, is that many of the large datasets available as context information for any study are numeric. The use of secondary data to help create or identify an appropriate sample (perhaps via stratification), to describe the pattern or problem to be explored by other methods, or even as a method in its own right, is growing. This is a trend encouraged by the funding councils, which allows cumulation and helps prevent the waste of resources involved in attempting research to explain non-existent patterns or problems. Existing statistics, whatever their limitations, provide a context for any new study, which is as important as the 'literature review' and the 'theoretical background'.

Consider this. I am not involved in running our university library, have never been to Newcastle and do not work for the Department of Education and Science. Nevertheless, without leaving the desk in my office, I could assemble within thirty minutes:

- a breakdown of the number and type of books borrowed at Cardiff University by the country of origin of all students (and therefore decide, for example, whether students from the western Pacific Rim read more books on statistics per year than those from the USA);
- an analysis of car ownership among the population of Newcastle broken down by the floor level of their permanent residence (and decide, for example, whether those living above first-floor level are less likely to own cars);
- a consideration of the rates of unauthorized absence from school

in each region of England in relation to the local population density (and decide, for example, whether 'truancy' in secondary schools is higher in towns and cities than in rural areas).

I could do this because the relevant figures already exist. As long as I can get access to them I can then run my own analysis. Now, of course, these findings may be of little interest to you and I have certainly never done any research on these topics. They are simply examples of using what is termed in this chapter 'secondary data', which is data used by a researcher who did not also collect it. Most researchers, especially new researchers carrying out small-scale studies on a limited budget, tend to go out and collect their own new (primary) data. It takes a little experience to appreciate the value of secondary (second-hand) information, and to know what to do with it when you get it. This chapter and the next help provide that experience. My prediction is that once you have experienced the power and economy of secondary analysis you will not want to design any further studies without incorporating at least an element of it. It can transform a post-graduate dissertation from something that gathers dust on a library shelf to a project worthy of further dissemination through publication and worthy of further attention by other researchers in your field. Yet it can take less time to complete and cost less to produce than a small questionnaire survey or a handful of interviews.

WHY USE SECONDARY DATA?

The call to make better use of existing records in social science dates back at least to the writing of Bulmer (1980) or perhaps to the 'statists' of the seventeenth century concerned to improve life chances for the very poor. In a loose sense of the term, all academics already use secondary findings in constructing their review of literature (Hakim 1982). The background to a new study, the relevance of the research questions and the importance of the findings are usually presented in relation to previous and existing work on related topics (often under the unappealing title of a 'literature review'). More recently, the drive towards creating research results with more impact has led to a demand for evidence bases (see Chapter One). The evidence in question has generally been seen as a precise and measured type of review of existing work, using a model derived from similar 'what works?' approaches in medical research. These are known as research 'syntheses' (see

Cooper 1998). A step beyond a synthesis is a meta-analysis in which the actual results of many studies on the same topic are arithmetically combined to provide an overall answer (Glass et al. 1981, see also Chapter Eleven).

The fundamental difference between all of these and a full secondary analysis as the basis for a project lies in the notion of originality. Most academic institutions lay stress on 'originality' for their students' dissertation work, and many students therefore assume that their data must be original as well. But in the same way as it is possible for a researcher to review previous work in any field and still go on to carry out original work, it is possible for a researcher to carry out a secondary data analysis and still go on to carry out original work, without necessarily collecting any further data. There are many reasons why you might decide to use secondary data in a project, and these are described briefly under five headings below (and illustrated in the remainder of the chapter).

Speed and cost
These are probably the most obvious advantages of using secondary data. Since the data already exists it is usually, by definition, quicker to 'collect', involving less travel and minimal cost. This means that the researcher can make a lot more progress in any given time period (such as the one year of a full-time Masters course). Some existing datasets do involve a financial charge for access, and some of these charges sound quite large when they are presented as a total. However, it is likely that even these datasets will end up cheaper to use than incurring the costs of travel, telephone, printing, postage and subsistence involved in carrying out primary data collection. In addition, there are very many valuable datasets available free of charge or with nominal administrative costs (see below).

Sometimes the distinction between primary and secondary appears a little blurred. In assembling the data for my early work on the socio-economic composition of schools (Gorard and Fitz 1998), I needed the annual census returns from schools for six Local Education Authorities (LEAs) for as many previous years as available. These records were held centrally (by the Welsh Office in this case) for the past two years only. To get any earlier records I had to negotiate access to the six LEAs and in most cases travel to their offices and spend half a day in a dusty cupboard full of the school census archives (for which opportunity I am still very ateful). Since this stage was the unfunded pilot for what became a much larger study, I used LEAs close to home wherever possible and arranged my visits to minimize wasted mileage. The end result was that I completed the study for a total sum of less than £100 for travel, postage and telephone. If I had ignored the existing archive material, not only would the ensuing result have taken longer and been more expensive but it would also inevitably have been of significantly lower quality. As it is, this £100 project, while still the subject of considerable debate, has changed the field of school choice research and attracted both media and political interest on an international scale.

Contextualization
Although I have been involved in several small studies involving only secondary data (see below for a further example), in most studies the power of secondary data is allied to the flexibility of primary data techniques. One way in which all studies can gain from integrating secondary data is to set the context for the primary data. Even relatively large-scale data collection cannot compete in size and quality with existing records, so re-analysis of these records can be helpful in a variety of ways. It can provide the figures for each stratum in a stratified sample (else how do you know what proportions to use?). It can be used to assess the quality of an achieved sample by providing some background figures for the population. These figures can then be used to re-weight the sample if there is clear bias in its composition (see Chapter Four).

Contextual secondary data can also be used to show that a problem exists that needs to be addressed using other techniques, and to begin to describe the nature of that problem (Gorard 2002a). If you intend investigating the causes of increasing crime in city centres or the reasons for boys' under-achievement at school, for example, you need to show via secondary data that these problems actually exist (and many such moral panics are based on misreading of the existing data). You can also show via secondary data something about the nature of the problem you are investigating. Is the increase in all categories of crime, and is it manifested differently in different cities? Are boys achieving lower school outcomes than girls at all ages and levels or only at the highest grades? Only then, once you have created your sample, justified your study and begun your examination – all via secondary data – would you sensibly move on to the primary phase of your investigation in an attempt to create a plausible explanation. I really cannot see how any researcher can evade the necessity to use secondary data for at least the early part of an empirical investigation.

Authority, quality, and scale

Extremely large, long-term and official datasets carry a certain authority, and this can be reflected in any further work involving the same data. A dataset like the Labour Force Survey (LFS) covers hundreds of variables relating to 150,000 people collected every three months and with the results from the last decade available in spreadsheet format. Whatever its faults, it is clearly of a much higher quality than anything most of us could ever hope to achieve in a small project. Therefore, analysis of these figures can lead us to higher-quality findings than we could achieve on our own, and we would be silly to try and collect any of the variables covered in this survey ourselves. Obviously, there may be biases built into any secondary figures we use (which are discussed below), and as with our own research we need to be aware of them and work around them. Nevertheless, if you claim, for example, that job-related training for over-35s has declined in Northern Ireland over the last ten years you are more likely to be believed (and quite rightly so) if your source is a re-analysis of the LFS than if it is a survey of 100 people. Yet it will be both quicker and easier for you to use the LFS data than to collect 100 survey responses.

Cumulation

If there is a purpose to discovering new knowledge it surely involves the use of that knowledge as the basis for further work, as well as for its immediate implications for policy and practice. So, apart from the need for replication (which is rarely met in social science research), it may become less and less necessary to do *some* forms of primary research since these have already been completed, and more important to build on previous work. Why 'reinvent the wheel'? It is also, at least in theory, becoming harder to carry out primary research to collect data that already exists. Funding bodies allocating publicly funded grants or commissioning research, such as the UK Economic and Social Research Council, require applicants to show that they have looked to see if the data they require already exists, and to present evidence that it does not. In addition, once a publicly funded project is completed the datasets generated must be lodged with a public data archive (see below), therefore increasing the chance that for each new proposal something similar already exists in the archive.

Cross-pollination and originality

It may seem odd to suggest that using 'old' data can lead to more original research than getting new data, yet I believe this to be precisely the case where what I have termed 'cross-pollination' of datasets is involved. I have lost count of the number of times I have found research students to be carrying out small-scale surveys of employers' attitudes, or interviewing a handful of headteachers' about the management of change in schools, or conducting a few focus groups on public perceptions of alcoholism. While the students always manage to claim originality by changing the institutional or national setting, I am afraid that I generally no longer expect the results to be definitive or even very interesting (and am therefore pleased when I am proved wrong).

Contrast this kind of small project to one that I carried out in one afternoon in my 'spare time' while a research student (see Gorard 1998b, 1998c). As background, it is important to realize that it has been a 'given' of educational policy in Wales for a long time that schools in Wales do not perform as well as those in neighbouring England. Children have, it is argued, been 'schooled for failure', and models of improvement in Wales have therefore been predicated on policy-borrowing from more successful schools elsewhere (Reynolds 1990). In raw-score terms, schools in Wales have until recently certainly had lower average public examination benchmarks (such as the percentage of pupils with five GCSEs grades A*–C) than schools in England. I set out to test whether the results for education authorities in Wales are actually worse than those of equivalent authorities in England. The key word here is 'equivalent', as Wales is a generally poorer and more sparsely populated region than England, with lower economic activity rates.

I needed, for the basic study, the examination results for each LEA in England and Wales for the past year (published annually in the series represented by DfEE 1994a and Welsh Office 1995a). From these I formed my outcome measures (GCSE benchmark, GCSE failure rate and so on). I also needed estimates of the proportion of children from families in poverty (those eligible for free school meals). These formed one of my input measures, and I obtained them from the same series as the results for Wales and from DfEE (1994b) for England. All of these booklets were in my local library. Among other input measures I used the population density, percentage of householders in each social class and the percentage of school-age children in fee-paying (private) schools for each LEA. All of these were obtained from the 1991 population census, available on-line at any level of geographical aggregation (see below). These figures suggested (and the conclusion has now been confirmed by more complex analyses at school level) that the schools in LEAs in Wales were producing results that were as least as good as those of LEAs in England that matched them in terms of the input measures.

The findings of this simple contextualized analysis ran contrary to the schooled-for-failure thesis. They defended children, teachers and schools in Wales, and met with considerable local media and political interest. The study is clearly very far from perfect but it made a key contribution to an important regional debate, and like many studies has led to further research (for example of the validity of international comparisons between educational systems). I therefore repeat what I said above. The complete study including data collection, transcription and analysis took me one afternoon at an additional cost of less than £10 for photocopying and access to census figures. I would have been very happy to have done this study for my Masters dissertation instead of traipsing around institutions conducting yet another survey (which is what I actually did). I would have saved time and money and produced more interesting results for my discussion section (something to get my teeth into). All that was involved was an idea, along with the cross-pollination formed by bringing together three existing datasets in a way that had not been thought of before.

LIKELY SOURCES

Once you have opened your eyes to secondary data, the difficulty is not so much whether what you want exists but where to find it. Suggestions of likely sources are made here for illustration, but the specific details, especially of Internet resources, are likely to date very rapidly. The sources below over-represent sites relevant to education (with which I am most familiar). Sources of interest will also vary between countries. Obviously the search engines and databases available in your library are a good place to start (librarians themselves can be very useful), along with the search engines available on the Internet (see Peters 1998 for an introduction to finding research material on the web, the structure of URLs and how to guess the address you want).

A key starting point when looking for existing data is the UK government's (Office for) National Statistics (Website: http://

www.statistics.gov.uk/default_content.asp). National Statistics hold a large and rapidly growing range of datasets, with the introduction 'You can download a wealth of economic and social data free'. They produce a large number of annual publications based on these figures and, perhaps most usefully at this stage, they produce catalogues of their data and publications. These catalogues are free on request and they include a brief guide to sources of government statistics with a list of relevant offices, publishers and contact details. Their public enquiry services will give you, by fax or email, the latest macro-economic statistics including tables and graphs within minutes of their official release time of 9:30 am. There is no room here for an exhaustive list of all publications handled by National Statistics, but they include the following.

The *Social Focus on Children* report is a summary of UK statistics relating to children, such as what they read, how they spend their money and what their leisure interests are (now updated for Wales as a *Statistical Focus on Children*, including poverty, welfare, health, population and lifestyle figures). *Social Trends* is an annual production in book and CD-ROM format giving figures on education, health, employment, leisure, transport and housing. As it is an annual produced since 1970, an examination of past figures allows the creation of trends over time. *Regional Trends* produces similar figures on policy and life in the UK broken down by regions. *Family Spending* reports the findings of the regular Family Expenditure Survey (again allowing the creation of trends over time), showing how households distribute their incomes between food, travel, housing and other demands. The *New Earnings Survey* is another annual report, allowing trends over time and regional analysis, and showing ages, occupation, sex, work hours and earnings of the UK workforce by occupation or industry. *Retail Prices 1914–1990* uses the retail price index and the earlier cost of living index to present monthly figures for the price inflation (and deflation) affecting UK consumers. *Statistics of Education UK* shows the annual figures for many education-related topics (with past years to 1972 for comparison) including the number of teachers and students by school and sector and participation and qualification rates for each age group of students. Information from various surveys run by the Social Survey Division of the office for National Statistics is now available on-line for the years 1941 to 2001 (http:// www.statistics.gov.uk/ssd/default.asp).

National Statistics also publish descriptions of public policy systems, such as education, in other countries, as well as annual reports of the first destinations of UK graduates, and trends and predictions for the supply of graduates to industry. Other key themes are crime, justice, offenders and terrorism. These are dealt with in the British Crime Survey and the Scottish Crime Survey. The NS site at http://www.statistics.gov.uk/themes/crime_justice/crime.asp links to existing datasets on crime rates, fear of crime, recorded crime, attitudes to crime and crime reduction. These are all broken down by area and type of crime, and allow the examination of trends over time. The Crime and Justice home page lists crime, police forces, the prison and probation services, drugs, the courts, and family and civil justice as major themes. On 27th May 2002 when I last accessed it, the NS content page (http://www.statistics.gov.uk/default_content.asp) also offered figures on agriculture, fishing and forestry, commerce, energy and industry, health and care, the labour market, natural and built environment, population and migration, welfare, transport, travel and tourism, the time-use survey and several other themes. It showed the weekly deaths recorded in England and Wales and the weekly cases of notifiable infectious diseases in Scotland, for example. Surely something for everyone there?

The 2001 population Census contained questions about type of housing (including number of rooms, access to bathroom facilities, floor level, heating and tenure), car ownership, household relationships, economic activity (including employment contract, length out of work, size of workforce, job title, supervisory responsibilities, nature of business, travel to work and working hours), health (long illness and provision of care), qualifications (academic, professional and vocational) and the individual (sex, age, marital status, change of address, birthplace, ethnic group and religion). In Wales, the Census also asked about ability in the Welsh language. Previous censuses have asked about fertility and marriage duration. The number and range of the questions creates a fantastic starting point for almost any social science investigation. Given that the Census questions are asked of everybody in the UK (or a 10% sub-sample in some cases), the scale of this information is hard to compare with 'normal' research. Many of these questions have been asked and anonymized responses are available for every ten years since 1841. There is considerable potential here to map social trends over time. And do not make the mistake of imagining that this has all been analysed and therefore the data will yield nothing new. The kind of analysis done depends on the nature of the question asked. If you can think of a new question, you can do new research with this old data.

Another useful starting place is the Economic and Social Research Council Data Archive (University of Essex, Colchester, Essex CO4 3SQ, UK), which keeps a copy of the 'quantitative' datasets collected by all past ESRC-funded projects. Other Research Councils have equivalent archives. The data in these archives is available to researchers on request (and usually a fee). Whatever aspect of social science you are interested in, the chances are that something similar has been done before. It is almost as important not to ignore this previous data as it is not to ignore the findings of previous relevant research in your own review of the literature. Recent acquisitions include large-scale surveys on adult literacy, patterns of lifelong learning and the new British Household Panel Survey. The archive retains older datasets, such as those from the Social Change and Economic Life Initiative (SCELI) and the ESRC 16-19 Programme. It also holds or has access to international datasets, including such diverse sources as Bulgarian microdata, US marital instability over the lifecourse, UNESCO Education Database, the Dutch Panel Survey and even the physical stature of Georgia convicts from 1770 to 1860, for example. The related website of the Teaching Resources and Materials for Social Scientists is at http://tramss.data-archive.ac.uk/, where data from large and complex social science datasets can be downloaded along with free analytical software for multi-level modelling.

Several of these publications involve a cost. The researcher might have to pay from around £5 to above £100 for a particular current survey (although past years often come free). However, these costs are small in relation to the real and opportunity costs of carrying out fieldwork. Many publications should anyway be available in your local library. The data from several of these surveys, including the ten-yearly Census of population, is available from the National On-Line Manpower System (http://www.nomisweb.co.uk/). Using this system, researchers have access to datasets such as the Labour Force Survey and 40 years of Census returns to generate reports for chosen geographical areas. The available geographical areas include enumeration districts, electoral divisions, travel-to-work areas and education authorities. Census data disaggregated to a local level is also available free of charge from the Manchester Information and Associated Services (or MIMAS at < http:/www.mimas.ac.uk// >). Using this system it is possible to calculate the Townsend Deprivation Index for enumeration districts and transfer the results to local digitized maps, for example. Again, the office for National Statistics (see above) offers access to a 'state-of-the-art' Geographical Information System which allows you to search a variety of large datasets at a level of geographical aggregation below electoral wards.

The Teacher Training Agency (TTA) has a website at < http:// www.teach-tta.gov.uk/itt/funding/alloc.htm > . This has its own search routines and a 'quick navigation menu' leading to figures on initial teacher training targets, funding and applications, for example. The Department for Education and Skills (DfES) has a website at < http://www.dfes.gov.uk/index.htm > . This has an index, search routine and news flashes, as well as sections on the Office for Standards in Education (OFSTED), the National Grid for Learning (NGfL) and Statistics. The Statistics section provides monthly figures back to October 1998 (at time of writing) on policies such as the New Deal, nursery provision, admission appeals against school placements, the destinations of leavers from higher education, work-based training, special educational needs, student numbers in colleges, teacher sickness absence, exclusions from school, National Curriculum assessments, teacher vacancies, pupil:teacher ratios and class sizes (among others). It is almost a one-stop shop for the beginning secondary analyst in education, containing everything that appears in 'league tables' of school examination results and much more.

The Office for the National Assembly for Wales (formerly the Welsh Office) produces the annual *Wales in Figures*, a summary of figures for population, economy, education and health. The Welsh Office Statistical Directorate, like National Statistics, publishes a catalogue of their statistical publications. These include the *Digest of Welsh Statistics*, the *Digest of Welsh Local Area Statistics* (with figures broken down for each of the 22 local authorities), the *Child Protection Register*, two annual volumes of the *Statistics of Education and Training in Wales* – one for schools and one for post-compulsory education and training – another on *Schools* (including their finance, number, size, type, meals service and a record of statements of special educational need) and an equivalent for *Further and Higher Education and Training*. The Welsh Office produce their own survey data, such as the 1992 *Social Survey* report on education and training (Welsh Office 1994), the 1994 *Education and Training Survey* (Welsh Office 1995b), the 1995 *Education and Training Survey* (Education and Training Statistics 1997), and the 1996 *Welsh Employers Survey* (Welsh Office 1996). The Welsh Office also produces a large number of statistical briefing papers, such as those measuring progress towards the national targets for education and training

(Welsh Office 1999). These last, along with several of the publications listed here, are free on request (and, of course, will mostly have been updated since I last used them). Equivalent publications are available for England, Scotland and Northern Ireland.

The DfES 'Skills and Enterprise Network' is free to join, and provides regular reports and statistics on work, lifelong education and training in England. These include a quarterly *Labour Market Report*, with figures for training disaggregated by age, industry, gender and so on, and with trends over time. There are also reports on graduate employment and comparative figures for basic skills. All are currently available from DfES Publications in Nottingham, or email dfes@prologistics.co.uk, and the Datasphere website is a gateway to data and commentary on labour market, learning and skills (see www.dfes.gov.uk/datasphere). Also available from the DfES and elsewhere are reports of large-scale surveys. See, for example, NACETT (1995 and later versions) for trends over time in progress towards national targets for education, or the Basic Skills Agency (1997) for an analysis of patterns of literacy and numeracy skills and their lack, or Beinart and Smith (1998) for a full report of the National Adult Learning Survey 1997. Equivalent publications are available in other areas of public policy.

Most developed countries have equivalent sources of national data. Some have longitudinal studies, such as the *US High School and Beyond Survey*, and the *US Cohort Study* similar to the *UK National Child Development Study*, which could make a very interesting comparison for a small project. The European Union produces a variety of statistical summaries allowing comparisons of most European public policy systems and the socio-economic systems from which they emerge. It is sometimes necessary to examine two or more of these publications to get a useful set of indicators, for example one on education and one on wider social policy (CERI 1997 and CERI 1998, or Eurostat 1995 and Eurostat 1998). The Organisation for Economic Co-operation and Development (OECD) also produces a range of figures on economics and education for developing and less developed nations, often in the form of trends over time (e.g. OECD 1993). OECD (2000) *Education at a Glance* is the latest (at time of writing) annual report of statistical information relating to the education and training systems of the members (plus 16 non-members). Some indicators therefore apply to over two thirds of the world population. It is both a yearbook showing trends over time and an encyclopaedia showing how things stand today in terms of: the national context of education in each country; the financial and human resources invested in education; access to education, participation and progression; the learning environment and organization of schools; individual, social and labour market outcomes of education and student achievement. Like all secondary data, especially at this high level of aggregation, the figures must be used with all the accompanying footnoted caveats in mind, and it is useful that the book includes three annexes showing how the indicators are defined, collapsed and compared over time. Nevertheless this is precisely the type of book that all of us should refer to more often for contextual figures.

WATCH OUT FOR LIMITATIONS

Despite the obvious advantages of using data that someone else has already collected, there are potential problems with this approach to research. Such problems do not, in my view, mean that we should spurn other peoples' work but that we should be aware of the limitations of what we are using. We should publish these limitations and take them into account in our findings. Even official statistics are not simple 'facts' but have been socially constructed (May 1997), so using them may involve an unconscious acceptance of their social values.

The availability of figures can determine what is considered researchable, rather than the other way around. In choosing to use secondary figures we are giving up access to the field notes and other incidental observations we may have made during the process of primary collection. Perhaps most importantly, prolonged 'desk-based research' may lead us to an unhelpful isolation from the subject of study and therefore to a lack of practical realism in the research findings. It is also the case that the very speed and cheapness of secondary data may be seen by some as a disadvantage. Sponsors and supervisors who believe that a project should take a certain amount of time may be reluctant to accept that a quicker and superior method is available. Ironically, researchers in need of grant-funding may prefer primary analysis, not because it is necessary but because it takes longer and therefore requires the services of more research employees whose salaries bring in overhead expenses to the university or research institution (although of course this is not a reason to waste public money).

Examples of the difficulties of using official statistics are endless. If the figures from the British Crime Survey depend upon the level of crime reported to the police, then changes in frequency over time could be due to changes in the level of crime or the level of reporting or both. Using secondary data we have no way of knowing which interpretation is correct (and there appears to be no simple way of deciding this point even with primary data). We need to treat secondary figures as we would any other research findings, with tentative scepticism. We would therefore need to know how the definition of unemployment has changed over time before accepting apparent changes in the official figures for that. In international comparisons of educational test results, we need to consider the conditions under which the tests were administered in each country. When looking at improvement in scores for Key Stage assessments in schools since their inception we need to recall the early disruption caused by teachers' lack of cooperation in the UK. When using examination figures in any way we need to recall the difficulties of ensuring comparability of standards between subjects, syllabuses, examination boards, years, modes of assessment and regions. A secondary analysis, done well, therefore requires a thorough examination of the pedigree of its raw materials.

A further problem is that we generally have no agreed methods for dealing with these large and often complex secondary datasets (Gorard and Taylor 2002a). It means that many of those researchers actually using secondary data today are 'pioneers' of one kind of analysis or another. There are currently debates between them over the precise way to measure trends over time, differences between places and how to deal with hierarchical data, for example. These debates need to be pursued with vigour so that relatively standard protocols can be produced for general researchers to use when simply wishing to conduct a 'smash and grab' on existing data in preparation for a new study. Nevertheless, the analysis of secondary data is still usually simpler than the analysis of primary data, requiring only primary school arithmetic (see Chapter Three) rather than the calculation of probabilities (see Chapter Six).

AN EXAMPLE OF USING SECONDARY DATA

A recent example of a project involving only secondary data was my study with colleagues of the impact of National Targets for Education and Training (represented by Gorard et al. 2000a, 2002a, 2002b). As a consequence of a report by the Education and Training Action Group (ETAG 1999) to the new National Assembly for

Wales, we were asked to predict progress towards the National Targets and make recommendations for modifying them where necessary. Although there was also an element of user consultation, the bulk of the project involved learning how progress towards targets was usually calculated and using secondary data from a variety of sources to model future rates of progress. I shall describe two findings here, one from each of these parts of the project. Both relate to the caution above to check carefully what is actually being measured by official statistics.

One finding was that, as far as we could tell, the setting of targets for lifelong learning has had no impact at all. There has been growth towards the target figures, but only because the targets are set for those of working age. Young people leaving education today and joining the workforce generally have higher qualifications than the older people leaving the workforce at retirement. So the workforce becomes more qualified without anyone of working age gaining any qualifications. If these changes are discounted, fewer people have actually been qualified as adults than was the case before the setting of targets. This is not 'lifelong' learning.

Another finding was that our own estimates of the qualifications of the workforce gained from the Labour Force Survey (LFS) were considerably lower than the figures published as official indicators of progress towards the targets. This difference was mainly accounted for by official assumptions about missing answers to the survey question about peoples' highest qualification. The DfEE and Welsh Office (as they then were) assumed that cases giving no response and responding 'don't know' could be allocated a qualification level in proportion to those cases giving a valid answer. Therefore, in their analysis, an equivalent proportion of those people not responding were 'awarded' a PhD as were reported as having no qualifications at all. Attempts such as these to rectify non-response appeared to be seriously inflating the actual reported levels of qualification.

Although both of these points are clearly methodological, they are also significant findings that should have been fed back to the post-16 committee of Assembly Members as affecting the then national debate about targets. In fact none of the members felt able to attend the dissemination organized for them by the Statistics Division of the Welsh Office. It was almost as though they did not want to hear what we had to say!

This chapter has looked at some of the advantages and potential problems in using secondary data. For further discussion of these points try reading Dale et al. (1988) or May (1997). The next chapter continues by examining some simple methods for analysing secondary data, as an introduction to the world of descriptive statistics.

Simple analysis?: index wars and other battles

This chapter introduces some basic approaches to working with the kinds of data discussed in Chapter Two. It should not be treated as a complete guide to calculation or to the use of a statistical package on a computer. There are already many of these (see below). Rather, it considers some of the key issues in analysis. Chief among these is the relationship between the methods of analysis used and the substantive conclusions reported, for 'the conclusion drawn by the investigator ... is often only vaguely related to the actual results' (Rosenthal 1991, p. 13). I would go further and say that different methods of analysis *can* produce contradictory results using the same data. In such examples the research findings are totally dependent on the method chosen and therefore not at all dependent on the data actually collected. This chapter begins to explain how and why this can be so.

THE PRELIMINARIES

Analysis usually proceeds via the essential, but mostly trivial stages of coding, transcription and cleaning of the dataset generated by your study. Coding of data involves converting observations and responses into scales or measurements. Descriptions of peoples' occupations might be converted into occupational class categories, or peoples' description of their familiarity with the Internet might be classed as 'High', 'Medium' or 'Low', for example. This stage should be relatively simple since the actual coding scheme is usually inherent in the design of your data collection (see Chapter Five). Designing your coding scheme is a complex and important issue, but not one to be faced after data has been collected (except where a reappraisal is required in light of experience). In secondary data, of course, coding has usually already been completed for you and, as you may imagine, this is both a benefit and a source of frustration.

The key virtue in coding is consistency. Some 'authorities' argue that coding should be made into an entirely separate stage, by writing coded responses on to individual completed questionnaires, for example. However, for an individual researcher (rather than a large team) I can see no great disadvantage in typing these codes directly into a computer spreadsheet or statistical package. In fact, there is considerable potential advantage in this approach since the data is then transcribed once only, rather than twice (once to the questionnaire and once from the questionnaire to the computer). As you will recall if you have ever played the game that I learnt as 'Chinese whispers', the more times a piece of data is copied the more likely it is to get garbled. So be prepared to ignore and defend yourself against the coding 'fundamentalists' who will try to insist that you code and transcribe separately.

The key virtue when copying your results on to another medium is accuracy. So keep going back and carrying out spot checks on the figures entered as a form of quality control. My advice would be to carry out the transcription yourself, in a systematic way, in concentrated batches, with no one else in the room and no distractions like background music (however much you might believe that music helps you to concentrate!). Note that even if you want to use a package like SPSS but do not have it at home, you can still do the lengthy entering of data at home into a spreadsheet file, which can then be opened by a more sophisticated package at work, college or library. Again, in secondary data this stage has usually already been completed, so your alternative task is to learn as much as you can about a coding and transcription process that has already taken place.

Cleaning your data is a slightly more complex task than coding, but less so perhaps that it would usually appear from reading research textbooks. The essential point in cleaning is to ensure that the data you eventually use in your analysis is the correctly coded version of the measurements that you took in your fieldwork. It is a long and probably never completed process. Long but not difficult. The spot checks carried out during transcription are part of cleaning. If you find that the figures on one form or questionnaire response do not match what you have entered into a spreadsheet at that point, then stop. Now trace back and find the mistake. It could be a simple typing error in that one case, but very often the mistake is a symptom of a bigger problem (your sheets are in the wrong order, you have turned over two pages at once, etc.).

Much of the rest of the cleaning process, other than simply

reading or looking at your completed dataset, takes place during simple analysis using many of the procedures described in the remainder of this chapter. Techniques such as drawing graphs and producing frequency counts, means and standard deviations can be useful when presenting data but they can also highlight further mistakes in the data coding and data entry procedures. These are easiest to spot when extreme or otherwise unrealistic scores are reported in your analysis. If the oldest person in your (alive) sample is 768 years old, then you need to go back to the original source and correct the error. Again, note that you cannot simply assume that the problem is isolated. You may have misunderstood the coding scheme for a secondary dataset. You may have entered the respondent's monthly income as their age which probably means that you entered their age as their highest qualification and so on. Anxiety and pedantry on your part can be accounted virtues at this stage.

The reason that some writers make cleaning appear more difficult is that they conflate this simple but arduous error-checking with the decision to remove inconvenient data from their dataset. This issue is discussed in Chapter Ten. The point I wish to make here for the beginner is that cleaning must take place, and it involves the rigorous checking for the accuracy and consistency of coding and transcription. Once this is done, there may be responses that you do not believe (such as a 12-year-old with two A-Levels, a qualification commonly taken at age 17 or 18) but this is another issue entirely. If the most original form of the data available to you codes into what you have in your final dataset, and the figures are all at least possible, then that is as much as you can do at present. If you start deleting/amending figures because you do not believe them then you will need a good argument to convince me and other readers that you are not on a slippery slope towards falsifying your data or simply making convenient results up. You would be unlikely ever to be surprised by your results, since if they are not what you expect you will, presumably, ignore them.

TWO TYPES OF DATA

This discussion of simple analysis continues by drawing a tentative but useful distinction between two types of numeric data. Although too much is often made of fine distinctions between numbering scales (or levels of measurement), the novice 'quantitative' analyst must learn to recognize the differences between descriptions of categorical information and real numbers. These differences relate in an important way to the organization of the rest of this book. Chapter Six considers the analysis of two or more categorical variables, Chapter Nine considers analyses involving both real and categorical variables and Chapter Ten describes approaches to analysing two or more real variables.

'Real' numbers are those that it makes sense to do arithmetic with. So a simple test of identification would be: does it make sense for me to add or subtract these numbers? The number of years a steelworker has been employed in a factory is a real number. To find the difference in experience between two steelworkers we could subtract two numbers of years and find how many years more one steelworker had been at the factory. We can do this because the scale we use to measure time has *equal* intervals all the way along. The difference between 99 years and 100 years is the same as that between one and two years, for example. A year is a year, wherever on the scale we look.

Categorical information, on the other hand, relates to categories only, and individual cases therefore cannot be subject to arithmetic operations. The sex of a doctor is a category and we cannot subtract a maleness of one doctor from the femaleness of another to find their difference in gender. This restriction applies even where the categories are expressed as numbers. Whereas the length of my foot is a real number, my shoe size is a category (shoe sizes do not represent equal intervals as children's sizes increase in smaller stages than adults'). We could add two lengths but not two shoe sizes. Arithmetic operations can, however, be conducted using the frequencies of categorical data. We could, for example, find a difference by subtraction between the number of male and female steelworkers in a factory, or find the total number of people with either of two shoe sizes. In fact, most social scientific data has elements of both types expressed as the *number* of things of a certain *category*.

Other authors give much greater attention to measurement theory and the issue of scales than I intend to do here (see for example Siegel 1956). For me the first and clearest distinction is the one just introduced between numbers we can add together and numbers used to label categories or types of things. On reading a traditional statistical textbook you will be introduced early on to measuring scales called 'ratio', 'interval', 'ordinal' and 'nominal'. But both ratio and interval measures are real numbers and I promise that the difference between them will never make any practical difference to you. There are very few interval measures (the frequently cited example of a temperature scale actually being the only one in common use, although rarely used in social science anyway), and the kinds of statistical procedures you would use, at least for the beginner, are identical to those for ratio measures anyway. So why worry about the distinction? Both ordinal and nominal scales are categorical in nature, but in many practical situations analysts use ordinal data as though it were based on real numbers (see Chapter Nine), and no real harm comes from treating ordinal data as nominal in nature. Let's worry about further niceties when and if we encounter them.

SUMMARIZING FIGURES

This section gives a brief account of standard methods of presenting summaries of your basic figures, whether real or categorical.

Frequencies and percentages
When data is categorical in nature the standard methods for summarizing and describing it involve frequencies (how many cases in each category) or percentages (what percentage of cases is in each category). These summaries can be represented in a bar chart or possibly a pie chart (but these tend to be over-used and are not that easy to read, in my opinion). All of these can be produced easily using either a spreadsheet or a statistical package such as SPSS. Table 3.1 shows the frequencies and equivalent percentages of people who had watched a particular programme on television, in an imaginary sample. Watching a programme or not represents a categorical variable with two categories. Table 3.1 is both precise and easy to understand. The percentage shows how many cases in every 100 have a particular characteristic. There is an at least informal assumption that percentages therefore refer to figures collected from hundreds of cases.

Table 3.1: Frequency of people who watched a certain TV programme in our sample I

Category	Number	Percentage
Watched the programme	217	29
Did not watch	542	71
Total	759	100

Figure 3.1 shows the same values in a bar chart. This and all subsequent figures were drawn using a spreadsheet. For more on how to do this see Solomon and Winch (1994). The bar chart has the advantage of making it slightly easier to see the proportion of responses in the two categories but with the disadvantage that it is now harder to read off the actual values for each with any precision (although the percentages could be placed at the top of each bar, for example). As the number of categories grows so the value of a bar chart increases (and makes it easier to read off the values of the 'mode' and 'median' averages, see Explanation of Terms).

Figure 3.2 shows the same results again but this time as a pie chart. Although there are many advocates of these graphs, I cannot see much advantage over the bar chart and it makes reading off any figures impossible (and so necessitates the insertion of the frequency values anyway).

Simple analyses of frequencies such as these are a very useful place to start getting to know your data. In particular, they can help you identify particular features or problems in your dataset (and this applies whether you are using secondary data or have collected the information at source). If there are empty categories in your coding

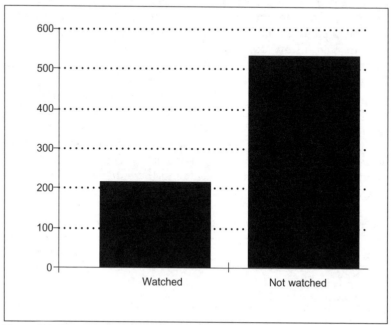

Figure 3.1: Frequency of people who watched a certain TV programme II

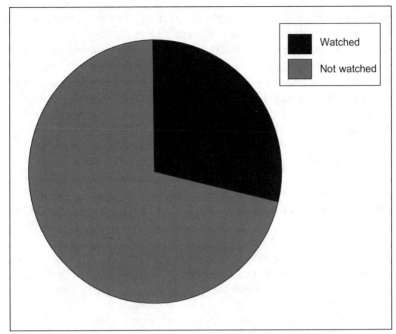

Figure 3.2: Frequency of people who watched a certain TV programme III

system, then you can delete these categories and so simplify your future analyses and presentations. If, for example, there are three types of occupation that the individuals in your sample could have but no one actually has one of these types, then your analysis will proceed with only two types (and this could have important implications for the nature of your analysis, see Chapters Six and Nine). If there are entire 'variables' with no variation then the variables themselves can be omitted from further analysis. If, for example, everyone in your sample owns a car then proceeding with any further analysis of car ownership is a waste of time.

Simple analyses of frequencies are also very useful to detect 'outliers'. An outlier is a value that is clearly out of the range expected or observed for a particular variable. You will not, for example, have expected any children at school today to have been born in the nineteenth century, nor would you have expected a 73-year-old to be still employed as a steelworker (see section on cleaning above). What you do about such outliers is a tricky decision. You should never adjust the data without good reason and without making your changes explicit. Cleaning up data is good research practice. Falsifying data is cheating. The difference can be very slight. In the two examples here, the nineteenth-century birth date is clearly a mistake. If you cannot correct it, then you will have to ignore it (by deleting the case perhaps). The 73-year-old steelworker sounds very unlikely but this, in itself, does not allow us to ignore the finding. If we make a practice of abandoning unlikely-sounding findings, then we can no longer be surprised by our research and are therefore, in my opinion, not actually doing research any more. We are seeking empirical-sounding justification for our existing prejudices.

Means and deviations
When data is in the form of real numbers, these can be presented as frequencies and percentages just like categorical data. This is often done to examine the distribution and to spot outliers (see above). Obviously this involves converting the real numbers into categories. For this purpose, we might change a set of individual ages into a set of categories such as those aged 16–20 years, those aged 21–25 years and so on.

Standard arithmetic operations are also possible with real numbers (unlike categories), and these are generally simpler and more powerful and use more of the information within the data than when working with frequencies. Standard techniques for summarizing numbers include the mean average (total of all values divided by the number of cases) and the standard deviation (a measure of how spread out from the mean the observed values are). Both the mean and standard deviation will be calculated by a computer package for you (see below). Some authorities also advocate the use of inter-quartile ranges, stem and leaf plots, or box and whisker plots to help show the distribution of data. While these have advantages on occasion, they seldom tell you more than a high-quality tabulation of the frequencies would (and there is a tendency for them to be over-used by novices). Use whatever techniques you feel comfortable with to get to know each dataset before doing the serious analysis.

Suppose we obtain the following set of scores from 12 shoppers, and each score represents the amount of money they spent on one trip to a supermarket (see Table 3.2). The mean is 50, computed as the total of the scores for the 12 cases (600) divided by 12. This gives us an overall idea of the size of the numbers and the central value around which they are distributed.

Table 3.2: Amount spent in one shopping trip

Case	1	2	3	4	5	6	7	8	9	10	11	12	Total
score	39	45	76	34	51	51	67	46	23	49	62	57	600
deviation	−11	−5	26	−16	1	1	17	−4	−27	−1	12	7	0
absolute deviation	11	5	26	16	1	1	17	4	27	1	12	7	128
squared deviation	121	25	676	256	1	1	289	16	729	1	144	49	2308

The row labelled 'deviation' shows how far each score is from the mean (and the sum of these is 0, by definition). If we ignore the sign (+ or −) of the deviations then the sum of these absolute deviations is 128, giving us a mean deviation of 10.67 (i.e. 128/12). The mean deviation gives us some idea of how spread out the 12 scores are. Traditionally however, people use the standard deviation for this. In order to find this, the deviations are squared (multiplied with themselves to eliminate negative values), and the *standard* deviation is defined as the square root of the sum of these squared values, all divided by the number of cases (or, more commonly, divided by the number of cases minus one to make an arbitrary allowance for sampling error). Don't panic about this — remember that the actual calculation is done by the computer. In the example the standard deviation is $\sqrt{[(2308)/11]}$, or 4.37. This also gives an overall idea of how spread out the actual scores are. Thus, the standard deviation (SD), by describing the amount of variation, gives an idea of how representative the mean (M) is. Four of these scores are within one standard deviation of the mean (i.e. between 45.63 and 54.37), six of the scores are within two standard deviations of the mean (i.e. between 41.26 and 58.74), and so on.

As another example, the mean of the three scores 1, 1, and 118 is 40, but in this case 40 is not a very useful or accurate representation of that set of numbers. It does not give the reader a good idea of the 'central' value in this distribution of numbers. The mean deviation of the three numbers is 52 (i.e. 156/3). The standard deviation of the three numbers is 47.77. So, in the first example the mean was 50, the mean deviation was 10.67, and SD was 4.37 (SD was much smaller than the mean), suggesting that the mean is a reasonable summary figure. In the second example the mean was 40, the mean deviation 52, and SD was 47.77 (SD was larger than the mean), suggesting that the mean is not a reasonable summary of the figures in question. It is for this reason, above all, that whenever a mean is quoted it should be accompanied by the standard deviation (or the mean deviation, if you want to try and establish an alternative trend!). Treat the two numbers as a pair of inseparable friends.

As I started writing this book there was an advertisement on UK television for Marks and Spencer clothing claiming, 'if you're not average you're normal'. This peculiar-sounding statement actually makes a lot of sense. The average number of bedrooms in a household may be 2.33 but no one actually has that number of bedrooms. The average annual earnings of UK actors in the union Equity was £15,000 in 1999, but 60% of actors earned less than £4,000 and 3% earned more than £100,000 (Matthews 2000). In both cases the average is not a good guide to what is normal. It is for this reason, of course, that parents should not worry unduly if their child does not talk by the average age for such a development. If the average is a good one, then almost by definition we would expect around half of all children not to talk by that age. That is 'normal'.

THE POLITICIANS ERROR

The remainder of this chapter considers the slightly more complex analyses necessary when examining changes over time or differences between things. Since the emphasis of the book so far has been on secondary analysis, an assumption is made for the rest of this chapter that we are not concerned with probability or significance tests as such (these are introduced in Chapter Six). Rather, we shall be concerned with the apparently trivial (until examined) issue of getting our arithmetic correct. The first issue, termed here the politicians error, relates to a widespread misunderstanding in using frequencies when expressed as percentages. The importance of this misuse would be hard to overestimate.

Imagine a country of 100 million adults, of whom 50 million are male and 50 million are female. There are 1,000 members of parliament (MPs or elected representatives), and all of these are male. The employed workforce is 50 million of whom 25.5 million are male. No great analytical skill is required to see that this imaginary country has a considerable political bias towards males. Similarly it is easy to see that the country also has a slight employment bias towards males but that the political bias is much greater than the employment bias. There are no MPs among the female half of the population, whereas 49% of women are in employment. Of the male population .001% are MPs, and 51% are in employment. I repeat, because of the importance of this point, that the ratio of male to female MPs is 1,000:0 (equivalent to an infinite amount) whereas the ratio of male to female employed is 25.5:24.5 (equivalent to 1.04). Therefore the inequity among MPs is far greater than among the general employed workforce. Why am I emphasizing this point? Because the most common 'method' used to analyse such data comes to the opposite and totally wrong conclusion. This so-called method is used very widely in areas of social science research, in the media and most frighteningly of all in policy documents and policy-making. It is the method of differences between percentages.

The argument goes like this. The percentage of male MPs is .001% and the percentage of female MPs is 0%, so the difference between them is .001%. The percentage of males in employment is 51% and the percentage of females is 49%, so the difference between them is 2%. Since 2% is much larger than .001% the lack of equity in general employment is greater than among MPs. This is a totally ludicrous argument making several related arithmetic mistakes, yet I would guess that all readers will have accepted this kind of 'analysis' at face value on many previous occasions. This is precisely the kind of example that leads me to argue (see Chapter One) that all researchers, indeed all good citizens, require some knowledge of what are termed quantitative research skills. So we won't get fooled again. Perhaps you do not believe that people get away with such nonsense. Consider another imaginary example, this time written as the start of a newspaper story.

Girls leave boys in their trail!

The new GCSE results for England and Wales have just been released and they do not make pretty reading for the families of boys. While general levels of qualification continue to rise, the difference between the performance of girls and boys is growing to crisis proportions. Five years ago 35% of girls obtained the government benchmark of five good GCSE passes while only 25% of boys did. This year 63% of girls got five good GCSEs and only 50% of boys did. The gender gap has grown from 10% five years ago to 13% this year, reflecting the increasing problem of boys' under-achievement that faces the education system. In fact, the minister for schools was quoted last night as saying that the growing under-achievement of boys at school was one of the most serious problems faced by our society today . . .

Such stories, using precisely these types of figures, are common-place in the media (see Gorard et al. 1999a, 2001a for a fuller list of examples). Once you have recognized the genre, try replacing boys and girls with different ethnic groups or regions of the UK. Try replacing GCSEs with access to health care or car ownership. Look for an example in this week's news coverage. Can you see that the logic is the same as the example of the MPs above? In order to decide what is happening we cannot simply subtract two sets of percentages and compare the results. One of the main reasons for this is that the difference between two percentages is not itself a *percentage*. In the newspaper example girls are not doing 13% better than boys this year; rather they scored 13 percentage points higher than boys. The distinction is crucial. If we look at the figures as ratios, as we did for the MPs, we see that the proportion of girls to boys with five good GCSE passes five years ago was 35:25 (equivalent to 1.4, or a 40% gap in favour of girls). This year the proportion was 63:50 (equivalent to 1.26, or a 26% gap in favour of girls). What the newspaper figures actually show is that the proportionate gap between girls and boys has fallen over time. Put another way, the scores for boys have doubled over five years (100% increase), while the scores for girls have increased by 80%.

Of course, part of what is seductive about the percentage difference approach is that one can apparently see the gap changing over time on a graph. In Figure 3.3 the distance between the two bars is greater for the current score than for the previous score. This approach is used quite widely in some respected research reports, books and journal articles. In some cases this is done even after the error has been pointed out, and with no attempt to explain why (e.g. Gillborn and Youdell 2000). Of course, an equivalent graph for our hypothetical example of elected and employed men and women (.001 to 0 and 51 to 49) would show an even more extreme difference in distance, but still signifying nothing. Since all of the numbers change in size from one case to another, the question is not whether any percentage point difference has grown but whether it has grown more or less than the numbers between which it is the difference. Or, put more elegantly, 'The drawback with using the absolute difference in proportions to evaluate social reforms, however, is that the measure is largely driven by changes in the overall totals' (Heath 2000, p. 318).

Dawes (2001) makes a similar complaint concerning the use of symptoms in medical diagnosis. Imagine an illness that occurs in

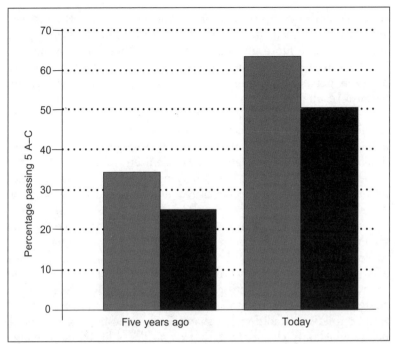

Figure 3.3: The 'growing' gap between girls and boys

20% of the population and has two frequent symptoms. Symptom A occurs in 18% of the cases with this disease, and in 2% of cases without the disease. Symptom B occurs in 58% of the cases with the disease, and in 22% of cases otherwise. Which symptom is the better predictor? Many commentators would argue that symptom B is more useful as it is 'typical' of the disease. There is a 16% gap (18-2) between having and not having the disease with symptom A, whereas the gap is 36% (58-22) with symptom B. Symptom B, they will conclude, is the better predictor. But while it seems counter-intuitive to say so, this analysis is quite wrong because it ignores the base rate of the actual frequency of the disease in the population.

In a group of 1,000 people, on average 200 people would have the disease and 800 would not. Of the 200 with the disease, 36 would have symptom A and 116 symptom B. Of the 800 without the disease, 16 would have symptom A, while 176 would have symptom B. Thus, if we take a person at random from the 1,000 then someone with symptom A is 2.25 times as likely to have the disease as not, whereas someone with symptom B is only 0.66 times as likely to have the disease as not. Put another way, someone with symptom B is more likely *not* to have the disease. What we need for diagnosis are discriminators, rather than typical symptoms. The more general conclusion is therefore the same as in the examples of MPs and of boys and girls. Simple differences between percentages give misleading and potentially extremely harmful results.

Are percentage point differences linear?
Another reason why simple comparisons between percentage point differences do not work and are labelled 'errors' here is that the figures on which they are based may not function as straight lines (Fleiss 1973). Using the notion of real numbers referred to earlier in the chapter, we would say that the percentage points used in the two examples here are not 'equal interval' in form. To be real numbers, the interval between 10% and 20% (10 points) would have to be equal to the interval between 20% and 30% (10 points), for example. This is not always the case, so the kind of arithmetic used to create the politician's error is wrong again. Rather than being a straight line, many patterns, trends and relationships in social science follow a traditional S shape. This consists of a threshold, below which any change in the x-axis produces little or no change in the corresponding value for the y-axis, then a line, where changes in x are linked to changes in y, and finally saturation, above which any change in the x-axis again produces little or no change in the corresponding value for the y-axis. A practical example of saturation is a difference of 50 percentage points between 40% and 90%. If the lower figure grows to 60% then the difference between it and the higher figure cannot be 50 points any longer, however much the higher figure grows. 100% intervenes as a limiting factor.

A similar logic applies at the other end of the percentage scale. The frequency of any population characteristic, such as the number of GCSEs per student, in any sizeable group is likely to be approximately normally distributed (i.e. to follow the traditional bell-shape, see Chapter Four). In Figure 3.4 representing a hypothetical school, exactly 50 of 100 students gain five or more GCSEs. If all of these students had gained one more GCSE then every bar on the graph would shift one place to the right, and the benchmark figure for the school would rise to 70%.

In Figure 3.5 representing a lower-attaining school, only 4 of 100 students gain five or more GCSEs (the actual pattern of frequencies for Figure 3.5 is the same as Figure 3.4 but moved three places towards the origin of the x-axis and therefore 'squashed' up by the

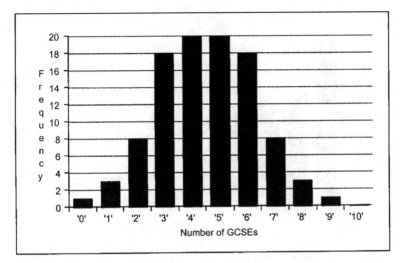

Figure 3.4: Distribution of GCSEs among candidates (high score)

limit of zero). In this case, even if all students gained one more GCSE, then the benchmark figure for the school would rise only to 12%. Increases in terms of absolute percentage scores are clearly much more difficult for low-attaining schools (but this phenomenon is never acknowledged by policy-makers or school 'improvers').

A similar problem occurs at the other end of the attainment spectrum, when comparing an average and a high-attaining school. This gives the GCSE benchmark score the typical S shape rather than a straight line growth. Many other social science phenomena are similar in having the 'threshold' and 'saturation' phase created by the limits of 0% and 100%, which means that they must be handled with care. At the 50% mark, where the distribution is taller, a small movement along the x-axis (representing a change in the number of GCSEs per student) would produce a disproportionately large change in the percentage attaining the benchmark. At either end (near 0% and 100%), a much larger change on the x-axis would be needed to produce the same effect. A more technical way of summarizing this whole section is that 'method' of differences between percentages, like differences between raw-scores, is not 'composition invariant'. If we cannot use differences in percentages (or simple frequencies) to measure differences between groups or changes over time, then what can we use? The standard reputable approach in social science is to use indices.

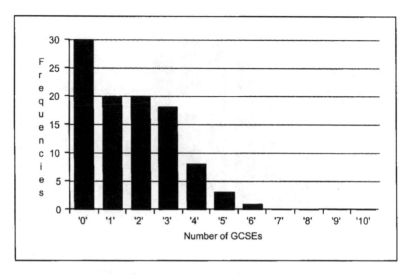

Figure 3.5: Distribution of GCSEs among candidates (low score)

THE INDEX WARS

Consider the following example. A researcher collects secondary data from a government department about the number of students from each ethnic group (as defined by the Registrar General for the population Census, see Chapter Five) at universities in England and Wales over the last five years. The researcher is also given access to the total number of students attending universities over the past five years. The intention of the research is to decide whether universities have widened participation rates for students from ethnic groups other than those classified as 'white'. The researcher calculates the percentage of the total student population who are in each ethnic group for each of the five years. The researcher finds that the percentages at university in England and Wales of all ethnic groups other than 'white' have increased, while the percentage classed as 'white' has declined in each of the five years. These findings are published as evidence that participation by ethnic minorities has widened, such that the student population is now a better reflection of the total population of England and Wales. Can you see why this conclusion is unsafe? If so, you are well on the way to understanding a further reason (stemming partly from the politicians' error) why we often need to use special approaches to analysing secondary data (indices).

The researcher in the example above should actually be tracking *two* trends over time. The first is the proportion of ethnic groups in universities, and the second is the proportion of the same groups in the total population. It is, of course, possible for the proportion of white students at university to decrease but for the proportion of white members of the population to decrease even faster, meaning that universities are actually increasing their over-representation of the white population. What is needed is a way of comparing the number of white students (w), the number of white members of the population (W), the total number of students (t) and the total number of people in the population (T). One formula (for the segregation ratio, see Gorard and Fitz 2000) is: $SR = (w/t) / (W/T)$. If SR equals 1 then the group in question is perfectly represented. If it is less than 1 the group is under-represented, so that .5 means that the group has only half the expected representation. If the ratio is greater than 1 the group is over-represented, and so on (you may prefer to use the logarithm of the ratio, so that divergence from 1 becomes an equal-interval value). Once you have grasped this useful proportionate approach you can see that you could substitute males and females (or any categories you want) for white and non-white. You could substitute owning a house or requiring heart surgery (or again any measure you want) for attendance at university. The segregation ratio is a general measure of unequal representation, which can be used to make safer comparisons over time, place and other categories because it takes into account changes in both of the proportions involved.

In our example, the segregation ratio has a key problem, which is that it can only tell us about the overall figures. It may be that the number of white and non-white (or male/female or whatever) students was a perfect reflection of the population composition (where 80% of the population and 80% of students are white, for example). The segregation ratio is, therefore, 1. But there could still be considerable inequality in the system if the two groups were disproportionately represented in different universities (in the old and the post-1992 universities for example). What is also needed is a measure of the distribution of the two groups across all institutions. One formula (for the segregation index, see Gorard and Fitz 2000) is: $S = \Sigma[|w_i/W - n_i/N|]/2$. Here we are considering the pattern of distribution between the universities, rather than simply comparing the population of all universities with the total population. The value w_i is the number of white students in University i, W is the total number of white students in all universities, n_i is the number of students in University i, and N is the total number of students in all universities. The | | symbols mean that we are interested only in the absolute difference between w_i/W and n_i/N (termed the residual), ignoring negative signs. The Σ symbol represents the sum of this difference for all cases.

Using the hypothetical values in Table 3.3, the segregation index is half the sum of the residuals (ignoring their signs). 80/300 minus 100/600 equals .1 and so on. The total of these residuals is .33 (one third) and half of that is around .17. This is a measure of how segregated this imaginary university system is. Strictly speaking it is the 'exchange proportion', which is the proportion of the white students who would have to be exchanged with others in order to achieve a perfectly balanced distribution in all universities. In this example, half of all students are white. If these were evenly distributed then University 1 would have 50 white students (not 80), University 2 would have 100 (not 120), and University 3 would have 150 (not 100). If the 30 'extra' white students in University 1 and the 20 'extra' in University 2 were exchanged with non-white students from University 3, then there would be an even distribution of both white and non-white students. Since 50/300 is equal to .17, which is our calculated value for the segregation index, this tells us that the overall system is 17% segregated (or that 17% of white students would have to be moved to eliminate all segregation). As with the segregation ratio, this approach can be used with other categories (male/female, pass/fail etc.), other organizational units (such as hospitals or occupations instead of universities) and any number of cases. It is a general measure of unevenness, which can be used reasonably safely for comparisons of inequality across time, place and other categories.

As can be seen, both of the indices described so far are based on a comparison between the proportion of one group and the proportion of the total population in each unit of analysis. In my

Table 3.3: Worked example of segregation index

	White students	Total students	Residual
University 1	80	100	80/300 − 100/600
University 2	120	200	120/300 − 200/600
University 3	100	300	100/300 − 300/600
Total	300	600	.33

experience these are the closest to what we mean when we talk about segregation or inequality. The segregation index is also identical in its properties to the Hoover index for income inequality, to the achievement gap, and, if the measurements are real numbers rather than categories, then also to the mean deviation (the sum of the differences between the mean score and each case, divided by the number of cases – see above). However, other indices have been proposed and some of these are also in common use (such as the dissimilarity index, which compares the proportion of one group with the proportion of its inverse group). Since the 1930s many social scientists have been involved in 'index wars', fighting over the relative merits of each. Even measuring the strength of association in a simple two-by-two table gives rise to controversies that span generations and still fascinate sociologists of science today (MacKenzie 1999). Pioneers in statistics, such as Pearson and Yule, could not agree how to perform this (apparently) simplest of calculations. The importance of this is, again, that the precise nature of your findings is often dependent on your selection of an appropriate index. Clearly you cannot use differences between percentages. What you use instead requires a deeper consideration of what precisely you are trying to measure. See Gorard and Taylor (2002a) or Massey and Denton (1988) for a summary of many different available indices (including rho, odds ratios, Yule's Q, and the matching marginals technique).

A FURTHER EXAMPLE OF SECONDARY ANALYSIS

An example of a project with significant findings using only secondary data and taking only ten days to complete is my work with several colleagues on the differential attainment of boys and girls (represented by Gorard 1999a, 1999b, 2001a, Gorard et al. 1999a, 2001a). The findings are still the subject of some debate, but they have clearly changed the field of research in which they appeared. Thus, as with the example in Chapter Three, they demonstrate the power and economy of working with secondary data. Having been commissioned to do the study by ACCAC (the Qualification, Curriculum and Assessment Authority for Wales), we were provided with some really powerful datasets by the Welsh Joint Education Committee and the statistics division of the Welsh Office (as it then was). These contained the public examination results for all children of the appropriate age to cohort at school in Wales from 1992 to 1997 inclusive, and summary figures back to

1970 where possible. The figures were broken down by each Key Stage, GCSE or A-Level grades, subject title and gender. This dataset was of higher quality than those used in many previous studies for a number of reasons, most notably because it contained only the results of the traditional 15-year-old cohort for GCSE, not including the figures for adult returners, for example. As with any official dataset there was still a considerable amount of cleaning and preparatory work to be done (see above). However, the stages of cleaning, analytic design, analysis and reporting took me no more than ten days of work in total (while my colleagues worked in parallel on other aspects such as the literature review and policy analysis).

The background was a 'moral panic' in the UK over the apparently growing under-achievement of boys at school and the introduction of a plethora of suggested remedies. My conclusions were contrary to this panic. These were that in examinations at all Key Stages, GCSE and A-Level there was no gender gap (i.e. no difference in overall patterns of attainment) at the lowest level of attainment in any subject. Approximately the same proportions of boys and girls of the relevant age were gaining the lowest level of each qualification (such as Level 1 at KS1 and grade G at GCSE). This was good news for the assessment system, but bad news for those who were then trying to explain the gender gap in terms of boys' laddishness and poor attendance at school. The gaps, where they appeared, were greatest at the highest level of attainment, mostly affecting a small proportion of the ablest boys and girls.

An overall gap 'in favour' of girls existed in every year back to 1970, meaning that for as long as records exist there is no evidence that boys have ever done better than girls up to GCSE level. From 1970 to 1986 this gap was small and approximately the same every year. From 1986 to 1988 the gap grew very rapidly, so rapidly in fact that this change cannot be due to changes in society, culture or pedagogy. Again, cultures of laddishness, seating arrangements in schools, mixed or single-sex classes and so on cannot be to blame. My tentative opinion is that the rapid change arose from the flurry of policy, curriculum and assessment changes (particularly the introduction of the GCSE, the change in standardizing results and the growth of coursework) at that time. Since 1988 this gap between the achievements of boys and girls has remained relatively static but declining somewhat over time. Therefore, there appears to be no empirical justification for the recent annual panics about under-achieving boys. The gaps between other social groups, such as by first language or between rich and poor, are anyway much larger than the gender gap. The gender gap in qualification, such as it is, also declines and even reverses among adults in later life. One interpretation of these findings is that a considerable amount of government and other money is being wasted in attempting to solve a problem of boys' under-achievement at school that does not in fact exist, while much larger systematic inequalities in education are being ignored.

I repeat, these findings were controversial when first published in 1998 (and probably still are). Nevertheless, my approach to the analysis of data in this field, coupled with the quality of the data I was given, means that the findings have had some impact on a debate of national importance. Yet the work cost me very little to do, and was mostly completed using a computer in my own home. No fieldwork. No statistical analysis in the sense that we normally mean when we use the term. I did not use anything more sophisticated than multiplication in my analysis (I used a combination of the approaches outlined in this chapter). Secondary analysis has a lot going for it.

COMMON PROBLEMS IN SIMPLE ANALYSES

This section presents what I consider to be some of the most common problems in the research literature when presenting simple summaries of numeric data (aside from the ubiquitous politicians' error discussed above). Several of these problems also relate to percentages – a genuinely useful but much abused way of presenting proportions.

- Using presentation to conceal numbers
- Saying the opposite to data presented
- Bogus averages
- Missing comparators

Using presentation to conceal numbers
Numbers have a rhetorical appeal all of their own, thereby giving apparent authority to a numeric presentation or article. Given this, it is very easy to allow the presentation of numbers to obscure the

actual evidence supposedly being revealed. Sometimes this may be unintentional on the part of the author, while on other occasions there may be a deliberate intention to deceive. An example is the appeal to 'accuracy' stemming from the presentation of numbers to an unjustified number of decimal places. I have seen a score for an attitude scale (see Chapter Five) presented as '4.29341', representing a mean from a series of integers based on a sample of 20. Is the author really wishing to argue that their scale is accurate to five decimal places?

I recently read a report which stated that 60% of the population have a computer at home, and that 40% of these had access to the Internet at home. The word 'these' is used ambiguously. Later in the same piece, the figures were used in a way that made it clear that the author believed that 40% of the population had access to the Internet (not the true figure of 24%, or 40% of 60%). The first is certainly what some political observers have taken it to mean.

In another example, Swadener and Hannafin (1987) converted the responses of the 32 'subjects' in their study into percentages, so that each individual's response is reported in the paper as 3.1%. Having effectively obscured the small size of their sample from the casual reader, they then proceed to divide the cases into two groups by level of attainment on a test, and then divide each of these groups by sex. Eventually they have some groups with as few as five cases. When they compare the resulting four groups in terms of their responses on the main variable for the investigation (the perceived usefulness of computers) they find no significant difference (between the groups of five people). This is then reported in the abstract as their overall finding – that gender and ability make no difference to use of computers! The finding should not be seen as convincing since the numbers involved are too small, but I suspect some readers, perhaps even some referees of the paper, remained unaware of this owing to the authors' use of percentages for very small numbers. I believe that 'percentage' implies 'in every hundred', so as a rule of thumb I recommend only using percentages for cases numbered in hundreds.

Another common example of disinformation, this time from psychology, appears in the labelling of graphs. In a paper by Pike and Forrester (1997) seven ostensibly similar graphs are presented. Six of these have the origin of the y-axis at zero, but the seventh has the origin at 3.4. No reason is given for this, but the effect is to make the variations in the seventh graph appear much greater. Watch out for this, as it is a common problem (especially in media reporting). The seven graphs are presented as line graphs. The lines connect two points on the x-axis representing, for example, 'use of stories' or 'textbooks'. These two points are categories, and the line is therefore misleading, whereas a bar chart should be preferred (see above). Other problems in the paper include the lack of specification of: the population, the method of sample selection, the number of schools in the study and the size of each of the age groups involved. These serious omissions are not due to lack of space, since a large amount of apparently irrelevant information is given instead. As with the previous paper, the authors' main conclusion was the absence of an effect between groups. Yet with six unspecified groups from a total sample of 62, perhaps little else could be expected (see Chapter Four). This paper had been peer-reviewed before publication in the journal *Educational Psychology*, and was a report of a study funded by the ESRC. It therefore represents work supposedly near the pinnacle of UK social science today.

Saying the opposite to data presented

There are many examples of reported results in which the findings presented in tables are not in agreement with the accompanying description written by the researcher. These could be due to misprints or to the inefficient working together of a team, in which one person does the calculation and the other the writing, or to simple slips. Slips are common when working with notions like occupational class and socio-economic status. Where class is measured on a numbered scale it is traditional for more prestigious ('higher') classes to be denoted by lower numbers (see Chapter Five). So where a figure for class gets lower (i.e. smaller) it actually represents a move towards a higher class. This could explain what happened in Waslander and Thrupp (1997), for example. They claim in their text that certain schools have moved towards a pupil body with a more prestigious class profile, whereas their tables make it clear that the opposite happened (see Gorard 2000b for more on this and other examples).

Bogus averages

Perhaps because computers/calculators are so accommodating and will find the average of any column of figures we want, the use of bogus averages is frighteningly common. These arise when figures are added together and divided by the number of figures, even where each figure is not of equal importance (or even where they are not real numbers). For example, if the average number of cases of a particular disease was 12 from 1995 to 1999, and the average was 18 for 2000, it is not the case that the average for 1995 to 2000 is 15 calculated as half the total of 12 and 18. The average should be (5x12 + 18)/6, or 13.

In an example of this type of error, Noden (2000) calculates the local level of socio-economic segregation in secondary schools using a specialist index of the type described above. This is fine. He then proceeds to calculate the national level of segregation by finding the average of all of the local figures. Noden adds the indices for each Local Education Authority (LEA) and divides the total by the number of LEAs regardless of the size of LEAs (and it should be recalled that the smallest LEAs have one secondary school and the largest have hundreds of schools). Therefore, if Merthyr Tydfil LEA (four schools) had a segregation index of 0 (no segregation at all) while Essex LEA (380 schools) had a segregation index of 1 (total segregation), then their 'average' according to Noden would be 0.5. The 'average' of these two areas should actually be close to 1 (the score for the majority 380 schools). If after a number of years, the index for Merthyr was 1 and for Essex it was 0, Noden would conclude that average segregation had not changed and was still 0.5, while it would actually have reduced considerably from near 1 to near 0. A simple arithmetic slip such as this leads to clearly bogus 'findings', but this (and it was not the only serious error) was not picked up by the peer-review system for the distinguished journal in question.

Missing comparators
One of the most pervasive and hard to eliminate errors in simple data analysis is the omission of a crucial comparator. This allows writers to present one set of results as though they were in contrast to another, as yet unspecified set. If done smoothly, many readers will never notice the error. Studies with missing comparators are widespread, almost by design, in a lot of what is termed 'qualitative' research. Social exclusion, for example, is commonly investigated through a consideration of the supposedly excluded group by itself, giving the reader no idea of how different the experience of this group actually is from the implicit 'included' group (who are often not even defined). This leads to very similar problems to that involved in using typical rather than discriminating symptoms in making a diagnosis (see above). However, this fatal flaw underlying almost all work reporting 'qualitative' analysis is not our principal concern here.

As a simple example of the power of this error in dealing with numeric data, look at the following question: 'A large survey discovered that fewer than 5% of 21-year-olds who had passed one or more A-Levels were unemployed. Why is this not necessarily evidence that passing A-Levels helps people to avoid unemployment?'. When I used this as part of an examination for a cohort of 245 second- and third-year Social Science undergraduates I received some very imaginative replies about the difficulties of establishing comparable qualifications for A-Levels, and alternate definitions of unemployment depending on whether full-time undergraduates themselves could be included in the study. All of these answers gained some credit. Only two candidates pointed out that they would, in any case, require the equivalent rate of unemployment for 21-year-olds *without* A-Levels. Only two. That is the power of the missing comparator (I therefore suggest no general criticism of the ability of these students). So widespread has this error become that it can almost be accounted a technique, used most prominently by politicians and by the media in reporting crises in public policy (e.g. Ghouri 1999).

As a more complex example, imagine being faced with the following realistic problem. Around 1% of children have a particular disease. If a child has the disease, then he or she has a 90% probability of obtaining a positive result from a diagnostic test. Those without the disease have only a 10% probability of obtaining a positive result from the diagnostic test. If all children are tested, and a child you know has just obtained a positive result from the test, then what is the probability that he or she has the disease? Faced with problems such as these, most people are unable to calculate a valid estimate of the risk. This inability applies to relevant professionals such as physicians, teachers and counsellors, as well as researchers (Gigerenzer 2002). Yet such a calculation is fundamental to the assessment of risk/gain in a multiplicity of real-life situations. Many people who do offer a solution claim that the probability is around 90%, and the most common justification for this is that the test is '90% accurate'. These people have confused the conditional probability of someone having the disease given a positive test with the conditional probability of a positive test given that someone has the disease. The two values are completely different.

Of 1,000 children chosen at random, on average ten will have this disease. Of these ten children with the disease, around nine will obtain a positive result in a diagnostic test. Of the 990 without the disease, around 99 will also obtain a positive test result. If all 1,000 children are tested, and a child you know is one of the 108 obtaining a positive result, what is the probability that he has the disease? This is the same problem, with the same information as above. But by expressing it in frequencies for an imaginary 1,000 children we find that much of the computation has already been done for us. Many more people will now be able to see that the probability of having the disease given a positive test result is nothing like 90%. Rather it is 9/108 or around 8%. Re-expressing the problem has not, presumably, changed the computational ability of readers, but has, I hope, changed the capability of many readers to see the solution, and the need to take the base rate (or comparator) into account.

The same approach of simplification can also help us to overcome what has been termed the 'prosecutor fallacy' (Gigerenzer 2002). In judicial proceedings (and media reporting), forensic evidence (such as a fingerprint or DNA profile) is used to make a match with a suspect. Prosecutors tend to use the probability of such a match (e.g. 1 in 10,000) as though it were the reverse of a probability of guilt (9,999 in 10,000). However, they have to also argue that there is no human error in the matching process, that the match signifies presence of the suspect at the crime scene, that presence at the scene necessarily entails guilt, and so on. Above all, they have to demonstrate that the number of potential suspects is so small that a 1 in 10,000 chance is the equivalent of 'beyond reasonable doubt'. If the crime took place in a city of 1 million people, and if we make the favourable assumption that potential suspects are limited to residents only, then 1/10,000 means that 100 residents will have just such a forensic match. Thus, the suspect has a 1/100 probability of guilt (on this evidence alone). This is much higher than for an average resident of that city (and therefore germane to the case without being conclusive) but much lower than 9,999/10,000. The importance of this error and others like it is hard to overestimate in law, medicine and beyond. But again, presenting the probabilities as frequencies makes the calculation much easier to follow.

This chapter has considered some elementary forms of analysis, leading to descriptive statistics. As you will already have seen, there are serious debates and misunderstandings even at this simple level of analysis (and we have not even begun looking at what most people think of as 'statistics'). Please do not be scared by this statement – rather the reverse. Be empowered. If you have followed most of the book so far then your understanding of 'quantitative' research is already far higher than that of the majority of social science researchers. If, on the other hand, you found it difficult then remember that you are not alone. For a reminder of simple calculation techniques and an introduction to probability, the use of spreadsheets and simple descriptive statistics see Hinton (1995), Creighton (2001) or Rowntree (1981). Phillips (2000) explains statistical concepts using examples of each from political science, psychology, education, social work and sociology. For more on the initial use of SPSS see Solomon and Winch (1994), for example. For a simple introduction to statistical tests see Clegg (1992), and for more on SPSS see Pallant (2001) or Norusis (2000). Dale et al. (2000) give practical advice on using software with the small area census. The next chapter looks at the process of sampling.

—4

Sampling: the basis of all research

In *How to Lie with Statistics* Huff (1991) quotes a report from one of the early Hispano-American wars. During this conflict the casualty rate in the US navy was approximately 10 in every 1,000. During the same period the number of deaths among inhabitants of New York was approximately 20 in every 1,000. A newspaper reporter might therefore conclude that it is generally safer to fight in a war than it is to live in New York. If you can see why such a conclusion is invalid then you are well on the way to understanding the significance of the material in this chapter. In many cases the apparent conclusions of our research are determined less by the social reality under investigation and more by the nature of the samples we use to collect data from. Sampling is therefore the basis of all research.

WHY DO WE USE SAMPLES?

I may have exaggerated slightly in calling sampling the basis of all research but not by much (see Gilbert 1993). It is true that a high-quality sample alone does not guarantee a successful piece of research and that many 'famous' pieces of work have not used particularly impressive samples. Piaget and Freud are widely used examples, but whether their contributions are empirically meritorious would have to be the subject of another book. In order for your work to have the widest appeal it is important to work through several stages, at least informally. It is also important that you refer to the decisions you make at each of these stages when you subsequently publish the work.

The first and perhaps most commonly omitted stage in sampling is deciding why you need to use a sample at all. Not all research is based on samples. Even discounting solely theoretical writing, it is not clear that all empirical research should involve a sample. Much of my own work has not involved sampling in a strict sense, using instead data relating to whole populations. In many respects, and wherever possible, it is preferable to use such complete datasets rather than to introduce the additional bias and error involved in selecting a sample (although a good sample can be better than an inaccurate set of figures for a population). This approach has been considered further in Chapters Two and Three.

The main reason that samples are used is to save time and money for the researcher. Sampling is a useful short-cut, leading to results that can be almost as accurate as those for a full census of the population being studied but for a fraction of the cost. Most studies are subject to a law of diminishing returns, in that after a certain number of cases/individuals have been involved each successive case is likely to add little to our understanding and do little to change any emerging patterns. A second reason for using a sample is that many methods of formal data analysis are based explicitly on sampling theory. Most notably, all the statistical tests of significance described in later chapters of this book assume that the data was collected from a sample drawn independently and randomly from a previously defined population. In the absence of secondary data relating to the entire population, a high-quality sample is a necessary precondition for the pursuit of high-quality and therefore safe research findings.

In conducting research bear in mind throughout the sampling procedure that you are using a sample because you are unable to use the entire population for a range of pragmatic reasons. Choosing to use a sample is the first in a series of compromises that you are bound to make as part of the research process. Keep a log of your reasons for using a sample and rehearse them whenever you publish your work. As with all such decisions you will not be able to persuade all readers that they would have done the same as you (if population figures for your variables are already freely available, for example), but you can at least make them aware that you have considered the alternatives and rejected them for substantial reasons.

DEFINING THE POPULATION

The purpose of sampling is to use a relatively small number of cases to find out about a much larger number. The group you wish to study is termed the 'population', and the group you actually involve in your research is the 'sample'. When you have collected results from the sample you will want to generalize (or apply) your results to the population. Since the population is the group to whom the results can be generalized it should always be defined in advance as the target of your research (e.g. social workers in New Zealand, or third-year university students in Scotland, or anyone working in the US steel industry). It is also perfectly possible to have a population consisting of institutions such as prisons or commercial companies, or artefacts such as examination papers, for example. Whatever your unit of population, the same logic as described below applies, but your 'respondents' would represent the prisons and so on, rather than individuals. For simplicity it is assumed in most of this chapter that your population and sample consist of individual people.

It is only from your previously defined population that the sample will be drawn, and of which the sample will be representative. Therefore if, for example, you have the resources to carry out research in the immediate area of your home or institution only, you cannot have a national or regional population. Anything you discover in your research will apply only to your immediate area. A sample drawn from the nurses in one Health Authority has nurses in that Authority as its population. This may sound obvious, but is easily overlooked in practice. Other Health Authorities may note your findings with interest but logically there is no contradiction if they deny that the results are relevant to them (because many of the local socio-economic conditions differ between Authority areas perhaps). The researcher sets out to generalize only to the population from which the sample was drawn.

In an ideal study you will be selecting cases from the population at random (by chance) to form your sample. Thus, you need to start with a list of all cases in the population and give each of them a non-zero chance of being selected. Any case that, in reality, has zero chance of being included in your study is not in fact in the population. This is another way of defining the population to which your results generalize. It is the list of all the cases which could be, or could have been, picked as part of your sample.

The list of all these cases is called a 'sampling frame'. One reason why it is given a special name (not population list) is that in real life (not an ideal study) your sampling frame will be an incomplete list of the population. You may know or suspect that the best list you can achieve has gaps, but you may not know how to rectify these gaps. For example, a household survey based on the electoral register will lead to several discrepancies and omissions. The register will be out of date, for however recent it is at least some people will have moved since, and it will always be incomplete since some people simply do not return the form for the register. Similarly, a survey of pupils drawn from those present in school on the day of the study will lead to notable omissions, such as the long-term sick, those excluded or suspended from school and those with a pattern of unauthorized absences. The first survey is likely to under-represent the most mobile elements of society, whether 'transients', travellers, or professionals who tend to work in national organisations and structures. The second survey is likely to under-represent those least committed to attending school. In both cases, these limitations to the sample should be published with the results and their likely impacts taken into account in assessing bias. This may be a key sign of 'slippage' between the ideal and the actual.

As your sample design progresses these slippages will increase, and each one weakens the force of your findings, and this is only for the sampling stage, not counting the compromises you will also be forced to make in collecting and analysing the data. Some researchers appear to behave as though the existence of these compromises means that rigour is impossible and they can therefore do pretty much as they like. On the contrary, I am advocating being realistic about slippages from the ideal, documenting them, publicizing them and above all worrying about their effects. Anxiety is therefore a very natural and healthy (for the research at least) state of mind for a good researcher.

In a possibly apocryphal PhD viva in my department a candidate studying truancy from school was asked whether he thought in retrospect that talking to the pupils at school on the day of the fieldwork only had been a mistake. The candidate did not get a PhD and the supervisor did not get any more candidates. This type of problem is frighteningly common for very practical, but rather lazy reasons. Captive audiences make convenient pseudo-samples. For example, almost the whole field of participation studies in adult and continuing education has been based on data gathered from participants in adult education (often from the same institutions as the researcher). The resulting notions of widening access to participation in adult learning by breaking down barriers such as cost and travel are therefore based solely on the views of those who are already participants. Rarer and more expensive studies of non-participants who can be contacted only via door-to-door work reveal a somewhat different picture (see Gorard et al. 1999b).

In some approaches to sampling it is not necessary to have an actual list of the entire population, which may be too long or too expensive to obtain (but note that some companies maintain commercial databases of addresses). The important thing is that such a list is at least possible. If obtaining a full sampling frame is too difficult, an acceptable compromise alternative is to characterize the population in terms of groups created by theoretically important variables. In this approach, rather than simple random selection of cases the researcher is working towards a clustered or a stratified sample (see below). These are both weaker alternatives, flouting the cardinal principle of statistical analysis that is computed on the basis of random sampling (see Chapter Six). Nevertheless, properly done, both clustering and stratification can lead to effective results.

THE SIZE OF THE SAMPLE

The third major issue of sampling concerns size. The sample must be large enough to accomplish what is intended by the analysis, and perhaps of the order of five or ten times the number of variables used. Small samples can lead to the loss of potentially valuable results and are equivalent to a loss of power in the test used for analysis (Stevens 1992). Cases in the sample will be lost at several stages of a study, and so redundancy needs to be built in. Surveys will have forms not returned, some questions not answered, some answered unintelligibly and some transcription errors, for example. Therefore, data will be lost before the analysis is even started. As soon as data is cross-tabulated, to look at the responses by gender, for example, the number of cases drops again, often at an alarming rate. All of these issues are considered in this section.

How large should a sample be? There are several methods to help decide on an appropriate sample size, but my general advice is to have as large a sample as possible. There are many reasons for saying this, but consider first my astonishment and appreciation when I started my research career at how easy it is to find people and organizations willing to take part in research. I once had a very brief job selling fire extinguishers door-to-door and it has produced in me a terrible fear, or terminal embarrassment, of approaching people in a 'cold' situation. Yet, I have learnt that approaching someone as a researcher, while still scary, is a lot easier and a lot more successful. So be ambitious in your sample size.

It is also the case that the actual number in your sample is not always the best determinant of your time or cost. You will naturally have to code and transcribe all cases, but this stage is a very small part of the research. Talking to ten people in one institution does not take ten times as long as talking to one person, because of the time taken to negotiate access and travel. Using a computer to add up a list of 1,000 figures takes no longer than using a list of ten cases. Posting 100 envelopes or sending 100 e-mails does not take proportionately longer than posting ten, and so on. In fact, once you have written an access letter, designed your research instrument and planned your analysis, then the actual process of collecting data can take very little time in comparison.

If you are looking for a difference or pattern among the data you have collected from a well-designed study, then your success or failure is determined mainly by four things. First: there is the effect size of the phenomenon you are studying (or, of course, its rarity). In social science research effect sizes are often very small. For example, studies of the impact of social work interventions have struggled to find evidence of any beneficial effect at all. Studies of the impact of schools on student examination results suggest that around 85–95% of the variation in results is due to the prior attainment and characteristics of the individual students. Only 5–15% at maximum is due to the impact of teachers, departments and schools and of any error component. Therefore, looking at differences *between* schools in terms of curricular development or management style involves examining small differences within what is already a fairly small difference between schools. In both cases, you would need a very large sample in order to have a chance of finding an impact of social work or schools.

Second: there is the variability of the phenomenon you are studying. The more variable is the thing (or things) you are studying, then the larger the sample needed. Imagine you were trying to find the average height of a group of people. If they are all of the same height then you need a sample of only one to be perfectly accurate in your measurement, but the more variation there is in the heights of this population the more people you need to measure to make sure the first few are not extreme scores. As another example, if you are interested in comparing the examination results by sex in two schools the results may be quite similar in many respects. The difference between the highest and lowest achievers in either school is likely to be much larger than the differences between the schools or between the sexes. If boys and girls are gaining fairly similar results in both schools, then the effect size you are looking for (difference between sexes) is small in comparison to the overall variability of your chief variable (examination results).

Third: there is the 'power' of the statistical test that you use to discern the pattern (power is explained more fully in Chapter Nine).

In summary, power is an estimate of the ability of the test you are using to separate the effect size from random variation. Fourth: there is the sample size.

To summarize: successful identification of social patterns is assisted by a strong effect, measures of low variability, using a powerful test and by having a large sample. A change in any one of these factors is *equivalent* to a change in any others. Increasing the effect size therefore has the same effect as using a more powerful test or decreasing the variability of the measure. However, of these four aspects only the sample size is clearly under the control of the researcher. Research questions are driven by importance, relevance, curiosity, serendipity and autobiography. Researchers do not decide what to research because of its variability or its effect size. Similarly, you will generally use the most powerful test that your design allows. Selecting a large sample is therefore the only chance you have to influence directly your chances of success. Note that even if you were to find *no* pattern this lack of pattern will be convincing to your audience only if the sample was large enough to have found one if it did exist.

In addition to these considerations, cases will be lost to attrition at every stage of the design. If you set out to get 100 respondents, maybe only 50 will agree to take part. Many of these will have missing variables (questions not answered, official records not found, etc.), and other cases may be lost at coding or transcription (researcher error or unreadable responses). You may actually achieve only around 30 fully completed responses for analysis. This emphasizes the same point about sample size. Whatever size you choose is simply the maximum you could achieve. From that point on your sample can only get smaller. So again, be ambitious.

Another important factor in choice of a sample size is the number of sub-groups needed for your analysis. Most social science research is not particularly directed at measuring the frequency of variables in a population. Rather, it is concerned with the distributions of those variables among identifiable groups in the population – occupations by sex, patterns of participation by age, absenteeism by socio-economic status. Once the population is broken into two or more groups then all of the comments made so far about sample size also apply to the size of the sub-sample for each group. Therefore, the more sub-groups used for the analysis the larger the overall sample needs to be, and this is one of many reasons why the researcher must design the analysis at the start of the project.

In my PhD work (see Gorard 1997b), although the total number of respondents (parents and children) was 1,267, only the 543 adults were asked about their religion, and only 272 of these gave intelligible responses to one of the other questions to which responses were made on a three-point scale. If parental religion is coded on a seven-point scale, the table cross-tabulating the two questions has seven by three (or 21) entries known as 'cells'. Any analysis of responses to the second question (about religion, put to adults) therefore has fewer than 13 cases per cell on average, making any test of significance very weak (see Chapter Six). It is quite frightening how suddenly the number of cases for analysis can 'melt' away. Such alarming calculations highlight the need for a very large initial sample, in order to draw conclusions of a bivariate nature. In designing your sample, you could start from the minimum number of cases required in each cell, multiply by the number of cells and then add 50% (and then some). As long as this is equivalent to several times the number of variables in the study, it should be a good sample size.

For the simplest bivariate analysis such as a chi-square test (see Chapter Six) it is recommended that we work with at least ten cases expected per cell. Using this base and multiplying by the number of cells in the most complex analysis required can produce a 'rule-of-thumb' guide to the size of the sample required (which assumes an even distribution of responses among categories). For example, if the most complex analysis is to be bivariate with one two-category variable (gender) and one seven-category variable (social class), then the table for analysis has 14 cells. If each cell is expected to have a minimum of ten cases (assuming nothing is known about the likely distribution between the categories yet), then the sample must have at least 140 cases. This kind of estimate is part of the reason why a detailed scheme for analysis should be created at an early stage (long before data is collected). It can be imagined how quickly the number of cells grows, and therefore how large a sample is needed, if a multivariate (more than two variables) analysis is attempted (see Chapter Ten).

In sampling theory the most important determinant of sample size is the required 'confidence interval' for the findings. The intention of the sampler is to generalize the results to the population of interest, and the confidence interval gives an indication of the accuracy of the findings as estimates for the population. For example, if I measure the age of one person in a crowded room this may be a poor guide to the average age in the room, but the more people I measure the better my estimate is *likely* to be. The larger the sample the more accurate the results are likely to be as an estimate for the population, and the smaller the corresponding confidence interval will be. This interval is defined in terms of a 'standard error'. The standard error is equal to the standard deviation (a measure of the variability in our sample, see Chapter Three) divided by the square root of the number of cases in the sample.

To make this clearer with an example, imagine we are looking at a numeric variable such as the age of the respondents. If we were to create lots of different high-quality samples taken from the same population, then each sample is likely to have a slightly different average age. The average age of each sample would be an estimate of the actual average of the population we are studying. Sampling theory suggests that the distribution of these sample averages will follow a well-known pattern known as the 'normal distribution' (the famous bell-curve, see Fielding and Gilbert 2000 for more on this). The characteristics of this distribution are known, and one of the things we know about it is that 68% of its area is within one 'standard error' of the population mean, 95% is within two standard errors and so on. Thus, if we take only one sample for our research (as we would usually do) this means that we could be 95% confident that the actual population average is within two standard errors of the average age we obtain for our sample.

So finally this is the point of the last two paragraphs. When taking a sample we can never be totally sure that what we find is actually very representative of the population, but we can control how *confident* we are about it. Since the quality of our result (e.g. the sample mean) depends on the variability of the item we are measuring (over which we have no control) and the size of the sample, it is clear that we can control the quality of our results only by varying the sample size. Suppose a sample produces a mean of three and a standard deviation of two on a particular variable, then the standard error is two divided by $\sqrt{N}$ (where N is the sample size). In this case, 95% of any sample means we could collect would lie between $3 - 1.96 \times 2\sqrt{N}$ and $3 + 1.96 \times 2\sqrt{N}$. If our sample size N is 9, then the sample mean of 3 tells you that the population mean probably lies between 1.7 and 4.3 (so we should not be very confident about our result). If N is 100, the sample mean of 3 tells you that the population mean probably lies between 2.6 and 3.4. But if you want to be within 5% of the likely population mean (i.e. from 2.85 and 3.15) then you need nearly 700 cases. See Hinton

(1995) for further details of using the standard error to produce confidence intervals.

When the standard error is plotted against the size of a sample (in this example for a variable with a standard deviation of one), it is immediately clear that increasing the size of your sample leads to a lower standard error and so to more accurate estimates of values (parameters) for the population (Figure 4.1). For samples less than 20, the standard error is very large, while for samples of 60 or more the standard error is very much smaller. After 80 or so cases, each addition to the sample size makes relatively little difference to the accuracy of your sample. So this visual representation helps to clarify the distinction between large- and small-scale research. Small-scale research could be defined as having a sample so small that the reliability of any results are too small for orthodox analysis, and where the addition or subtraction of one or two cases makes a considerable difference to the results (fewer than 30 cases perhaps). Large-scale research could be defined as having a sample of at least 60 cases for each group in the main analyses (i.e. 120 for a comparison of mean age between two groups, 180 for a comparison between three groups, and so on).

As noted above, your resources for the research, including the time and money available, are probably a strong influence on your chosen sample size but do try not to exaggerate their importance.

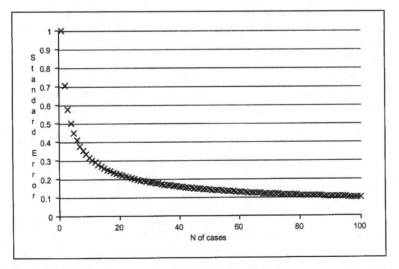

Figure 4.1: Standard error decreases with size of sample

On the other hand, if your consideration of other factors suggests that you need to use a sample size that simply cannot be achieved with the resources available to you, then the study must be modified. Do not go ahead in the knowledge that your sample size is totally unsatisfactory for the work you are doing. Incidentally, one of the factors you do not need to consider is the size of the population. The quality of a sample bears little relationship to its size proportionate to the population. A sample does not have to be a certain proportion of the population. If a sample of 100 cases was appropriate for a particular study, it would be appropriate whether the population was 1,000 or 1,000,000. Note, however, that if the sample to population ratio is high (because the population of interest is very small perhaps), then an equally effective sample can be designed with fewer cases (see Henry 1990 for details of this 'finite population correction').

An increase in the size of your sample is equivalent to an increase in the power of any statistical test or model that you use. Power, remember, is a measure of the test's ability to separate out genuine effects from random variation. In theory, you can try and estimate the sample size required more precisely via a 'power analysis'. In practice, power analyses are unrealistic – they need to be conducted in advance for each possible variable in the study, and require that the variance of each measure is known in advance (somehow). Any statistician who devised a new and more powerful test whose use with existing data was able to settle the debates that social scientists have been having for decades, or conversely to throw doubt on established explanations would be rightly famous. Improvements in method are thus often the precursor to an improvement in knowledge. Yet you could achieve exactly the same effect as this by using a larger sample than you anticipated or than is normal in your field. Be ambitious. In practice, you may find that tradition, your hunches, the number of sub-groups, your desire for accuracy and power and your resources will all point to a similar size of sample.

SELECTING THE SAMPLE

If you followed the steps above you now have a reason for using a sample, a defined population, a description of the population, either as a list of cases or as a summary of characteristics, and a target sample size. You are now ready to select cases from the population.

Random selection

In theory − sampling theory, that is − there is only one way to go about selection of a sample. A random number generator (computer, table, die, top hat with pieces of paper in it, etc.) should be used to select cases one after another from the sampling frame. In using a random number table or generator you number the cases in the population, start anywhere in the table or list and take the numbers and therefore the appropriate number of cases in sequence (ignoring any numbers out-of-range). This means, of course, that the sample could be very strange and non-representative of the population. However, the probability of this is small (by definition, since extreme distributions are less likely than representative ones). The larger the sample is the less likely such a 'freak' selection is.

Random sampling has two key advantages. It is free of the *systematic* bias that might stem from choices made by the researcher, and it enables the analyst to estimate the probability of any finding actually occurring solely by chance. Also, as discussed above, the sampling error can be used to estimate confidence intervals only where random sampling is used. Apart from the practical problems of obtaining an accurate list to work from and maintaining the sub-list of selected cases (which task can in any case be delegated to a computer), the technique of random sampling is also very easy − perhaps the easiest method available.

Probably the chief reason that simple random sampling is used so infrequently in social science research is that it produces a scattered sample (such as a few cases in every town). Where travel is involved in the fieldwork, clustered sampling is therefore often preferred (see below). Another slight problem emerges with the issue of replacement. Researchers generally do not want the same case to appear more than once in the sample, yet this is the possible outcome of true random sampling. A case is selected at random from the sampling frame and copied to the sampling list. When a second case is selected there is nothing to stop the randomizer from picking the same case again (equivalent to rolling two sixes in succession with a die). Generally the researcher prevents this by deleting selected cases from the sampling frame (equivalent to pulling raffle tickets from a hat) or rejecting any cases already selected. This solution, known as sampling 'without replacement', could be seen to bias the true random sample and so lose us some of the statistical 'high ground' that such samples occupy. However, if the sample is small compared with the population (i.e. the sampling fraction is low) then the probability of repeated selection is very low and the issue of replacement makes little practical difference.

Alternatively, either systematic or stratified selection can produce a sample very similar to a good random one. Systematic sampling is the simpler of the two, and more convenient. It involves selecting a random starting place on the list of potential cases, and then choosing the sample cases at equidistant points on the sampling frame (e.g. every 17th case from the list of cases in the population). Beware of periodicity (choosing the sixth apartment on every floor in a block with a multiple of six apartments per floor, for example). As long as the list is in no particular order, through having been shuffled, for example, then the process is equivalent to random sampling without replacement. This approach is even more convenient if used hierarchically, the researcher making systematic selections at progressively lower levels of aggregation. For example, you may select wards in a city, then streets in a ward, then households in each street (as long as the chances that each ward and street selected are proportional to its size). Already you should be able to see that this approach is more complex than simple random sampling.

Stratified samples are even more complicated. Here, cases are selected in proportion to one or more characteristics in the population. For example, if sex is considered relevant to the study and the population is 58% female, then the sample must be 58% female. In effect, the researcher creates two populations (men, from whom 42% of the eventual cases are selected, and women, from whom 58% of cases are selected). Within each stratum such as sex the cases still need to be selected randomly or systematically, else the sample merely becomes a quota one (see below). The number and type of characteristics used in this way (as strata) are chosen by the researcher on theoretical grounds of relevance to the study. The researcher must use or find expert knowledge to decide which characteristics of the population could be significant for the study findings, and then work out the pattern of distribution of these characteristics. This is not always an easy task, as the characteristics need to be considered in interaction, and the researcher may need to carry out a census anyway to uncover the nature of the population. So this approach to sampling is generally considerably harder than simple random selection. The researcher still needs a good reason not to use random sampling.

The stratified approach can lead to a high-quality sample by reducing the risk of a 'freaky' result, at least in terms of the strata characteristics. Its problems include the fact that it can require decisions about complex categories (race, occupation) or on sensitive issues (income, age). If several background characteristics are used then the selection process becomes difficult as each variable 'interacts' with the other. If both gender and occupational class are used, then not only must the proportions for gender and class be correct, but so too must the proportions for gender within each class (if 23% of the population are female and professional, this must be reflected in the sample).

For example, a study of motivation to become a teacher may be unable to obtain a list of all entrants to teacher training in a particular year (the population for the study). Many colleges will not release personal details to you, so you might decide to use as many cases as you can find that match, in aggregate, the characteristics of the population. Suppose that your knowledge of the field led you to believe that sex of trainees was an important variable, you would need to know the sex breakdown of all trainees (and such information is easier to obtain than a list of all trainees). If 40% of trainees were male, you would then set out to obtain a sample containing 40% men. Again, if you believe *a priori* that there will be different motivations for teaching different age groups then you need to know the breakdown of trainees between the post-compulsory, secondary, junior, infants and nursery sectors. If 30% of trainees were secondary-school specialists, then 30% of your achieved sample should be also. If 66% of secondary trainees in the population were male, you would also need to find this out (how?) and reflect this in your sample so that 20% (66% of 30%) of your sampled trainees were male secondary specialists, while the overall sample remained 40% male. If you also, quite reasonably, considered ethnicity, socio-economic status, prior qualifications or subject specialisms as important factors then the calculations would quickly become mind-boggling. You would need both to know the proportion of the population who were white, male, professional background, secondary, mathematics specialists with a first degree in a subject other than mathematics, and then you would need to reflect this in your sample. Such an example emphasizes two things. First: despite its lack of popularity, judging from its rarity in the literature, random sampling is actually a lot easier than stratified sampling. Second: even where the purpose of the study is to collect new data (on the motivation of trainee teachers, for example), it is often important to conduct a fairly detailed secondary analysis first in order to identify the characteristics of the population being studied (see Chapter Two).

Clustering

Using a clustered sample implies not so much a difference in selection procedures as a difference in defining population units. The cases we are interested in often occur in natural clusters such as institutions. So we can redefine our population of interest to be the clusters (institutions) themselves and then select our sample from them using one of the above procedures. The institutions become the cases, rather than the individuals within them. This has several practical advantages. It is generally easier to obtain a list of clusters (employers, schools, voluntary organisations, hospitals, etc.) than it is to get a complete list of the people in them. If we use many of the individuals from each cluster in our selected sample, we can obtain results from many individuals with little time and travel, since they will be concentrated in fewer places.

For example, in a survey of teachers we might select a random sample of 100 of the 25,000 schools in England and Wales, and then use the whole staff of teachers in each of these selected schools. As with systematic sampling, it is important that the odds of a cluster's being selected are in proportion to the number of individuals it represents (i.e. schools with more teachers should be more likely to be picked). Despite this complication in the calculation (and the need to have at least some information about each cluster), this approach is growing in popularity (see Chapter Eight). Its chief drawback is the potential bias introduced if the cases in the cluster are too similar to each other. People in the same house tend to be more similar to each other than to those in other houses, and the same thing applies to a lesser extent to the hamlets where the houses are (people in each post-code area may tend to be similar), and to the regions and nations where they live (and so on). This suggests that we should try to sample more clusters and use appropriately fewer cases in each cluster (and see Chapter Ten for another approach to overcoming this problem, known technically as 'auto-correlation'). As usual, the precise compromise between resource limitations and the ideal is a judgement by the researcher. Being aware of, and recording, this judgement is probably the most important safeguard against the undue influence of bias.

Other sources of bias

As we shall see, statistical analysis usually proceeds as though the cases in a study are independent of each other with an equal probability of selection, and that random sampling has been used.

Alternatively, clustering and stratification techniques can be used to select cases as outlined above, and produce a sample that is similar to a good random sample, in which all population elements have a known non-zero probability of selection. If any other method of selecting a sample is used, standard techniques of statistical analysis are inappropriate (Lee et al. 1989).

One apparent deviation from this principle of equal/proportionate probability of selection is where a boosted sample is used. In this design, the probability of selection is boosted for some rare sub-groups to ensure that sufficient of them are obtained for a comparison to be made (black ethnic groups in northern Scotland might be a current example of a rare sub-group, usually insufficiently represented in a regional poll for any serious analysis to proceed). This approach is valuable and perfectly valid as long as the then over-represented cases are re-weighted (see below).

A classic problem in sampling comes from bias through the use of 'volunteers'. Whether you provide an incentive for participants or use captive subjects, it is quite clear that those who are willing to devote an afternoon to taking part in your study could be very different from those who are not. Captive subjects are those forced to take part. On many university psychology courses, for example, undergraduates are required to sign a contract agreeing to take part in a certain number of studies as a condition of their acceptance. This can understandably lead to many problems such as sullenness and even the outright sabotage of experiments. At best it means that much of what psychology tells us applies only to the population of captive psychology undergraduates, and beyond specific groups does not have much external validity. Nineteenth-century psychology was often based on what researchers found out about themselves (introspection), while later twentieth-century psychology was chiefly based on what psychologists found out about each other. There are some hopeful signs that in the twenty-first century psychology is becoming more concerned with people at large.

NON-PROBABILITY SAMPLES

An implicit assumption has been made in the chapter so far that our sample will be what is termed a 'probability' sample, where cases will be selected either randomly or systematically. There are two good reasons for this focus. First: this kind of sampling is generally more technical than its alternatives, so requiring more explanation for a new researcher. Second: this kind of sampling is preferable in almost every way to any of its alternatives in all research situations. Thus, a simple guideline would be that probability samples should be used in all circumstances in which they are possible. A high-quality sample is crucial for safe generalization to take place (for high 'external validity'). Non-probability samples should therefore be reserved only for those projects in which there is no other choice.

The most common and over-used form of non-probability sampling is the convenience sample, composed of those cases chosen only because they are easily available. A researcher standing in a railway station or shopping centre or outside a student union and stopping people in an *ad hoc* manner would thereby create a convenience sample and not a random one. This approach is often justified by the comment that a range of people use such places, so the sample will be mixed in composition. The approach is sometimes strengthened, for example in market 'research', by determining quotas for groups of cases (such as men and women) and then deselecting people (e.g. by not stopping them) once the quota for each group is filled. Note that this is different from stratification where a *probability* sample is created within each stratum. I hope that by the time you have finished this chapter you will be clear how threatening a quota design can be for the security of your findings. Large numbers of people rarely travel by rail, shop in city centres or use a student bar. These people would tend to be excluded from your sample. The time of day could make a difference. Those in paid employment may be less likely to be in shopping centres during the day, while older people may be less likely to go out at night. The researcher may also make (perhaps unconscious) selections, by avoiding those who are drunk or who appear unconventionally attired or coiffured. Even with a quota system, therefore, convenience sampling introduces a very real danger of biasing the sample, and it does so unnecessarily in far too many studies.

Non-probability samples are more properly used for pilot studies (see Chapter Five), where the intention is to trial a research design rather than collect usable data. Even here, however, a first-class pilot study will trial the actual sampling method to be used along with the other components of the design. Sampling is so important as a stage in research that it is not clear why it is so often omitted from the pilot.

Non-probability samples are also more properly used when the intention is not to collect data on a general population but to use 'cultural experts' to help explain a social process. We might want to ask directors of health trusts how they allocate their annual budget, or headteachers how they allocate the places in their school. We may want to ask politicians about the background to a new policy. In each example we are approaching the informants as experts. In some studies the number of experts is so limited that we must use whoever is available to us, since there are not enough to select cases at random from a list. In these cases, we must accept that probability sampling is not possible, and so record our reasons and try to estimate the possible bias that will result from using our judgement concerning whom it is appropriate to select. *If there is no other way.* In the example of headteachers, of course, it may well be possible to produce a random sample even when our intention is to consult them as experts. The key issue is not what our sample is for, but how small the population of experts is. Of course, with a very small population, or a very high sampling fraction, we end up with an incomplete census and not a 'sample' at all.

Perhaps the clearest example of the appropriate use of a non-probability sample is where a snowball technique is necessary. In some studies, of drug use, truancy or under-age sex, for example, we are unable to produce a sampling frame even where the population of interest may be imagined as quite large. Indeed, one of our key research objectives may be to estimate the size of an unknown population. In such a project we might quite properly approach a convenience sample to get us started, and once we have gained their trust ask each individual to suggest other informants for successive stages. In this way, we hope that our sample will 'snowball'. As with small populations, difficult-to-reach populations can also make probability sampling impossible. We simply accept this and do the best we can with what is available. This approach is very different from using a convenience sample simply because it is... convenient.

There are advanced techniques available to help estimate the size of unknown populations. For example, an approach developed from ecological studies involves using the intersection between successive samples to gauge the size of the group from which they come (known as 'mark-recapture'). In ecology, a sample of a species of birds may be selected and tagged. Later, a second sample is selected. The proportion of already tagged birds in the second sample will be related to the total number of birds. If a high proportion are already tagged it means that the population will be not much larger than the sample size. If a low proportion are tagged, the population will probably be much larger than the sample size. Similar techniques (using more subtle tags!) can be used with homeless people or housebreakers, for example, to estimate the prevalence of these phenomena in society. However, we are then faced with several further problems, including the fact that the probability of any homeless person's being in the second sample may be affected by having been involved in the first, or that re-offending housebreakers may be simply less competent than those never caught. There are methods, known as adaptive sampling (Thompson and Seber 1996), to overcome these practical difficulties, but they are very complex and reinforce my message above. A probability sample is to be preferred, not only because it is superior in quality but also because it is generally easier to work with.

It is interesting that, despite their patent disadvantages, non-probability samples are by far the most common type in the literature, mostly used without any apparent justification at all. By way of example, the first four issues of the *British Educational Research Journal (BERJ)* in the year 2000 contained 28 articles. In my opinion, 14 of these were non-empirical or else non-systematic summaries of previous research (i.e. not research syntheses), ten used small non-probability samples without any attempt at explanation or justification, and only four used probability-type samples of any kind. The reports for these four contained substantially more about the nature of the samples and about their research design in general. *BERJ* is one of the most widely circulated journals in the UK, and one that insists on a substantial research content for all of its articles.

NON-RESPONSE

In an ideal world you, as a researcher, would select a high-quality sample, and all of those people selected to participate in the study would agree to do so. In reality this will not happen. Cases will be lost to non-response in at least two ways. Some cases will provide no data at all. People selected by you will refuse to participate in your experiment or will not return your questionnaire. Part-cases will also be lost where only incomplete data is collected. You may face people dropping out during an experiment yielding a pre-test score but not a post-test score (see Chapter Eight). People may return a questionnaire but omit some questions through lack of motivation, incompetence or ignorance of the answer (see Chapter Five). All of these examples will cause problems through bias, equivalent to using an inferior sample and similar to the problem of volunteer bias. There are proven systematic differences (some apparently trivial) between respondents and others. Respondents tend to be more highly educated and have higher incomes, for example, than those who refuse to take part.

Once you have selected your ideal sample, one of your main priorities for the rest of your research design should therefore be to achieve that sample and minimize any non-response. Relevant issues discussed in later chapters therefore include methods of delivering surveys, simplifying experimental designs, asking non-threatening questions, negotiating access, using incentives, following up missing cases and even choosing the right colour of paper. If you have designed a good sample you want it to be as close to the ideal as possible. Therefore, make it as easy as possible for people to take part in the study. Incidentally, what you should not do is decide that, as some non-response is inevitable, you do not need a good sample design in the first place because 'it will only go wrong after all'. As we will see, each further stage in your design requires compromises and, as we have already seen, each stage within sampling, such as listing the population, may require compromises. If we introduce unnecessary weaknesses as well, we are well on the way to arguing that, as accuracy is not possible, we may as well make the results up (and I have heard a distinguished sociologist of education state in public that accuracy was less important to him than producing shocking 'results'; see in Gorard 2000b).

While 100% is an ideal rate of response, even figures close to this may lead to significant bias since the small group excluded by a high response rate could consist of the most extreme cases with the characteristics of non-responders (the 'distilled essence' of non-responders, if you like). It should also be recalled that the sampling frame may have already inadvertently excluded some of the more extreme cases, such as those not on the electoral roll or without a telephone or without access to the Internet. Nevertheless, it is almost certainly true that the nearer you are to 100% response the better. Some textbooks have published very low expected rates of response, to surveys, for example, and novices may find these very reassuring. But these figures often include the rates for long-winded market research, 'cold-calling' on the telephone and other poorly constructed designs. Using the approaches described in later chapters of this book it should be possible for an academic researcher to obtain much higher rates, such as 70% or above as a minimum. If non-response is small and apparently random in nature then we can ignore it, but there is already clear evidence from previous studies that non-response is non-random.

Whatever you do, there is likely to be some non-response in your sample (and there have been suggestions that average rates of response to surveys are declining over time – through societal research fatigue perhaps). This means that you should record (and report) the rate at which this non-response occurs, try to estimate the bias introduced as a result and consider methods of ameliorating it. This is not easy, but you as the researcher are in the best position to consider the likely impacts and decide how to improve the situation.

Recording and reporting response rates is a relatively simple task. You should record the different response rates to each item or each component of a design. You may like to distinguish, where possible, between a refusal to take part in the study (by saying 'no' to an interview, for example) and non-response (by not returning a postal questionnaire, for example). This could be useful in helping you form an estimate of bias. For in the same way as those who do not respond may differ systematically from those who do, those who refuse to take part may tend to differ in key characteristics from those who do not respond. Those not responding to postal requests are more likely to be transient and therefore to come from the extremes of any classification of socio-economic status (by being either homeless or employed in a national-based profession involving travel or more regular house-moving perhaps). Those returning a questionnaire uncompleted may be busier or less literate, for example.

Not all institutions and individuals asked to take part in a piece of research will agree, often because they are too busy. By necessarily using only those prepared to take part, a study is therefore open to the charge of bias. Questionnaires may be more readily completed by those who are more literate, opinionated or confident or who have greater leisure time. If a popular newspaper published a finding that 95% of the population were in favour of the restoration of capital punishment for a particular crime, because that was the supporting proportion of its sample on a phone-in poll, we would be doubtful of the value of its sample. Aside from the issue of the self-selected readership and the fact that people may call twice and be double-counted, there is also the question whether those in favour of capital punishment are more motivated to call because they wish to change the *status quo*.

One approach to estimating the bias involves looking at the order in which people respond. An argument can be constructed that those who reply later to a postal survey, for example, are more like those who do not respond at all than are those who reply early.

Thus, we can estimate the character of non-respondents by looking at the difference between early and late responders. This is certainly worth a try, and there is no harm in recording when and how a response appears and how much cajoling/reminding was necessary. However, other studies have suggested that the empirical basis for this approach is weak (Giacquinta and Shaw 2000). Using late returners to estimate the sample bias induced by non-returners may not be very effective and may even lead to a poorer estimate than the original.

Another common approach to dealing with non-response is to find suitable replacements for the missing cases. If you are conducting a postal survey of 100 people and 30 do not respond even after a reminder, then you can preserve your sample size by adding another 30 cases. Unfortunately even if your sample is stratified and you try to replace like with like in terms of your strata, you will still be left with the possibility that those who do respond are more alike in some way than those who do not (see below for an example of this from my own work). Replacement is a useful approach, but should always be accompanied by scrupulous records showing the response rate of the initial sweep (the first 100 in our example) as well as of the final achieved sample. Otherwise you could continue the process of replacement indefinitely and always get a perfect 100% 'response' rate.

Perhaps the most effective, but too rarely used method of controlling for non-response is to use weights. Weights are adjustments made to correct for the perceived bias in your achieved results by using post-stratification corrections. If you know that the achieved sample differs from the population in some crucial respect you can use corrective weights to produce a better estimate of your result. In fact, many sample designs implicitly require such weighting, which are therefore not optional extras and can have a fundamental effect on the outcomes (Lehtonen and Pahkinen 1995).

For example, imagine that you have collected a stratified sample of 1,000 respondents, of whom 600 (60%) live in urban/suburban areas and 400 (40%) live in rural areas. However, you had set out to achieve a proportion of 80:20 urban:rural respondents because the census of population for the region tells you that this is the actual proportion in your area of interest. Your sample therefore over-represents rural respondents. One of the substantive questions you asked this sample was whether they had considered more than one political party when deciding on their vote at a recent election. The overall result was that 440 (44%) had considered another party, and therefore the modal average (most frequent) response for your sample is 'no' (56%).

You then separate these responses by area of residence, and discover that 60% of the urban inhabitants but only 20% of the rural ones had considered voting for another party. This is a very large systematic difference. What difference might have been made if your sample had fully represented urban respondents, and these extra urban cases had answered the question about voting in the same proportions as we actually found? This is what weighting tells us. If we had achieved a sample of 800 urban and 200 rural cases and both groups had answered the voting question in the proportions we found, then we would expect 60% of the hypothetical 800 urban cases (480) and 20% of the 200 rural ones (40) to answer 'yes'. On this calculation, since area of residence makes such a difference and our sample over-represents the views of rural residents, our best estimate of the population figure considering another party would be 520 per 1,000. Therefore, the modal average response is actually 'yes', even though our achieved sample appeared to suggest 'no'.

Although this seems rather fiddly, most researchers could cope with it since the actual calculations would be performed by a computer package. The key role of the researcher is to decide, on theoretical or prior knowledge, which of the background variables form important strata. This is another reason why the use of secondary contextual data (see Chapter Two) is an important skill for all researchers. As with the original stratification of a sample, the complexity of weighting arises in the interaction of the strata. If, in the example above, you decide that sex of respondent is another important factor, then you will need to consider separately the four groups consisting of: male and urban; female and urban; female and rural; and male and rural. If you add ethnicity, first language, level of education or social class, then the calculations become mind-boggling, and these are only some of the 'standard' contextual variables. Therefore, as with stratifying, you need to select a few really crucial background variables for your specific study, and work with those only.

AN EXAMPLE OF SAMPLING

A genuine fully random sample is rare for many of the reasons given above. I have tended to work with clustered random samples, perhaps using schools as the unit of sampling (see for example

Gorard 1996, 1997b), or with systematic stratified samples (see for example Gorard et al. 1999c, 2001a, Gorard and Rees 2002). In the second of these studies I was trying to collect 1,100 retrospective life histories from the populations of three contrasting local authorities in industrial south Wales. Although it is normal for a study of this size to select a diverse and well-spread sample, which can then be divided into gender or class categories, since the differences in local economic effects are so varied in the UK a more focused study was required to make these local effects explicit. Three sites were chosen to represent the range of experiences in industrial south Wales. Bridgend could be briefly characterized as an expanding town, Neath Port Talbot as an established manufacturing conurbation and Blaenau Gwent as a depressed coalfield valley. Three electoral divisions (wards) were selected within each site to reflect the range and diversity of their social and educational conditions as evidenced by 1991 population census data. Secondary analysis was used to characterize the nine wards, the three sites and south Wales in terms of a range of social and educational measures capable of disaggregation at each level. This data provided the sampling frame for the survey and part of the context for the primary analysis (Gorard 1997c). Households in each division were identified from the electoral registers, which were the most accurate and up-to-date available listings of addresses. These lists were considered appropriate since the target population for the first wave was only those adults aged 35 to 64.

Systematic sampling was an appropriate method to use, but to avoid problems of periodicity and special methods of variance estimation, *repeated* systematic sampling was used. The sample was also stratified in an attempt to reduce the sampling variance and to ensure sufficient cases in certain categories, and this stratification was proportionate (i.e. the sampling fraction for each stratum was uniform within wards). Stratification was appropriate as the sample: population ratio was large and the population was well character-ized (Lehtonen and Pahkinen 1995). Four points were chosen at random in each electoral division and every nth household after those points was selected for inclusion in the survey as a primary respondent, with the ten subsequent addresses set aside as potential reserve respondents. The sampling fraction $1/n$ was similar for each division but was determined by the precise number of electors. A quota was devised such that half of the respondents in each electoral division were male and half female, while one third were aged 35 to 44, one third were 45 to 54 and the remainder 55 to 64.

The primary address was visited three times at different times of the day in successive weeks (to allow for holidays and shift working) until contact was made with one of the householders. In a house with two or more householders, either was interviewed, according to quota and as convenient. If the house was clearly empty (having been 'gutted' by builders, for example) or all of the householders were out-of-stratum, the first house on the reserve list became a new primary and the process started again. If the primary householder refused to take part or was not contacted after three calls, the first house on the reserve list was used instead, followed, if necessary, by the second reserve and so on. In the latter cases the response was recorded as a reserve for accounting purposes. This procedure of repeated systematic sampling produced a set of respondents stratified by age and gender within electoral divisions chosen to represent the educational and socio-economic diversity of the three research sites, which were themselves selected as representatives of the range of socio-economic experiences in industrial south Wales over the past 50 years (Gorard 1997c).

A second wave of the survey was based in the same areas as the first and was also stratified by gender and age. Half of the respondents in the second wave were aged 15–24 and half were 25–34. These became the two younger cohorts, so that the sample as a whole represented training experiences throughout working life from just before finishing compulsory education to retirement. However, in order that the study could also examine family influences more fully the two younger cohorts were selected by repeated systematic sampling from the children of the respondents in the first wave. Several of the respondents in the second wave therefore no longer lived in south Wales or even the UK. This second stage was similar in many ways to the method of boosting a sample in order to obtain a higher proportion of respondents with certain characteristics (SCELI 1991). The survey was designed to include at least 800 respondents in the first wave and at least 200 in the second. From this grand total of over 1,000, around 110 were selected strategically for in-depth interviews.

In using sites and wards as administrative units to select the sample, the survey can be described as 'complex', so that some standard statistical procedures might not be appropriate without weighting (Lee et al. 1989). Weighting was possible since the entire sampling frame for the survey at each stage of this multi-stage design was known, at least in principle, and each element had a known non-zero chance of being included in the sample since a record was kept of the probabilities of inclusion at each stage of the design. However, the sample was automatically self-weighting at the ward level since the probability of selection within a ward was proportionate to the size of the ward. Similarly, within each ward, although each household of whatever size had an equal chance of selection, the sample was of householders only and stratified by gender, therefore it was not necessary to correct for the probability of selection in terms of the number of people in the house, as has been done elsewhere (Gershuny and Marsh 1994).

Weights were used in this survey for two main reasons: to attempt a correction for missing values and to form a more reliable estimate of the population characteristics for industrial south Wales, since even a self-weighting sample can have non-response and design errors. Where a questionnaire was incomplete or had other missing values, a simple method of imputing the missing value was devised, if possible, such as using the mean of all other cases. To attempt a correction for bias in the sample through self-selection, where this was related to demographic composition, and at the same time expand the data to fit the background characteristics of industrial south Wales better, the responses were re-weighted via a post-stratification adjustment factor. This factor adjusted for the different response rates within categories and adjusted demographic variables to those of the known population. The adjustment factor is the population distribution divided by the sample distribution for each demographic sub-group. For example, if the proportion of men aged 35-44 in south Wales is 12%, and the proportion in the sample was 10%, the factor is 1.2. Weighting and imputing were used only for the production of descriptive statistics and the estimation of current population parameters. The analysis of the determinants of life histories covers 50 years from 1945 to 1996, therefore no one set of population characteristics from a snapshot date would be appropriate to use as the basis of weights for that whole period.

I have described my sampling procedure in this project in some detail as an example of how samples can be reported, and to show that, whatever its peculiarities, considerable care was taken to draw it, and to record what happened in doing so. My colleagues and I achieved 1,104 responses with a primary response rate of over 75%, and a sample almost perfectly stratified by age, sex and geography. In retrospect, however, I am fairly sure that the techniques used combined to over-represent the long-term sick and disabled since these would be more likely to be at home when we called. I can only guess this from evidence of the subsequent interview details, since disability was not recorded in the survey (as in retrospect it is clear that it should have been) and could not therefore be stratified or weighted. Since the sample was so large the work was partially contracted out to a professional company. It is therefore possible that some interviewers (paid on piece-work rate) would have been tempted to use the reserve households more often than the design allowed (differences between sub-contracted researchers in large studies is another important source of bias). If so, this would have the effect of further increasing the proportion of relatively house-bound respondents. The battle against bias is never won.

COMMON ERRORS IN WORKING WITH A SAMPLE

The following section summarizes some of the common problems relating to sampling as encountered in the research literature and in the work of research students. I have not repeated here what I consider to be the worst example (see above) of omitting from the sample the very people under study, by carrying out a study of absenteeism within an institutional setting, for example.

> - Not reporting the sample size
> - Not specifying the population
> - Ignoring drop-out
> - Using an unjustified non-probability sample
> - Not using weights
> - Obscuring the response rate

Not reporting the sample size

A report on the quality of research in education (Tooley and Darby 1998) found that in the *Oxford Review of Education*, for example, around one third of the empirical articles did not report their sample size (i.e. there is no mention of it and therefore no way of telling how large or small the sample is), another third reported size but gave no information at all about the method of selection, and the final third gave some generally inadequate information about size and selection. Very few researchers discussed the possible limitations of their approach. I suspect that this practice is at least as common in other fields (see Huberty and Olejnik 2002). Hardly any academic reports allow authors the space to describe their handling of missing, deleted and outlying cases. It means that the published methods of most studies would not allow another analyst to repeat the same analysis even with access to the same dataset (and of course the situation for 'qualitative' work is far worse in this respect). Any afternoon spent examining the contents of current journal issues in your local library will confirm the scale of these defects. It means, of course, that when a researcher claims that a certain proportion or percentage of individuals responded in a particular way, without specifying the actual number, we can have no idea of the confidence of their finding, and should, in all probability, ignore it as unsafe.

A specific example is provided by the writing of Cheung and Lewis (1998). Their study of the expectations of employers of school-leavers was reported in 14 pages, including a reference list of two pages. They include seven pages of background/introductory material but only a paragraph on the methods used. It is therefore very difficult to judge how important or valid their reported findings might be. Most crucially, they do not report their sample size, while all of their frequencies are presented as percentages (implying that the sample was in hundreds). It is important to realize that putting the number of cases at the bottom of each table would have taken no extra space in the report, therefore suspicion should immediately be aroused that the sample size, if reported, would be inadequate for its purpose (i.e. not in hundreds – and I have subsequently confirmed that this is so). The benefit of the doubt here should rest with tentative scepticism.

Not specifying the population

Even more common is the absence in research reports of any reference to the population involved. The work of Reay and Lucey (2000) is typical, and far from the weakest of a whole genre of research that appears to evade critical reading by claiming to eschew quantitative analysis (while still basing their conclusions on arithmetic-logic, using terms such as 'majority', 'few', etc.). Their work describes a sample size, but it is not drawn from a clear population. In their own words, 'it focused on 90 Year 6 children (aged 10–11) in two primary schools in one inner-London borough, chosen because of its demographic diversity. Forty-four children were involved in focus group interviews and a further 20 children, 15 of their parents and three teachers were interviewed individually' (p. 85). Only a sub-set of these are cited in their paper, including 'five with parents' (p. 85). There is clearly an approach to the notion of sampling here in the mention of numbers, types and demographic diversity. But is the sample meant to represent the Year 6 in the two primary schools, or in all primary schools in the LEA, or inner-London LEAs, or all LEAs? How much can the authors generalize from this study? If the study focuses on 90 children why are there only 64 children involved (44 in the focus groups and 20 separately)? Are the 90 the total Year 6 population of these schools? Either way, how were the 64 selected for inclusion (we have seen above the potential bias in a non-systematic selection method)?

Perhaps we could argue that these questions do not really matter. The authors have used a non-probability sample (although without explaining why), and are interested only in the individual accounts they collect. They will therefore not seek patterns within, nor generalizations from this dataset. Unfortunately, this is precisely what they do attempt. Their abstract includes the following phrases – 'a strong pattern of class-related orientations to class', the 'vast majority of children' involved in choice, and 'less choice for black and white working-class boys than for other groups of children' (p. 83, my underlining). The full text makes it clear both that the authors have divided their already small sample into sub-groups for occupational class (of family), gender, ability level and ethnic group, and that they are keen to draw general conclusions about the differences between these groups. They conclude that 'despite the idiosyncrasies and cross-cutting inflections of personal characteristics and ability levels, a majority of the children operate within class-differentiated horizons of choice' (p. 98). We are given no indication of the relative size of the sub-groups, but given that the total sample is only 66 cases, dividing these by class, gender, ethnicity and so on means that the actual number of cases in any comparison must be very small.

This is most obvious in the discussion about parents, where the authors state that 'in the parental interviews, a majority of the working-class parents concurred with their child' (p. 90), and 'a significant deviation from this class trend was mothers of mainly black working-class boys' (p. 90). So, from their 15 interviews with parents the authors have apparently been able to analyse responses separately by class, ethnic group, gender of parent and gender of child. If we make a charitable assumption (and note that this should not be necessary since it would take little effort for the authors to have provided all the relevant details) that the 15 parents were roughly half mothers and half fathers, then there would be seven or eight of each. If we assume that the pupils were half girls and half boys, then there would be three or four parents in each gender group. Again, if we assume that half of each of these groups were middle-class and half working-class (and assuming that only two categories were used), then there would be one or two cases in each gender/class cell for comparison. Finally, if we assume that half of each of these groups were black and half non-black (again making the favourable assumption of only two categories) then there would be, on average, less than one case in each cell for comparison. When Reay and Lucey state that a majority of working-class parents agreed with their child they may be talking about as few as four parents from a sub-group of seven. There is no way that such a 'finding' is significant (see Chapter Six). When Reay and Lucey state that mothers of mainly black working-class boys differed from this pattern, they could be talking about one mother. If they are talking about *more* than one mother, this must mean that some of the other cells with which they make explicit comparison are actually empty (and therefore can provide no basis for that comparison).

For social science purposes this scale is clearly insufficient for any generalization, and as with some other examples cited in this book it is rather surprising that the peer-review process for the journal in which the paper was published did not pick some of these problems up. The reason could be the continuing and over-used dichotomy between quantitative research and other research. The referees involved may have been in sympathy with the methodological style (and perhaps the conclusions) of the paper, and not looked too carefully at the figures on which the authors base their case. The net effect is to allow authors to make unsafe 'generalizations' from one or two cases in a way that may propagate through the research literature, leading to an increasingly defective cumulation of knowledge.

Ignoring drop-out
We have already considered the potential damage caused by non-response, since non-responders may differ significantly from those individuals taking part in a study. The same problem arises during sampling designs based on repeated use of the same cases (see also Chapter Eight on subject 'mortality' in experiments). Some studies use longitudinal approaches (tracking people over time), including some of the famous large surveys mentioned in Chapter Two (the Youth Cohort Study, for example). Each time the researchers return to their sample, sometimes after a number of years, some of the

cases will drop out. Some may be out of contact, have died or emigrated or simply be unwilling to continue. The percentage dropping out is nearly always reported, but less often are the full implications of this thought through. A good example is presented by Huff (1991) where a university follows the careers of its graduates into later life and advertises their average annual income. If they can trace only 75% of the cohort from a particular year, although 75% is a high 'response rate', do you think this could lead to an over-estimate of the average income? How many of the missing cases are likely to be national politicians, consultant heart surgeons or sporting or cultural superstars, for example?

Using an unjustified non-probability sample
Aside from a very few studies, for example where the snowball technique is necessary, all researchers are faced with an early decision to use or not to use a probability sample. This applies to those interviewing cultural experts as much as those doing large-scale trials. There is no obvious reason, other than necessity, why most researchers would choose to use a non-probability sample. Whatever the sample size and purpose, a random or systematic or stratified sample is better than a convenience, purposive or quota one. Yet the majority of the social science research literature reports the use of non-probability samples, and no good reason is given for their use. The questions of representational bias and whether to use corrective weights generally do not arise in the literature. I have a feeling that many authors are using the technical term 'sample' to mean simply 'the cases I involved in my research'. By using the term 'sample' they gain some of the associated prestige and an apparent ability to generalize from their findings, without any of the difficulties of actually using a properly selected sample from a previously defined population.

Not using weights
As shown above, the existence of post-stratification weights is very good news for the researcher. They mean that even if your sample deviates radically from an ideal and is clearly biased in some respect, you can estimate some corrections even after collecting your data. As long as the number of variables used for weighting is kept to a minimum of the really crucial ones for your study, and you use a computer for all of the hard work, then corrective weights are fairly simple to operate. It is therefore quite surprising how seldom they appear in use in the social science

research literature. Not using weights can lead to significant misrepresentation of your findings, and if further more complex analyses are performed using the same data then the representation errors will propagate, sometimes alarmingly (see Chapter Ten for a discussion of error propagation).

Obscuring the response rate
It is important to keep a close eye on the number of cases in your (and others') research. This number (often reported as 'N') can have several meanings. Is it intended to be the number of responses, the number of usable responses or the number of responses used in a specific table of results? Does it include those people contacted who were ineligible (too old, for example), who terminated the interview or who were not at home when you called? Decisions such as these can affect your apparent response rate.

A large-scale survey called 'Future Skills' was carried out in Wales in 1998 to coincide with the creation of the new National Assembly when Wales was given a limited form of self-governance. It was carried out by MORI for a group of public sector clients, including the government. The results attempted to match available workforce skills and future employer demands, to determine a national strategy for training and reskilling. These results were extremely influential in the setting of National Targets for Lifelong Education and Training and in the policies formed by the post-16 education committee. It is the only empirical evidence used in the Education and Training Action Plan for Wales (ETAG 1999). The sample was carefully constructed, stratified, and corrective weights were used. The summary of the main report (the document likely to be used by politicians and other policy-makers) does not include the response rate, however, although the figure in general use is 45% for the survey of employers, for example. While less than impressive, this 45% is sufficient to demand some respect for the results. This response rate is calculated as the number of achieved interviews (5,790) divided by the total of the number of achieved interviews (5,790) plus the number of refusals (6,528) and the number of interviews terminated (607). The appendix to the technical report describes this as the 'valid response rate' (Future Skills Wales 1998). In the terms used in this chapter this is not really a response rate at all, but a non-refusal rate.

The survey actually drew a sample of 29,952 employers to contact. The researchers did not contact 6,207 of these because they were not needed to fill quotas. Therefore the survey contacted

23,745 employers and held successful interviews with 5,790 of them. This is a response rate of 24% (or 19% of the initial sample drawn). The reasons given for not including the remaining 10,820 employers include finding a telephone number engaged, not recognized or unobtainable (1,866), discounting firms that have too few employees or do not carry out recruitment themselves (2,330), and excluding employers who made appointments (1,222). Each of these reasons, as well as others like them, could clearly lead to bias in the achieved sample. Small businesses, for example, may be more likely to fail and therefore no longer have the advertised telephone number. Therefore, excluding any cases who cannot be contacted by telephone may over-estimate the views of medium and large employers. There may be little that the researchers could have done about this, and in a sense they have given sufficient information about it for the benefit of the reader prepared to wade through the technical appendices. This example is used to show the importance of reading 'between the lines'. The actual response rate to this influential survey is around half of that advertised. This may affect our impression of the significance of the findings, or it may not. But we, as consumers of research, should have this information and be able to make the decision ourselves.

SUMMARY: THE STAGES IN SAMPLING

- Decide whether to use a sample, and why.
- Define the population of interest (be as precise as possible).
- List the inhabitants of the population (create a sampling frame), or characterize the population.
- Estimate the size of sample you need (consider sub-groups, stability, power, effect sizes and resources). Make it large.
- Choose a method of selecting population elements (consider random, systematic, stratified, clustered or non-probability).
- Decide on methods of correction (consider response rate, refusal rate, weighting).
- Characterize the achieved sample and compare with the ideal (or the population).
- Apply corrections if necessary.

This chapter described the key stage of deciding who participates in our research. In summary: a good sample is representative of a wider population, large and with a high participation rate. It is risky to accept the generalizations made in previous work, without first considering their sampling strategy and the potential biases that this introduces. If, after reading this chapter, you would like to know more about sampling some useful starting points would be Stuart (1968), Henry (1990), Bernard (2000), or Cohen and Manion (2000). The next chapter looks at ways of collecting your own data via a survey questionnaire.

Surveying the field: questionnaire design

WHY DO A SURVEY?

Many new researchers appear to assume that their project must be based on a questionnaire survey (in the same way as many appear to assume that it should be based on semi-structured interviews). Indeed, the practice is so widespread in social science research that some commentators appear to equate quantitative approaches only with surveys. However, the 'decision' to use a survey is often quite hard to justify (Gillham 2000a considers the relative merits of interviews and surveys). Surveys are generally inferior as a design compared with experiments, as they are less well-theorized (see Chapter Eight). Even good ones cannot hope to establish a causatory explanation for any observed phenomenon (see Chapter Seven). Surveys are also generally less complete than official statistics, providing data of poorer quality (see Chapter Two). Their use is therefore far from automatic, and should be as reasoned as any other stage of the research design.

The use of a survey is indicated when the data required does not already exist and the research questions are not susceptible to experimental trial for practical reasons such as lack of resources or ethical constraints. Surveys are better at gathering relatively simple facts (such as respondents' current occupation) or reports of behaviour (such as how often the respondent misses a day at work) than at gathering opinions, attitudes or explanations. Viewed in this way, a survey is not a positive solution to a design problem but almost a position of last resort (and much the same comments could be made about the equally common approach of completing a couple of dozen interviews with a 'grounded theory' analysis). According to Gillham (2000b) no single method has been so abused as the questionnaire – 'the quick fix of social research methods'.

Since even good ones tend to generate much poor data, when the are used it is perhaps better that they are used as part of a larger study also involving other approaches.

SAMPLING

The intricate steps involved in selecting a sample (see Chapter Four) should come before the other stages of survey design. Obviously the sample does not actually have to be selected first, but you should at least have made all of the sampling design decisions first. Most importantly, you need to make a preliminary decision about the population, sample size and method of selecting cases. Many of the problems in survey design that follow have no best solution, but must be considered in relation to the sample required.

For example, if the population of study is five-year-old children then a postal questionnaire is not likely to be appropriate and a face-to-face interaction may be preferable. Since face-to-face delivery is more costly in research time than postal, the sample size may therefore need to be smaller. On the other hand, if the population is all of the householders in the country and the method of selection is random, then a postal delivery would seem more efficient. Face-to-face delivery would be very difficult since there would most likely be a widely scattered sample in geographical terms, necessitating arduous travel to remote areas for rather small clusters of cases. The research process is therefore iterative and messy, and not linear like following the steps for an instant cake mix. Your sample depends in part on your instrument, which depends in part on how you intend to analyse the results, which depends in part on your research questions, etc.

For simplicity this chapter assumes that the respondents are people, but a survey does not have to be of people. It could be of books or buildings, for example (and most of the comments made here would still apply).

METHOD OF DELIVERY

A key decision affecting the likely response rate, cost, speed, sample size and length of your questionnaire is how you intend to deliver it to your sample. There are many variations, but the most common choices are between face-to-face, self-administered and technology-based. In the following discussion of each these are, by implication, being compared with each other.

Face-to-face

Face-to-face delivery takes place when the researcher is present while the questionnaire is being completed, and can therefore record the responses herself. This approach is very useful in allowing a wide response that includes those with low levels of literacy and those with visual challenges, who would find a self-administered questionnaire very difficult. Face-to-face, the researcher can read the questions aloud, explain any difficult points if necessary and record the responses in as much detail as desired. Since they are present, the researcher can also check who is answering the questions (i.e. that it is the right person) and can stop him or her answering the questions in a non-standard order (i.e. by flipping ahead to see what is coming).

Conducting a door-to-door survey, where you are invited into someone's home, given tea and seated on their sofa, can be a very rewarding experience. It is also possible to take a longer time, for a fuller set of questions, than you might achieve in requesting, say, a postal response. As well as being on hand to explain difficulties, you can use cue cards and visual mnemonics easily (lists of possible multiple-choice responses, perhaps), and can even add an element of multi-media via a laptop computer if this is deemed helpful. In their own homes, respondents can also check the accuracy of their answers by reference to their personal records such as certificates, diaries and so on. Maybe the single most important advantage of being present at the administration of a survey is the potential for observation, field notes and *ad hoc* interviews that other methods of delivery deny you. You can see facial expressions, type of house, age of car and a hundred other little details that might help you interpret your findings. You can talk to other people on the way in and out of the interview, and these 'staircase' meetings can be very fruitful for new ideas or contacts. Once you are on the road, everything becomes data.

The biggest single drawback for this form of delivery is the length of time it takes with all its practical consequences. Whereas postal surveys, for example, allow parallel mailings far afield, a visit requires travel and so constrains the nature of the sample used. Travel is more expensive than sending a questionnaire the same distance. This also creates a greater temptation to shirk on the call-back procedure for those not available at first (if you have to travel 300 kilometres to see someone and they are not there, will you really go back and try again next week?), and so leads to an even greater possibility of bias in the sample. Also, if the research takes a long time to complete then the nature of the phenomenon under investigation may change (owing to new legislation, the natural ageing of children, etc.).

If the time problem is solved by having a team of researchers working in parallel, the design now needs to ensure consistency between them in terms of their administration of the questions. It is clear even from work with tight experimental designs (see Chapter Eight) that the presence of the researcher can give unconscious cues to the other participants. This point is even more important in the more relaxed design of a survey. Respondents will react to the appearance, manner, body language and tone of a face-to-face interviewer in a way that is simply not possible using other methods of delivery. Other actors in the scene can also play a part. I once piloted a household questionnaire that asked the householder about the number of life partners they had had prior to their current relationship. It became quite clear, and seems obvious in retrospect, that the presence of their current partner making us coffee in the next room was creating a constraining influence. Finally, and quite importantly for the individual novice researcher, there is the personal safety aspect. Although unlikely, respondents might be abusive or threatening and, whereas abuse by letter or telephone is unpleasant, such a breakdown of communication face-to-face is extremely alarming. All of these potential advantages and disadvantages could be taken into account before a decision is made on the most appropriate compromise.

Self-administered
Self-administered (by the respondent) questionnaires are usually mailed. There are also considerable opportunities for dropping off and collecting forms in batches at institutions such as hospitals or schools, thereby reducing the cost of postage and travel. If the respondents complete the survey form themselves there are several key advantages. There is much less of the reactivity effect or interviewer bias that can be created by the presence of someone who has a vested interest in the results. It can be arranged that the responses are not only confidential (which is standard practice) but also anonymous (so that even the researcher does not know to whom each returned form belongs). This can help create an atmosphere of trust, and therefore lead perhaps to more truthful answers. This method of delivery is easier if the questions come in batteries of similar types with the same scaled response (e.g. from agree to disagree), or where the list of possible multiple-choice

responses is very long. Both of these designs are difficult to handle efficiently face-to-face without resorting to at least some elements of self-administration (such as show cards). Self-administered questions can also be created in a form, such as optical marks, that are already computer-readable, so avoiding the time and potential errors involved in coding and transcription. They can also be sent and returned via email with many of the same advantages (see below).

There have been claims that the average response rate to postal surveys is low (20% perhaps), but these claims tend to conflate figures from market 'research', which are generally lower than those from academic studies. If you follow the advice given in this chapter you should obtain much higher rates than those generally quoted. Aim high. Bernard (2000) suggests there is little real difference between the response rates for face-to-face surveys (80%) and for well-designed mail surveys (73% +).

If the researchers are not present at administration they cannot check the identity of the respondent or for frivolous treatment of the questions (Gillham 2000b). They cannot preserve the order of reading the questions, and therefore the secrecy of later questions, and they are not available to explain the meaning of questions or to answer questions about the use to which the data will be put. Self-administration is clearly impossible for those unable to read or write effectively.

Technology-based
To a large extent, the use of ICT and technology-based delivery represents a compromise between the previous approaches. This is most obvious in the use of telephone surveys where no travel is involved and the interviewer is depersonalized to some extent (although not in terms of accent or speech patterns), but is still available to explain questions and help motivate the interviewee. Although there is a charge for telephone calls, the cost of these is falling relative to mail delivery and travel, and with an appropriate sample can actually lead to the cheapest form of questionnaire delivery. There are no problems of gaining access via security guards, receptionists, 'doormen' for apartment blocks, etc. The use of random digit dialling is very convenient, does not require a list of telephone numbers to start with, and can avoid the bias introduced to such lists by ex-directory and other unlisted numbers. As your research career takes off and you find yourself running a survey with several investigators, the use of a telephone schedule with a

switchboard will allow you to monitor centrally the quality and consistency of the work of each interviewer in your team.

Email approaches are even better in some respects, leading to cheaper use of telephone lines (or digital television), easier access to worldwide samples and at present an atmosphere of camaraderie and friendly informality. Response rates to email surveys may also be better than by telephone (Selwyn 2002). Selwyn and Robson (1998) cite examples of 50-90% response rates using email and they compare this to rates of 20–50% in conventional mail surveys (Frankfort-Nachmias and Nachmias 1996). The times taken to respond are excellent (almost instantaneous) and the responses can be returned in an already computer-readable format.

The disadvantages of using technology to collect your data are relatively obvious. Random digit dialling cannot distinguish between the number of telephone lines for each area code, thereby over-representing those from rural areas. Not all potential respondents have a telephone and not all who do have a telephone appear in published lists of numbers. In Wales, for example, as many as 10% of people in the year 2000 did not even have access to a shared public payphone at home (Gorard et al. 2000b). As many as 67% of people in Wales in the year 2000 did not have access to a computer (never mind whether it is email-capable) either at work or home. In addition and in general, those who do not have access to telephones and computers are systematically different from those who do. Any of these forms of technology are less likely to be available to those who are older, unqualified or economically inactive. The potential bias from this is considerable when using email in particular, so in order to obtain the response rates suggested above, any remotely delivered questionnaire must be brief (see the example below). The choice of email as a method is also not simply about delivery; because of the tendency of respondents to use a simplified register of language, or even symbols for expressions, the form of data collected is altered (Gorard and Selwyn 2001). In addition to all of these problems, anonymity of the sort possible in mail surveys is often just about impossible (else how do you know the telephone number or email address?), but much of the tacit information available face-to-face is lost.

If I had to have an overall preference it would be for self-administered questions delivered either by mail or, preferably, by the researcher to natural groups of respondents (such as school classes, see Gorard 1997b). This approach is generally better if the respondents are literate and well-motivated, and have no clear need for individual attention. Whichever method you consider for the delivery of your questionnaire, bear in mind the issues described above, such as cost, time, geography, length, complexity, control of the question order, visual aids, the use of respondents' personal records for reference, rapport, sensitivity, sample bias, response rate, response bias, knowledge of non-responders and so on. Perhaps a combination of methods can maximize the advantages to you as the researcher.

TYPE OF SURVEY

Another topic for brief consideration before we get to the design of the actual questionnaire instrument is the type of survey you are planning. You may find thereby that there are constraints imposed upon your design. What is the goal of the survey? Is it, for example, to describe something accurately or to test one or more hypotheses? Is it to be a one-off snapshot of a certain period or will it collect historical information? Is it to be repeated in the future or will it repeat questions from previous studies?

A longitudinal (repeated) survey allowing prolonged study of the lives of one group of respondents has many attractions. Data from such a study could be richer, may be more accurate and could help us to understand the process of change over time. However, it would also be expensive and time-consuming and might entail many compromises. It can lead to complex statistical problems, so longitudinal data is often collapsed into a format of one or more cross-sections, or 'snapshots', for analysis anyway (Crouchley 1987). Long-term studies also suffer from respondent attrition, with the result that even the best ones may end up with an overall response rate that clearly suggests bias through self-selection in the sample (Dolton et al. 1994). For example, Banks et al. (1992) had response rates of between 60% and 70% for the first sweep of their study, but if this response rate was similar on each occasion that they attempted to contact the original respondents in successive years, then the overall response rate for the third sweep could easily be less than 25% of the original target sample. The respondents in the Banks study became proportionately more middle-class in each wave. Similarly, only 45% of the respondents in the Youth Cohort Study took part in all three sweeps to 1991 (Whitfield and Bourlakis 1991). Long-term studies also face a threat to internal validity coming from the necessity to test and re-test the same individuals (Hagenaars 1990, see also Chapter Eight).

One way around this is to use a trend design collecting data from different groups for each sweep, but this design does not allow a consideration of change in individuals. Also, since the second sample is not from the same population as the first, in the statistical sense, then this causes problems in looking for changes in population parameters over time. A compromise, which might have the advantages or the disadvantages of both, is to use a rolling sample, whereby a proportion of the sample for each sweep remains longitudinal. For example, the Labour Force Survey (see Chapter Two) contacts 80,000 households every three months, of which 60,000 have also been used in the previous quarter.

Longitudinal studies also face problems of comparability over time (Glenn 1977). In educational research, for example, the modes and titles of certified public examinations change over time (Gorard 2001b). Even where equivalencies between them are established it is not clear that their value-in-exchange actually remains constant. An A-Level may have meant a lot more in 1970 than in 1990, not because it was any harder to attain, but simply because there were fewer of them. Similar issues arise in most fields of research. However, such considerations are even more difficult for a long-term study since the instrument to be used for all sweeps has to be designed before the changes that it needs to encompass (a nearly impossible task), or else has to be changed between sweeps, exacerbating comparability problems and opening researchers to the charge that the study is not actually longitudinal as the questions have changed.

A retrospective study, asking respondents to recall past events, has the advantage of hindsight. A retrospective study, as opposed to a simple cross-sectional study, also avoids many of the other problems noted above. Retrospective employment histories, such as the 1984 Women and Employment Survey (Martin and Roberts 1984), and learning histories, such as the National Training Survey 1975/76 (Greenhalgh and Stewart 1987), are much used by economists (McNabb and Whitfield 1994). They are not, of course, immune to criticism since a wide range of life variables and events may be difficult for the respondents to recall (although the use of household records can be encouraged). Among these variables are attitudes, which are notoriously unreliable *post hoc*, and some figures such as income and health measurements.

All of these factors need to be considered before designing an instrument for replication, retrospective or longitudinal work, or a snap-shot picture (and they obviously also have implications for drawing the appropriate sample).

INSTRUMENT DESIGN

Before writing actual questions it is useful to consider the overall design of your questionnaire instrument. Perhaps the most crucial issue here is the order in which items will appear. This applies to the order of the questions in each section and the order of each section within the whole. A good example of the importance of the first of these points is provided in the novel *Yes Prime Minister* (Lynn and Jay 1986), where the prime minister's cabinet secretary is demonstrating to a colleague how surveys can be designed to produce whatever result a government official wants. If, for example, the government want support for their plans to reintroduce compulsory National Service in the armed forces, they might ask their sample the following series of questions.

1. Are you worried about the rise in crime among teenagers?
2. Do you think there is a lack of discipline and vigorous training in our schools?
3. Do you think young people welcome some structure and leadership in their lives?
4. Do you think young people respond to a challenge?
5. Might you be in favour of reintroducing National Service?

Here, there is strong encouragement to answer 'yes' to question 5 to maintain consistency if you have answered 'yes' to the previous questions. Then, of course, only the responses to question 5 are published under the heading 'Majority of public support National Service'. If, on the other hand, opponents of the government wish to obtain a contrary view they might ask the following series of questions.

1. Are you worried about the danger of war?
2. Are you unhappy about the growth of armaments?
3. Do you think there's a danger in giving young people guns and teaching them how to kill?
4. Do you think it is wrong to force people to take up arms against their will?
5. Would you oppose the reintroduction of National Service?

Here, there is strong encouragement to answer 'yes' to question 5 again, even though it now says the opposite of the version above. Again, only the last responses might be used and published under the heading 'Majority of public oppose National Service'.

Now, I am not advocating that either of these approaches be used or that you use leading questions at all. But this example does show how sensitive our responses can be to the precise ordering of questions in a questionnaire. Other than being aware of the problem, the best defence may be to use more than one version of your questionnaire with differing question orders. You can then allocate these versions randomly to your sample and analyse their responses in terms of the sub-groups faced with each version. If there is no obvious difference in the response patterns between groups then you can report with some conviction that order has been eliminated as a possible confounding variable in your results. If there *is* a difference between responses to different versions, then at least you can use this difference as an estimate of the size and direction of the bias.

The sections of a typical questionnaire might include an introduction (to secure the cooperation of respondents), a question or two about the respondent (as a selection, identification or quota check to make sure you are addressing the right person), the substantive questions (about the research) and background questions (concerning respondents' personal characteristics). This list is in a logical order. The introduction is first. The selection check ensures that no time is wasted answering questions unnecessarily. The substantive questions come next as they are the most interesting and are, after all, what the respondent has agreed to answer. The background questions come last because, although important, they can appear intrusive. Therefore, having them at the end encourages people to start the questionnaire, and once started they are more likely to complete the task. It also means that even if they drop out at this section you still have their responses to the substantive questions (and you may not need background data from everyone).

The introduction should be brief and easy to follow. It might contain the purpose of the study, who is conducting it, who is paying for it, why it is important, what will happen to the results and why the respondent has been selected. Rather than having a complex introduction, it is preferable to use a separate covering letter. This letter could briefly explain the nature and purpose of the study, how the respondent was selected, why their help is needed and how to return the completed form (or even the incomplete one). If you know the respondent's name it is probably better to use it, but reassure them of the confidentiality of their answers (so if the form has any identifying marks these should be explained). Some authorities suggest using stamps on the pre-addressed return envelopes. This can be expensive, especially for an unfunded study.

Alternatively, try and arrange to use FREEPOST (through your department perhaps). In this way you will have to pay postage only on those forms returned, and potential non-respondents will not be tempted to steam off your unused stamps.

If possible, do not put any questions on the front cover, but have a title and the name and address and lots of space. Similarly, on the last page you could have a simple word of thanks and lots of inviting space for any open-ended comments on the survey as a whole. Although the use of incentives for completing the form are sometimes advocated, I prefer to encourage a full response by making the instrument easy to complete and stressing the value of each response to the study. It is also useful and courteous to offer to supply all respondents with a summary of your eventual findings. Curiosity about research is a key motivator, especially in areas of public policy like health, crime and education where everyone feels they are an 'expert'. Generally, the use of the words like 'University' early on in the document are useful to establish that there is no sales or advertising threat to follow. For similar reasons, words such as 'study' and 'research' are more attractive to respondents than 'survey'. The use of photographs or elaborate logos on the front page is dangerous. Whatever you intend them to signify, such illustrations carry multiple messages and are easily misinterpreted. The first substantive question in the instrument should be relevant to all respondents (since if it applies only to some then this can be demotivating for the others), easy and interesting (so put harder or duller questions towards the end), but non-threatening and probably closed in format (see below).

I recommend a questionnaire of eight core pages as a maximum, preferably less for self-administered instruments. Or looked at another way, do not go much above 100 separate questions (and even this figure presupposes that most questions use the same response format). Use a standard paper size (A4 in the UK), printed in black on a white background (although some authorities suggest that light green is the most attractive paper colour). Questions should be grouped as far as possible into topics, with spaces between them. Each question should have no more than two sentences of instruction, and a different typeface should be used for instructions and questions. Using a different typeface to emphasize instructions is a good idea, as long as both typefaces are similar. Varying between capitals, bold, underlining or italics, or even a different font size can be effective – the instructions in capitals and questions in lower case, for example. Use a normal-sized reading font (12 or 14 point). Changing the font entirely (e.g. Times and Courier) rarely works aesthetically.

Minimize, or eliminate entirely, the use of skip an questions or branching instructions that ask respondents to ⌐ve to a question other than the next in sequence. I have seen branching questions go badly wrong with even the most motivated and educated respondents (try getting all under-graduates even in their final examinations to read and follow an examination rubric that is not like the one in the sample paper!). For similar reasons, although it is tempting to save paper, use only one side of each sheet. I once found that the responses to a six-side questionnaire from an entire school covered only the three sides that faced them as they flicked through the instrument. That was a very false economy for me. Again, for similar reasons do not split a question between pages.

Like many readers (I suspect) I very rarely use the grammar checker on my word processor proactively. It just appears to insist on criticizing my use of the passive voice. The one occasion on which I would thoroughly recommend it to the full is when designing a questionnaire. The grammar involved should be simple and clear, the spelling standard for your audience, and the meaning of each sentence easy to understand. Most checkers will provide you with a readability report, including measures such as a Flesch Index of readability. Make sure that the questionnaire is of an appropriate readability for the age and literacy of your entire target sample. If you are working in one language and translating your instrument into another language before completion (a common process for overseas students), then use the technique of back-translation as well. In this, the translated version is translated back into the original language by a third person as a check on the preservation of the original meaning. See Birbil (2000) for advice on what to do if there are still deficits in the translation.

Finally, where possible it is useful to have the responses pre-coded on the actual form, but also to allow space for respondents to make further comments (which are often the most interesting part of the response). Above all, do not cut corners. If, and this is a big 'if', a survey is to be your main method of data collection then you need it to be successful. Don't be mean with the photocopying, paper or postage. If you cannot afford to carry out a proper survey, then do not attempt it.

QUESTION DESIGN

As with projects involving secondary data (see Chapter Two), it is important to realize that you do not have to start any questionnaire from scratch. Many questions are 'old favourites' (see below). Also, many instruments are available commercially and many are available from academic and other public archives. For example, the ESRC Data Archive (University of Essex, Colchester, Essex CO4 3SQ) has the complete instruments used in much of their publicly funded social science research in the UK. The Centre for Applied Social Surveys (CASS, National Centre for Social Research, 35 Northampton Square, London EC1V 0AX, UK) has a large question bank formed from past studies (whose current address is http://qb.soc.surrey.ac.uk). The Social Survey division of the Office for National Statistics also have on-line information on survey methods and quality, and they publish a methodology bulletin twice per year (http://www.statistics.gov.uk/ssd/default.asp). The advantages of using such previous instruments and questions are clear. The instruments will have been piloted and used before, probably on a far larger scale than you could envisage. They will be mature and ready to use. They may carry some extra authority for your readers. Most usefully, they will enable you to compare the responses in your study with those gained previously, to show changes over time or between locations perhaps. Looking at other questionnaires also helps you see what is good and bad about them, and this should give you confidence since even many famous instruments look terribly imperfect in retrospect.

Good question design is the key to easy survey analysis. You do not commit yourself to any particular form of analysis just by thinking about it before designing your questions, but you do restrict the kinds of analysis available to you by the design of your instrument. Therefore, as I have already emphasized, consideration of analysis is more like the first rather than the last stage of research design. You do not want to ask any question that you cannot analyse, otherwise you will waste resources in preparing the question, waste the respondents' time in answering it (so endangering the response rate) and waste more of your time coding and entering the responses. Even worse, you may need an answer to a particular question, but have asked the question in the wrong form (or even the wrong question). Each question should therefore have an explicit purpose. Once you have formed the question you need to consider whether the respondents could know the answer, can report their answer, whether they would want to answer or whether they might be tempted to lie or pretend, or whether they would be in a rush and so make a mistake? Thinking about these five issues might then lead you to change the format of your question.

There are many different forms of questions. They include requests for information (such as 'how many...?'), tick-box categories ('yes or no'), multiple choice ('which of these...'), scales ('how strongly do you feel...?'), ranking procedures ('put the following in order'), grids or tables (for multidimensional questions) and open-ended questions. Each of these is discussed below:

One of the biggest problems you will face in designing a question is likely to be that you end up using the wrong metric or level of measurement (see Chapter Three). This will affect the power and type of statistics that you can use later. You can sometimes convert from one scale to another but this can introduce bias and measurement error, so it is better to ask the questions in the form in which you are intending to analyse them. At best, using the wrong metric loses power and is therefore equivalent to using a smaller sample. Poorly designed questions therefore have much the same effect as throwing away responses.

The best metric to use is a real number such as age, number of children or years in employment. This generally allows the use of all/any statistical tests, including the most powerful. The weakest but the most common formats in social science are categorical variables, such as gender or family religion. Sometimes these categories are artificially devised, such as occupational class (see below). If the use of categories is unavoidable, then I advise keeping the number of categories per question to a minimum. Thinking that using more categories leads to greater accuracy is a fallacy, and I have too often seen students collect answers on a seven-point scale and immediately collapse the responses to the three-point scale they intended to use all along. Why bother, and why make respondents worry about seven points?

Open-ended questions
Perhaps the easiest types of question to design are those using an open-ended format. They are easy because they are the most natural way of expressing a question in everyday conversation. This ease does not necessarily make them the most appropriate for a questionnaire, but it may tempt researchers to over-use them. Their biggest drawback comes when they are subjected to systematic

analysis. Simple closed scales (such as those described below) mean that the respondent is the main source of measurement error, but open-ended questions with *post hoc* classification of the results adds another layer of measurement error due to the researcher. Open-ended questions are best used in two situations: where it is already clear how the responses will be analysed or where the responses will be used not to create a statistical pattern, but to help explain it.

Such choices of question design are far from trivial. Farrall et al. (1997) found that the reported fear of crime was much greater in surveys using closed rather than open-ended questions. Therefore, the results of your study depend on more than simply its face validity (i.e. looking like the right question). People may also respond more sensitively to open-ended approaches. Since there may be so little similarity between responses to forced-choice and open-ended questions it is probably advisable to mix the types of questions in any instrument. Vocabulary and precise phrasing are also more generally important in question design. In a large survey in the US it was recorded that a much larger number of people were in favour of assistance for the poor than were in favour of welfare. The terms you use should be neutral, as far as possible, and familiar but not patronizing. This can lead to problems when you are dealing with very different sub-groups such as parents and their children. Should you change the wording for each group, and run the risk of asking different questions of each, or should you find a common wording and run the risk of patronizing one group?

In early studies of school choice, which tried to identify the reasons reported by families for using a particular new school, there were two main approaches. These involved giving respondents a list (or menu) of choices or else giving them a blank sheet and asking them to list their reasons. Where a list of these potential reasons is presented to respondents for them to tick or rate as appropriate, the list is usually incomplete, not containing all possible reasons for choosing a school. This can lead to serious omissions in the responses, which may well bias the study (Kim and Mueller 1978) by making other criteria appear more important than they truly are (Maddala 1992). For example, a survey by Dennison (1995) used 25 choice criteria but excluded religious preference and the size of the school, which have both been shown to be important to some families in other studies.

Direct evidence of the importance of such omissions from a questionnaire comes from my own study of choice (Gorard 1997b). In one of my focus schools, I mistakenly issued a set of questionnaire forms with one page, containing 25 of the 73 suggested reasons, missing. The criteria accidentally left out included 'good public examination results', 'firm discipline' and 'small classes', which were all found to be very important overall. Although there was a section for respondents to write any other reasons not covered by the list, not one of the affected respondents suggested any of the 25 missing reasons, and so presumably without the prompt did not notice their lack. This would have the effect of increasing the apparent importance of other variables. Yet few researchers in any field can truly claim that they have tried to make their lists as complete as possible, and it is strange that this phenomenon is not more widely discussed in the literature. A pre-fixed list may also suggest reasons to respondents which they might, in retrospect, feel are important, but which they did not, in this example, consider at the time of making a selection of schools.

On the other hand, the method of asking respondents to create their own list of reasons for choosing a school (for example) by asking an open-ended question relies more heavily on the imperfect memory of the respondents, will over-represent the views of the more literate and highly motivated (Payne 1951) and is likely to produce as many differently worded responses as there are respondents (Oppenheim 1992). This makes them very difficult to analyse. Some groups of respondents, those with the most education for example, may produce more reasons each. Therefore, even if all reasons can be assumed to be simple and unrelated constructs, which they patently are not, but which should be a necessary precondition for their frequencies to be computed, they cannot all be given equal weight. It is not reasonable to assume that both of two reasons given by one respondent are each as important as one reason given by another. Neither can it be assumed that each is only half as important. Such considerations begin to give a clue to the complexity of the analysis of open-ended questions.

If you want to collect real-number answers (in many ways the ideal), then a simple form of open-ended question is one aimed at the apparently straightforward collection of facts. Examples might be, 'How many years have you worked in this factory?', or the simpler, 'How old are you (in years)?', or even simpler, 'In which year were you born?'. In each of these examples the respondent simply writes a number. Three common problems with this type of question are lack of clarity, lack of knowledge and intrusiveness. Lack of clarity can usually be sorted out at the pilot stage. One example would be lack of clarity about the units involved, such as in, 'How tall are you?'.

Should the answer be in feet or metres? Another would be lack of clarity about parameters, such as in, 'How many people are there in your university?'. Does this mean today or on the roll? Does it mean students or staff or both? Does it include service staff? If the question is, 'How many schools have you been to?' does this refer to attendance as a student or visits? Lack of knowledge arises when you ask someone about something they cannot possibly answer. Most children do not know their parents' incomes, for example, and many parents would not know the full range of subjects taken by their children at school. Some commentators believe that direct questions such as these are anyway very intrusive, and suggest that closed questions should be used instead. People may find it easier to tell you their annual income to within a certain range than to give you a figure, either because they do not know exactly or because they do not want to tell you.

Closed questions
Close-ended (or closed) questions are somewhat harder to design well than open-ended questions but should then be much easier to analyse. The reasons why they are hard to design can be experienced in those semi-serious tests that appear in magazines with titles such as, 'How compatible are you?' or, 'Are you a thinker or a doer?'. Whenever I attempt one of these (only at the dentist's, obviously), I can hardly answer any of the questions since all of the possible responses are not right for me. Imagine possible answers such as, 'Do you a) whisk your partner off to Paris for the weekend; or b) sulk for the next three weeks and then buy your partner some chocolates?'. You see my difficulty. What if it is Rome and not Paris, or only one week, or a CD rather than chocolates? What if my response is something completely different? Of course, these are trivial examples but even 'proper' research can lead to questions that appear to exclude the very people they are aimed at by denying them the chance to tell us what they know. Closed questions should ideally be as inclusive and flexible as open-ended ones. Herein lies their difficulty.

Make sure that each question allows for all possible responses, but without overlap. This would usually involve adding categories for 'don't know' (in my opinion a perfectly valid answer to most questions) and for 'other, please specify'. You should try and make this last option of 'other' redundant by making other categories as inclusive as possible, but still retain it as a fail-safe (at least for your pilot study). Consider the difference between these two versions of the same question.

a) What is your highest qualification?	A-Level or equivalent (or above)
	GCSE or equivalent
	None

b) What is your highest qualification?	A-Level or equivalent (or above)
	GCSE or equivalent
	None
	Don't know
	Other (please specify) ...

While neither version is perfect the second is preferable to the first in allowing everyone to answer something, whereas the first will lead to some null responses.

Avoid also the use of negative statements if possible (which are surprisingly confusing) and double-barrelled questions (or two questions in one). Making questions easy to answer involves avoiding hypothetical situations, jargon, technical language and ambiguity. Avoid the danger of assuming a falsely shared premise. To aid recall by your respondents do not ask for more information than you need (or than you are intending to analyse). If, for example, you wish to know how many different jobs a respondent has, then it is not necessary to ask him to list all of his previous jobs.

The following example questions could all lead to problems. The first does not allow respondents to separate their reactions to the two parts of the question. The second (very common in style) is asking something that most people would have no evidence about and therefore should not answer. Note, however, that the added danger of asking such questions is that people may respond even when they have no knowledge. The third is ambiguous. Does it refer to the respondent or to his/her partner as well? Does it refer to each child separately or to all of them together? Does a verbal reprimand count as punishment? And so on.

| c) How do you rate the new government for achievement and presentation? | [high/medium/low] |

| d) Are people better educated today than 10 years ago? | Yes/No |

e) How often do you punish your children?	Never
	Monthly
	Weekly
	At least daily

Although it is also usually recommended that questions are not 'loaded', this technique can occasionally be useful to provoke responses in difficult situations. If this is what you intend then build it into your design and your later description of the method used. An example might be when you know that respondents have been selected because they have a characteristic that they may wish to cover up, and you want to let them know both that you know about it and that it is all right (e.g. 'How many times have you been arrested?').

Scales
By 'scales' I refer here not just to closed questions in general, but to the use of batteries of similar format questions using a standard scale aimed at the indirect measurement of an underlying concept. A very common example of such a concept would be attitude. I have already stated that, in my opinion, questionnaires are not good at gathering anything other than the most straightforward information about respondents. Therefore, it should come as no surprise to realize that I am not a great fan of this particular use of scales. I will not go into great detail here, but for those interested there is further discussion of these in Oppenheim (1992) and elsewhere.

Complex scales are multiple indicators, often used to measure things like stress, political stance, attitudes or prejudice. They should only be used when a single or even a proxy (substitute) measure is not possible. Their use requires considerable care, since we are not even sure exactly what these things are (if they exist), and are even less sure how to measure them. Simply putting a lot of similar questions together and treating the responses to each question equally (as in scoring a multiple-choice examination) does not automatically lead a social scientist to an underlying variable. There is a lot of make-believe in this technique, since multiple responses are not necessarily any more accurate than a single one. A good multiple scale requires a lot of work and much testing. Their creators often use ordinal scales such as 'strongly agree' to 'strongly disagree', in which respondents, especially less-educated ones, have a tendency towards agreement whatever the associated statement. These responses in ordinal form are then often treated as real numbers (see Chapter Three), which has led to 'intellectual pollution' in the opinion of some writers (e.g. Mitchell 1994). Mitchell claims that the legacy of Spearman (a famous statistician) is a pseudo-science, combining contempt for real information with a worship of false quantification, and ignoring the fact that epistemology and logic are more important than statistical technique. The users of complex scales are therefore often like the second 'villain' in Chapter One, determined to work with numbers at any cost, and convinced of their authority regardless of their substantive meaning (see Prandy 2002).

The old favourites

Many questionnaires you see or design will ask standard background questions about the age, sex, social class and ethnicity of the respondent (and perhaps also the family religion). These are some of the old favourites of social researchers, because they can almost always be relied upon to point up systematic differences in the responses to the more substantive questions. There are not many large-scale studies that do not report differences in employment, educational attainment, attitude, participation, or confidence in terms of young and old, men and women, middle and working class, or white and a minority ethnic group. Questions for the first two of the standard questions are relatively simple to devise. If you feel that asking people their age is too intrusive you could ask instead for their date of birth, or year of birth if that is all you really need. Practical problems arise in forming questions about the other two, so much so in fact that I have never seen (much less devised) a satisfactory version of either question. This may be partly due to lack of clarity in the concepts and the lack of an agreed meaning for either term. On reflection, what is astonishing is that, despite these flaws, the many systematic differences between these groups (however they are defined) are so great that even a poorly designed question will usually identify them.

Many social class schemes are actually based on occupational prestige. Until 1971, the UK Registrar-General's class scheme used in the population Census and other official figures was an ordinal classification of occupations according to reputed standing in community (Rose 1996). In 1980, this notion of prestige was exchanged for levels of skill, which sounded more objective but were in some ways more confusing. There are other scales in common use, based on both nominal and continuous variables (in particular look at the Cambridge/Cardiff scale, www.cardiff.ac.uk./ socsi/camsis, for a radically different approach). There are also Standard Industrial Classifications (SIC) and Standard Occupational Classifications (SOC), appropriate for different purposes. However, the RG scale remains the most widely used. Originally designed to relate to measures of infant mortality and adult fertility, the traditional scale looked like this (Table 5.1).

Table 5.1: The Registrar-General's class scheme

I	Professional occupations (e.g. medical doctor, lawyer)
II	Managerial and technical occupations (e.g. company director, teacher)
IIIN	Non-manual skilled occupations (e.g. clerical assistant)
IIIM	Manual skilled occupations (e.g. craftspeople, plumbers)
IV	Partly-skilled occupations (e.g. lathe operator)
V	Unskilled occupations (e.g. litter collector)

As can be seen, this list represents a mixture of both skill and occupational prestige. For many analytic purposes you may prefer to work with only three divisions – Service class (I + II), Intermediate class (IIIN + IIIM) and Working class (IV + V) – since this may lead to fewer difficult decisions in classifying cases and produces more cases per cell for analysis (see Chapter Six). The scale is primarily male in focus, and thus works less well with what are predominantly women's jobs. Using the scale for women tends to inflate their class since fewer are involved in manual work. It is questionable to suggest that simply working in an office makes a person middle-class (Intermediate). The scale also does not recognize unpaid labour, and makes it difficult to classify those without employment.

The newer social class categories introduced in 1998 are based not on skill or prestige but employment conditions, and so overcome some of these problems. This 'socio-economic classification' generally makes it easier to classify the jobs of women, by giving less emphasis to the distinction between manual and non-manual jobs (Table 5.2). Where people do not have a job, you can ask them about their usual occupation or about the occupation of their parents. You will also need a category of 'Unclassified' for students and for no valid response. A self-coding version of this is available from National Statistics (see Chapter Two), suitable for postal surveys in which you do not want full details of the respondents' jobs (following the principle restated throughout this book of not asking for unused detail, but rather asking questions in the format that they will be analysed).

The other standard question that gives the researcher a great deal of trouble but which is worth persevering with relates to the ethnic background of respondents. There is perhaps even less agreement about what this constitutes than there is about social class. Again, the standard question would be based on that used by the Office for

Table 5.2: The Registrar-General's class scheme 1998 (used 2001)

---

1. Higher professional and managerial occupations
   a Employers and managers, company directors, health service and bank managers
   b Higher professionals, university and college lecturers, scientists, doctors, teachers, librarians, social workers, clergy
2. Lower professional and managerial occupations, laboratory technicians, nurses and midwives, journalists, artists, actors and musicians, police
3. Intermediate professions, secretaries, dental nurses, electrical equipment installers, piano tuners
4. Small employers and own account workers, farmers, publicans, restauranteurs
5. Lower supervisory, craft and related jobs, plumbers, butchers, train drivers
6. Semi-routine occupations, shop assistants, security guards, hairdressers
7. Routine occupations, waiters, cleaners, couriers
8. Never worked, and long-term unemployed

---

the Population Census (Table 5.3). As can be seen, this list is a peculiar mixture of skin colour, other racial characteristics, country of 'origin' and primary state religion.

The situation was improved somewhat in the classification for the 2001 census (Table 5.4), largely by the addition of the 'mixed' category. It is still not clear whether a respondent with white skin born in India would be 'Indian' or 'White other'. With the addition of 'Irish' (and 'Scottish' in Scotland, but not 'Welsh', in Wales) as opposed to 'Born in Ireland', it is no longer clear whether these categories are intended to be based on area of birth, residence, language or self-attribution. Can someone be Black *and* Irish (or Welsh) for example? The same applies to Asian British and Black British. Is 'Indian', for example, a description of birthplace, parental birthplace, or something vaguer? How can 'British' be a sub-set of White and also a modifier for 'Asian British', for example?

Table 5.3: Ethnic groups 1991 census

Main group			
White	White		
Black groups	Black Caribbean	Black African	Black other
Indian sub-continent	Indian	Pakistani	Bangladeshi
Chinese/other groups	Chinese	Asian other	Other
Born in Ireland	Born in Ireland		

Table 5.4: Ethnic groups 2001 census

Ethnic group				
White	British	Irish	Other White	
Mixed	White and Black Caribbean	White and Black African	White and Asian	Other mixed
Asian or Asian British	Indian	Pakistani	Bangladeshi	Other Asian
Black or Black British	Caribbean	African	Other Black	
Chinese or other	Chinese	Any other		

Most crucially, how mixed does one have to be to be classified as mixed? Are we not all mixed to some extent? Consider the fact that as I have two parents, four grandparents, eight great-grandparents and so on, then 40 generations ago I had 2^{40} antecedents, or over one trillion (one thousand billion) people. If each generation, for the sake of argument, reproduced on average after every 25 years, then 40 generations represents 1,000 years. Therefore, I had more ancestors 1,000 years ago than there were people alive at that time (more even than everyone who has ever been alive). Put another way, as recently as 500 years ago (the era of the Tudor monarchs and 'discovery' of the USA perhaps), everyone in the entire world must have been related to me. The notion of 'pure' ethnic groups in terms of genetics or ancestry is therefore somewhat unrealistic. If, on the other hand, ethnicity is defined by our shared local cultures and patterns of behaviour, this means that a change of lifestyle (or country) could lead to a change of ethnic group (meaning therefore that we can alter our ethnicity by altering our circumstances). Perhaps the concept of ethnicity has become so complex and delicate that it has passed its usefulness. Yet, as with social class, however poorly thought out your question, the categories you use will appear to approximate to a social process so powerful that you will still find significant differences between them.

Other issues
A further difficult issue relates to clearly sensitive questions. Often as researchers we wish to consider emotional and controversial topics since these are also often important and interesting. The key technique here is to be clear and unemotional in wording questions.

My advice is, however long you make the preamble to a difficult question, keep the question itself short. Avoid all pejorative or leading words (even commonly used terms such as 'truancy' for unauthorized absence imply something about the views of their author). I once asked a large group of students how many had been present at or involved in committing a crime. None had. I then asked how many had been present at or involved in shop-lifting, speeding in a car or the use of illegal drugs. More than half had. Responses are horribly sensitive to the precise phrasing of the question. If you want respondents to be prepared to report dangerous or possibly incriminating matters, then a number of designs that have been worked out could help. How much help they actually are is something you can decide in your pilot study (see below).

A simple example might run as follows. If you wish to ask a difficult question, use a preliminary question such as, 'Toss a coin, if it is heads answer the next question, but if it is tails toss again and then put "yes" for the next question if it is heads and "no" if it is tails'. In theory, therefore, half of the people answering the next question 'yes' or 'no' are genuine and half are talking about their second coin toss. You do not know which is which (so their anonymity is secure) but you do know that the chances of heads or tails is 50:50. So you need to subtract a quarter of your total sample from the 'yes' responses and a quarter from the 'no' to the next question to be left with the genuine answers (assuming you have a large sample). Please note that I have never tried this and, although it sounds fine in theory, there is an awful lot that can go wrong. The question just seems too complicated to work in real life.

Other notoriously tricky questions involve grids or two-dimensional tables, and those questions where respondents have to rank a set of responses, and indeed any question where the respondent can legitimately respond more than once. These questions are often so difficult to analyse that they are not worth including even if they seem the natural way to ask the question. They are also difficult to complete, and so might endanger your response rate. I suggest you keep away from these until you are more experienced. I have not managed to make one work successfully and have resolved in future to find another way of getting at the same information.

⅃T STUDIES

All research designs need to be piloted or pre-tested, so the comments made here about surveys could apply equally well to experiments, observation studies, interview schedules and so on. Researchers are always working to a deadline and so the temptation to skimp on the pilot study is very strong. Resist this temptation, at least until you are more experienced. Pilots are sometimes misinterpreted as applying only to the survey instrument. Rather, a pilot study should be seen as a full 'dress rehearsal' for the whole research design. Thus, a good pilot study involves selecting a sample in the same way as intended for the final study, negotiating access in the same way, delivering the instrument in the same way, calculating response rates and analysing the results in the same way. Problems will probably appear at every stage. This kind of pre-test does generally have two main differences from the 'real thing'. It will involve a much smaller sample, making it quicker and cheaper than the final survey, and it involves asking participants some supplementary questions about the design itself, making it slightly longer and more complex again.

I recommend a two-stage pre-testing process. First, try your questionnaire out on experts, friends, family and anybody else you can bully into helping. Ideally try it out in face-to-face interview or focus groups with a few people from your intended population (but not from your sample). Ask for comments and criticisms. Note where people are hesitant or do not understand the question. Note carefully any non-responses. Consider whether there are any pressures to produce socially acceptable or desirable answers. In particular, note if the respondents' first reaction is not actually an answer to the question (often a clue to a design problem). Fix any problems. And there will be problems. Anyone who tells you it is all fine is either lying or cannot be bothered to help. Then pre-test again. Remember to date each draft of your questionnaire so that you know which is up-to-date, but keep the earlier versions in case you change your mind again.

Second, move on to the full pilot. Analysing even four responses in the way that you will in the full study forces you to design this stage early on (so that at least you will not come to my office in six months' time with a pile of questionnaires, saying, 'so, what am I supposed to do now?'). It will also help you face up to flaws. Are the respondents really able to answer the questions? For example, do people know how many litres of petrol they used last year or how many employees work in the same company as themselves? Or are they guessing to try and please you?

If the pilot leads to a few changes, you might then proceed to the main study. If, however, things go seriously wrong then the changes you need to make are so major that you will need to pilot the whole thing again. This is the social science equivalent of your aeroplane design crashing on its first test flight.

AN EXAMPLE OF A SIMPLE QUESTIONNAIRE

The example questionnaire below comes from a pilot project investigating the relationship between the use of digital technology and patterns of participation in lifelong learning (the work is represented by Gorard and Selwyn 1999, Selwyn and Gorard 2002). It was sent to all of the users of a particular Internet-based educational course, in an attempt to garner information about their background (Figure 5.1). It was sent by email (acceptable given the nature of the population), and completed interactively by the recipients (thus reducing transcription). Our primary concern was with widening participation, and we needed to see whether the kind of people using web-based instruction were different in any significant way from those following more traditional courses at the same level. In essence, has technology broken down the barriers faced by those previously excluded from learning in adult life? Or has it reinforced them? We already knew that patterns of participation in traditional adult learning varied by gender, age, location, employment, social class and prior educational attainment. Therefore, this is what our questions asked about. The temptation to include questions about the nature of their learning experiences and other superficially interesting matters was very strong. We resisted it because we added one final question: 'Would you be willing to be interviewed as part of this project?' It was in the follow-up interviews with a sub-sample that we decided to approach questions about attitudes, learner identities, the nature of barriers and possible tranformative experiences. The questionnaire was intended to elicit basic 'facts' only.

As a result of the responses and follow-up interviews, we made some modifications even to this simple design. The responses about usual occupation were hard to classify, and the use of equivalence levels in the question about qualifications was not a great success. Nevertheless, I include this simple instrument to make the point that questionnaires do not have to be complicated to be useful to the

INFORMATION ABOUT YOUR LEARNING

1. How often do you use the on-line Welsh for learners website?	At least once per week Less than once per week No longer use it
2. Where do you access the Internet from?	Home Work Elsewhere*
if 'elsewhere' please specify	....
3. Are you still in full-time education?	Yes No*
if 'no', how old were you when you left full-time education?	....
4. Which of the following levels best describes your highest qualification?	Level three: 2+ A-Levels (or equivalent), GNVQ Advanced, NVQ3, OND, etc. Level two: 5+ GCSEs grade A*-C (or equivalent), 5 O-Levels, 5 CSE grade 1, etc. Level one: less than 5 GCSEs grade A*-C (or equivalent)

INFORMATION ABOUT YOURSELF

5. Sex	Male Female
6. Date of birth	....
7. Postcode (or area name)	....
8. Are you currently employed?	Yes No
9. What is your current or usual occupation?	....

Figure 5.1: Draft questionnaire on background to web-based participation

researcher (as this one has been). The information we requested includes the key predictors of adult learning patterns derived from our previous work. We did not need, in this instance, to ask any more questions. We did need more responses (but that is another story!).

COMMON PROBLEMS IN QUESTIONNAIRE DESIGN

There are many potential pitfalls in the design of a survey instrument, and several have been described in this chapter. Most can be avoided by careful proof-reading followed by a full pilot study. A selection follows.

- Asking the research questions
- Use of leading questions
- Making the instrument too long
- Asking pointless questions
- Use of offensive language

Asking the research questions

Some novices become confused between their research questions, which define what they are trying to find out, and the questions they use in an investigation to answer those research questions. Research questions do not generally make good test items. Suppose, as a simple example, you wanted to know whether most employers believed that graduates were genuinely more multi-skilled than non-graduates. You could not use the following item in a questionnaire to a sample of employers.

Do most employers believe that graduates are more multi-skilled than non-graduates?

(please circle your answer)   Yes

No

Don't know

Employers cannot answer for most employers, only for themselves. Your job as researcher is to aggregate the answers of many employers to decide what most of them believe. Even so, you probably cannot simply convert the question to, 'Do you believe that graduates are more multi-skilled than non-graduates?'. The question is still too much like the research question and therefore too complex. People may want to know more about what multi-skilling is or in what areas of employment this is meant to be relevant. People may feel resistance to answering either 'yes' or 'no', sensing that it is too extreme and wanting to assess different parts of a job differently. The proper development of survey items from research questions is a complex and rewarding business.

Use of leading questions

I have regularly seen introductions to surveys that 'give the game away' by leading the potential respondent to answer in a certain way or share some unnecessary assumptions with the researcher. For example, I recently saw a letter addressed to heads of schools starting, 'I am a student researching the current shortage of teachers . . .'. One of the objectives of the research was to establish whether there was a teacher shortage (although the student-researcher clearly believed that there was).

Less common, as it is easier to spot perhaps, is where the lead is in the question (as in the legendary, 'When did you stop beating your wife?'). I have paraphrased the following question slightly for anonymity, but the example is a genuine one from a PhD student whose dissertation I was examining:

'How important is the quality of music teaching to you when assessing a new school?
      1   some importance
      2   medium importance
      3   very important.'

This candidate, for whatever reason, could not conceive of someone not caring at all about the quality of music teaching when assessing a school.

Making the instrument too long
All of us tend to make questionnaires too long. I have seldom managed to analyse all of the questions in a piece of survey research. Despite planning and piloting, some of the questions simply do not work. Working in a team makes the situation worse as each team member tends to have 'favourite' questions that he or she wishes to retain. All these problems exist and must be faced. What is absurd, though, is any desire for length for its own sake. One of the most ridiculous things I have ever heard concerned a PhD student who was repeatedly criticized during his pilot study for having an insufficiently long questionnaire. The complainants did not point out any key issues that had been omitted, merely claiming that the current length was suited only for a Masters project. In their opinion, a government-funded PhD project required a more substantial instrument. While clearly laughable, there is a little of this attitude in many of us. Resist it.

Asking pointless questions
Typical problems here involve asking questions to which we already know the answer or asking for information that we can obtain more easily by other means. One example I have seen in real studies involved questionnaires sent to named individuals who had been selected on the basis of sex. The first question was, 'Are you male or

female?". Another involved asking teachers at named schools how many pupils there were in their school, where this information could be more accurately obtained from official statistics (see Chapter Two).

Perhaps the most peculiar example of a pointless question I have come across occurred in a paper by Coldron and Boulton (1991). They asked one group of people for their own views, and for their views of the views of others and then concluded that the 'two' (sic) sets of views were related. Even though the researchers were interested in the views of the pupils, only 'parents ... were asked to report their children's reasons for wanting to go to a particular school' (Coldron and Boulton 1991, p. 175). It is not clear, in this case, why the 11-year-old children were not felt able to speak for themselves. It is, however, hardly surprising that the authors concluded that 'from these figures it appears that children chose mainly on the same basis as their parents', since the two sets of views they were comparing were in fact both from the parents. A similar situation is evident in a study by West et al. (1995), in which parents were asked about their child's reasons for choosing a new school, and which found that 83% stated that the child wanted the same school as themselves. The inaccuracy of parent's and children's reports about each other has been shown several times (e.g. Pifer and Miller 1995), and so the value of findings like the two above are suspect.

Use of offensive language
Clearly no sensible researcher would set out to use deliberately offensive language in a questionnaire, so all of the examples I have come across have been unintentional. Sometimes the use of offensive language is the result of a misjudged attempt at informality and therefore approachability. While a questionnaire should not be pompous or use long technical words inappropriately, it is probably best to stick to a relatively formal style throughout to encourage a serious frame of mind in the respondent. Sometimes the use of offensive language is the result of naiveté or ignorance. Sometimes it is due to cultural or national differences. I have seen a question for teachers in the UK refer to a 'retard' or retarded pupil, and another for adults asking whether they were 'low class'. In both cases fashions in terminology had changed and made both questions seem unpleasant in tone. Be careful. Be up-to-date. I have seen questions use analogies and terminology from the drinking of alcoholic beverages in instruments for a general population

including Moslems. Why take the risk? Don't turn people away by your use of language.

This chapter has concentrated on the design of a survey instrument. For more on general survey design see Thomas (1999), Czaja and Blair (1996), Hakim (1992), Oppenheim (1992), Payne (1951) or Sudman and Bradburn (1982). See Bernard (2000) for examples of more esoteric survey designs. Chapter Six continues by describing some simple statistical techniques for analysing the kinds of data collected from a survey.

Simple non-parametric statistics: minding your table manners

To a large extent, the simple presentation of survey and other findings is dealt with in Chapter Three. More complex and powerful parametric approaches to analysis are dealt with in Chapters Nine and Ten. Here we are concerned with going beyond the presentation of data and its simple arithmetic manipulation, to consider patterns within it and differences between sub-groups in our sample.

ANALYSING SURVEY DATA

Suppose that one of the background questions in a survey using a random sample of 100 adult residents in one city asked for the sex of the respondent. The results might be presented as in Table 6.1.

Suppose that one of the substantive questions in the same survey asked the respondents whether they had visited their GP (doctor) in the past two years. The results might be presented as in Table 6.2.

Table 6.1: Frequency by sex in our achieved sample

	Number
Male	41
Female	59
Total	100

Table 6.2: Frequency of GP visits in our achieved sample

	Number
Visit GP past two years	53
Not visit GP past two years	47
Total	100

We know therefore that our achieved sample contained more women than men, and that slightly more than half reported visiting their doctor in the past two years. Both of these might be important findings given a good-quality sample of a clearly defined population. In many cases, however, our chief concern as social scientists is to go beyond these simple patterns and answer questions such as, 'Are men or women more likely to report visiting their doctor?'. In this case we need to consider the two variables simultaneously, and we can present our summary as a cross-tabulation using different rows for one variable and different columns for the other. The results might be presented as in Table 6.3 (note that tables such as these will be created for you automatically from your datafile by the cross-tabulation function in statistical packages such as SPSS).

Table 6.3: Cross-tabulation of sex by GP visit

	Visit GP	Not visit GP	Total
Male	24	17	41
Female	29	30	59
Total	53	47	100

Note that the 'marginal' totals are the same as in the simpler tables above. There are still 100 cases of whom 41 are male, 53 visited their GP, and so on. The table also now shows that more than half of the men visited their GP (24/41 or around 59%), while fewer than half of the women did (29/59 or 49%). For our sample therefore we can draw safe conclusions about the relative prevalence of GP visits in the two sex categories. The men in our sample are more likely to have visited their GPs. In Chapter Four it was argued that one motive for using probability sampling was that we could then generalize from our sample to the larger population for the study. If the population in this example is *all* residents of the city from which the sample was taken, can we generalise from our sample finding about the relationship between sex and GP visits? Put another way, is it likely that men in the *city* (and not just in the sample) were more likely to visit their GP than women?

In order to answer the question for the population (and not just for the people we asked by selecting them at random) it is very useful to imagine that the answer is 'no' and start our consideration from there. If the answer were actually no, and men and women were equally likely to visit GPs, then what would we expect the figures in Table 6.3 to look like? The number of each sex remains as defined in Table 6.1 and the number of people visiting GPs remains as defined in Table 6.2. In other words, our table of what we would expect to find starts with the partially completed Table 6.4.

Table 6.4: The marginal totals of sex by GP visits

	Visit GP	Not visit GP	Total
Male			41
Female			59
Total	53	47	100

From this outline we can calculate exactly what we expect the numbers in the blank cells to be. We know that 41% of cases are male, and that 53% of cases visited their GP. We would therefore expect 41% *of* 53% of the overall total to be both male and have visited their GP. This works out at around 22%, or 22 cases as shown in Table 6.5.

Table 6.5: The expected value for males visiting GP

	Visit GP	Not visit GP	Total
Male	22		41
Female			59
Total	53	47	100

We can do the same calculation for each cell of the table. For example, as 59% of the cases are female and 53% of the cases visited GPs, we would expect 59% of 53% of the overall total to be females and have visited GPs. This works out at around 31%, or 31 cases. But then we already knew that this must be so, since 53 people in our survey visited GPs, of whom we expected 22 to be male, so by definition we expected the other 31 to be female. Similarly, 41 cases are male and we expected 22 of these to have visited a GP, so we expected that the other 19 did not. We can now complete the table (Table 6.6). Note that in practice all of these calculations would be generated automatically by the computer.

Table 6.6: The expected values by sex for visiting GP

	Visit GP	Not visit GP	Total
Male	22	19	41
Female	31	28	59
Total	53	47	100

To recap, we obtained the figures in Table 6.3 from our survey (our 'observed' figures) and wanted to know whether the apparent difference in visiting rates for men and women was also likely to be true of the city as a whole. To work this out, we calculated how many men and women we expect to have visited GPs assuming that there was actually no difference, and obtained the figures in Table 6.6 (our 'expected' figures'). For convenience in Table 6.7 the observed figures in each cell are followed by the expected figures in brackets.

Table 6.7: Observed and expected values by sex for visiting GP

	Visit GP	Not visit GP	Total
Male	24 (22)	17 (19)	41
Female	29 (31)	30 (28)	59
Total	53	47	100

If there were no difference in the city as a whole between the rates of GP visits for men and women then we would expect 22 of 41 males to have visited but we actually found 24 of them. In each cell of the table there is a discrepancy of two cases between the observed and expected figures. Is this convincing evidence that men are more likely to visits GPs than women in this city? Hardly. In selecting a sample of 100 cases at random it would be easy for us to have inadvertently introduced a bias equivalent to those two cases. We should therefore conclude that we have no evidence of differential visiting rates for men and women in this city.

Did you follow that analysis? If not, try reading it again. The argument traced in Tables 6.1 to 6.7 contains just about everything that you need to know about the logic of significance-testing in statistical analysis. If you can follow the logic and are happy with the conclusion, then you have completed a statistical analysis.

I think that the argument is relatively easy to follow if you try, and is a form of logic that all social science researchers should be able to follow. There is, therefore, no reason why anyone reading this book should not read and understand statistical evidence of this sort. There is also no reason why anyone should not be able to complete such an analysis with different figures (and the help of a computer). Everything that you will learn about statistics is built on this rather simple foundation, and yet nothing in statistics is more complicated than this. Much of what follows is simply the introduction of a technical shorthand for the concepts and techniques used in this introductory argument.

MORE FORMALLY

For example, a concept that has little practical significance for us, now that computers handle the calculations, is that of 'degrees of freedom'. You will see this term used in books and cited in publications. In the example above the number of degrees of freedom tells you how many of the four main cells you (or rather the computer) would have to complete with an expected value before being able to work the rest out immediately. In the example above, once you have calculated that you expected 22 males to visit their GP, you could find the other three numbers immediately since they had to add up to the marginal totals. The degrees of freedom for the table is therefore *one*, meaning you need to calculate only one of the four numbers to see by simple subtraction what the other three must be. Only one cell in the table was free to vary. 'Degrees of freedom' is therefore a posh name for something you already understand.

As another example, consider the concept of a 'null hypothesis'. This is an assumption, merely for convenience, that there is no difference in the population between the two groups you are examining. In the example, our null hypothesis was that the GP visiting rate for men and women in the city was the same. We do not say that the null hypothesis is true, merely that it gives us a convenient base against which to judge our actual (observed) findings. We need the null hypothesis of no difference in order to be able to calculate our expected values. It is a matter of arithmetic convenience, no more than that. 'Null hypothesis' is therefore also a posh name for something you already understand.

Our conclusion above was that on the basis of the data collected we had no evidence that the visiting rates for men and women differed in the population. The rates did differ slightly in the sample we obtained but consideration of the null hypothesis led us to believe that this difference was too small to attach any importance to. What we did, therefore, was to try and distinguish between a real difference in data and one due to random error in the sampling procedure. This is the whole basis of statistical testing. Traditionally we use probability or likelihood to determine the difference between systematic and random events, and this is where the importance of random sampling comes from (see Chapter Four). Because of the nature of random events we can argue that the less likely it is that an event occurred by chance the more likely it is that the event reflects a real difference in the population we are examining. We could therefore be more precise in our example than we have been so far. It would be possible to calculate exactly, if the city's visiting rates for men and women are the same, how likely it is that any random sample would find the pattern we did, namely, men appearing to be slightly more likely to visit their GP. The calculation would be possible, but luckily for us we do not have to bother with it. All such calculations have already been done and are summarized in statistical tables.

We do not even have to bother to consult statistical tables, since a statistical package on a computer (such as SPSS) effectively has these tables in its memory and can tell us the precise probability. In our example the probability of obtaining the results we did (or an even more extreme set of results) if the null hypothesis were true is 0.36 (or 36%). The cross-tabulation function on SPSS has a 'Statistics' option, on which you can check (i.e. tick) a box for a chi-square test. This test will calculate the probability above for you (if interested, see Siegel 1956 or Clegg 1992 for a simple introduction to the chi-square distribution used). Apart from the cross-tabulation (i.e. like Table 6.3) the output will look something like this (Table 6.8):

Table 6.8 – Results of a chi-square test of significance

	Value	df	Asymp.sig. (2-sided)	Exact sig. (2-sided)	Exact sig. (1-sided)
Pearson chi-square	.855[b]	1	.355		
Continuity correction[a]	.520	1	.471		
Likelihood ratio	.858	1	.354		
Fisher's exact test				.418	.236
Linear-by-linear association	.847	1	.358		
No. of valid cases	100				

a. Computed only for 2x2 table
b. 0 cells (0.0%) have expected count less than 5. The minimum expected count is 19.27.

Now you can begin to see or remember why statistics has such a bad press! The important thing when faced with reports like this is not to panic. A lot of this output is easy to understand, and most of the rest of it is irrelevant to us at present. Computer statistical packages are notorious for producing lengthy reports even for relatively simple analyses because, presumably, they are trying to be extra helpful. I tolerate this because they are so helpful. They calculate for me the probability of observing what I observed if the null hypothesis is true, and therefore give me the basis for making a decision about the 'significance' of my findings (more on significance below).

The column headed 'df' we already know about. It tells us how many degrees of freedom there are in Table 6.3. The final row also tells us something we already know. It is the number of cases or individuals in Table 6.3. The five other rows are actually for five different tests of the same thing, which all appear automatically when we asked for chi-square. The one we are concerned with here is the first row labelled 'Pearson chi-square'. For each test the first column gives us the test statistic. It is this that is used by the computer to consult an internal statistical table for conversion into a probability. This statistic has no clear meaning in the real world and is therefore best ignored (although note that in some areas of social science traditionalists still insist that you quote this value – as a beginner I suggest you humour them). The numbers in the last three columns are all probabilities. The one that concerns us here is the shaded cell reading '.355'. This cell would not be actually shaded in practice, but I have emphasized it here because it is the key number in the report. If this cell contains a large number we have no reason to disbelieve our null hypothesis, whereas if this number is small we can reject the null hypothesis and assume that males in our population as well as in our sample are more likely to report visiting their GPs.

The key question is therefore how large or small this probability must be before we can decide either way? There is, of course, no clear answer to this. You, as the researcher, make the decision. As with all decisions about research design, sampling and analysis you will need a reason for your decision, and you must publish your decision and your reason with your results. Recall what you are trying to decide here. In our example the question is: if there is really no difference between men and women in terms of visiting GPs, how likely (or unlikely perhaps) is it that we found the small difference we actually observed? Our answer is that if we selected a sample and ran our survey many, many times and there was no difference between men and women in the population, then we would still find a difference as large as, or larger than, we found 36% of the time. This is a very large probability (roughly equivalent to throwing either a three or a four with one die, or picking a playing card of ten or more from a standard pack). Our observed difference is therefore not a safe one, and would be termed 'not significant'.

The most common value used as a cut-off point is 5% (or 0.05). Using this value for the present, our decision simplifies to: if the value in the shaded cell is 0.05 or higher then we retain our null hypothesis and report that we have no evidence of a significant difference in the population. On the other hand, if the shaded value is less than 0.05 we reject our null hypothesis and assume that there *is* a significant difference between men and women in our population. Our significance level, or threshold, is 5%.

If we had decided that our evidence did show a significant difference between the men and women in the city in terms of their reported frequency of visiting their GP, then we would need an alternative to our null hypothesis. The simplest alternative explanation of our results (other than chance, that is) is that there *is* a real difference. This may seem a rather laborious way to get to this point, but for the moment pause and check that you are still happy with the argument or logic of statistical testing, perhaps by reviewing the previous section before continuing. The next section introduces further important but interesting complexities.

SIGNIFICANCE AND SOCIAL SCIENCE

Before continuing with our conversion of the overall logic of statistical testing into a technical vocabulary, we need to consider the most important point of all analyses. In our city example, we now have a result and an answer to the question about statistical significance. In my experience, many newcomers to statistics treat this as the end whereas it is only the end of the beginning. The stages of design, sampling, data collection and significance testing are skilled activities but relatively technical ones. Of these stages, significance testing is the easiest to get right and the quickest to complete. If the design is a good one for the questions being researched, the sample is selected appropriately from a defined population, the method of data collection minimizes observer bias and measurement error, and the statistics have been used correctly, then we now have a social science finding to be explained. This is not the end. This is what we have been doing all that rigorous work for. What does our finding mean? Unfortunately this final stage is far from technical and not easy to teach as it is heavily dependent on the precise nature of all the preceding stages (but read the rest of this book for some tips, or Booth et al. 1995, and see Huff 1991 or Thouless 1974 for amusing illustrations of how not to proceed).

In our example we have two elementary-level explanations. One is that there really is no difference between visiting rates for men and women. The other is that difference exists but that our research is somehow defective (perhaps by using too small a sample or having a gender bias in the wording of the questionnaire). If we have any evidence for such defects we should, of course, record and publish it whenever we publish our results. However, the law of parsimony rules here. In the absence of evidence, even with defective research, we err on the side of caution and assume that the social world is as simple as possible (a principle known since the Middle Ages as Ockham's razor). Therefore, given no significant evidence of a difference we have to assume that there actually is no difference (the default position in any investigation). At our next level of explanation we need to consider why there is no difference between men and women in their rates of visiting GPs, or perhaps why other commentators might have expected there to be a difference.

If, on the other hand, we had found a real difference, we would have needed to begin to explain how this difference arose. Is it genetic or learnt or motivational, to do with self-confidence, or related to marriage or childbirth? Is it likely to be specific to this city in this country and era? Are there variations in the pattern between different age categories or between occupational groups? This stage of exploration is both creative and exhausting (and is very unlikely to be solely 'quantitative' in nature) but, as I have already said, this is the point that our research would have been building up to. The generation of social science knowledge provides our motivation for all of the foregoing stages.

A second important point to consider before getting a bit technical again is the meaning of the term 'significance' as used in statistical testing. It is unfortunate that this word has an important meaning in general writing as well, since the two meanings are easily confused. If we find a significant result using a test of significance such as chi-square, we mean that the null hypothesis can be rejected with relative safety. In other words, our difference between the two groups appears not to be a fluke. This does not mean that our finding is or is not of any interest or importance to the wider research community. If I took many samples of the table salt and the ground pepper sold in a national supermarket chain, analysed their components and found that salt and pepper were significantly different, then this result could be seen as less than exciting. If, on the other hand, I found no significant difference between salt and pepper and that the supermarkets were selling basically the same product under two headings, then this would be more interesting (worth a newspaper report, surely?). Similarly with social science research. Although we tend to get caught up in the flow of significance testing and look forward to a 'positive' result, a negative result can be just as exciting (and often more so).

Some examples of my own work in education illustrated in this book include the findings that different types of schools (fee-paying and comprehensive, for example) are no more or less effective than each other, that boys are not increasingly under-achieving in relation to girls at school, and that the use of targets and performance indicators has not led to the increased polarization of high and low educational outcomes. The reason that these findings are interesting is that many commentators believed the opposite to be true. The findings therefore contradict a moral panic in each area and are seen by some as counter-intuitive. This makes them interesting. The message here is not that you should seek out controversial findings (or the more common reverse of this, seeking out acceptable or confirmatory findings), but that you should seek findings that are as secure as possible. If this means retaining your null hypothesis of no difference/pattern then so be it. The key thing to remember about significance tests is that they do not test the rigour of your design, the quality of your data or the meaning of any differences between groups (Campbell and Stanley 1963). All of these other elements are up to you, and they involve mostly non-mathematical issues with non-mathematical solutions.

ANOTHER WORKED EXAMPLE OF SIGNIFICANCE TESTING

To reinforce the points made so far and continue our formalization of the logic of testing, I include another example of a chi-square test. This one is from real life or, rather, it ought to have been! Coldron and Boulton (1991), in a study published in a highly prestigious journal, made the following claim. They listed the reasons reported by parents for selecting a new school for their child, and then looked at differences in the frequency of responses from parents of boys and girls. They stated that for two of the groups of reasons, there were two differences worthy of note between parents of boys and girls. No null hypotheses or tests of significance were mentioned in the article. As an example of a difference 'worthy of note', they stated that 'the child's own preference of school was mentioned more by parents of boys (15) than of girls (7)' (Coldron and Boulton 1991, p. 173).

If true, this could be an important finding and it has accordingly passed into the research literature as a 'fact'. The finding has been widely cited by other authors, who like most of us tend to read only the summaries and findings of research reports, while ignoring the methods by which those summaries were reached. The actual finding is that 15 of the parents of boys but only 7 of the parents of girls in their sample reported taking the views of their child into account when selecting a new school. These figures are summarized in Table 6.9.

Table 6.9: Raw figures from Coldron and Boulton (1991)

Observed	Boys	Girls
Involved in choice	15	7

We cannot work out from Table 6.9 what we would have expected under our null hypothesis of no difference between the parents of boys and girls, and the authors did not do this or any other form of analysis. Their logic appears to have been that 15 is bigger than 7, so the finding is clear enough. Luckily, they do report their achieved sample size (but not their population, method of selection or response rate be it noted). They had 120 families of boys and 102 of girls. We can therefore construct for the authors a standard cross-tabulation of sex and involvement in choice (Table 6.10).

Table 6.10: Sex of child and level of involvement

Observed	Boys	Girls	Total
Involved in choice	15	7	22
Not involved	105	95	200
Total	120	102	222

From these figures we can now calculate our expected results under the null hypothesis of no difference between the two groups. The marginal totals are set, and we do not change them. The table of no difference by sex would have 12 of the families of boys expected to be involved in choice. This is calculated as in the previous example. The sample includes 120/222 (54%) boys and 22/222 (10%) of the children were involved in choice. Therefore we would expect 54% of 10% of 222 (or 12) cases to be in the top left cell. As the degrees of freedom are one, we can calculate quickly that 108 families of boys would not involve their child in choosing (since 120–12 = 108), and so on. Thus, we have Table 6.11 containing the observed values followed by the expected values in brackets.

Table 6.11: Observed and expected values for sex and level of involvement

	Boys	Girls	Total
Involved in choice	15 (12)	7 (10)	22
Not involved	105 (108)	95 (92)	200
Total	120	102	222

Although Coldron and Boulton have not performed these calculations for their 'analysis', what this table means is that they could have expected to find 108 of the families of boys uninvolved with choice if there was no difference in their population between boys and girls. They actually found 105. Is this difference significant? You would not think so, and the more you learn about the logic of significance testing the easier it will become to 'predict' the results of tests. In fact, when you get to that stage, statistical tests are not really that much use to you. If there clearly is or clearly is not a difference, then a test is not needed. If the difference is unclear, the statistical test will not reduce much uncertainty for you (but this is a more advanced consideration than we need at this point, see Chapter Nine). Returning to the example – creating a datafile that matches the two variables in Table 6.10 allows me to run a chi-square test, again using the SPSS package. I simply select the 'Analysis' menu, a 'Descriptives' sub-menu, a 'Cross-tabulation' sub-menu from that, and check the box for 'Chi-square' under the heading 'Statistics'. A selection of the output is as follows (Table 6.12):

Table 6.12: Chi-square test of sex and level of involvement

	Value	df	Asymp.sig. (2-sided)	Exact sig. (2-sided)	Exact sig. (1-sided)
Pearson chi-square	1.382[a]	1	.276		
No. of valid cases	222				

a. 0 cells (0.0%) have expected count less than 5. The minimum expected count is 10.

This report confirms that there are 222 cases, and that the 2x2 table has one degree of freedom. More importantly, the chi-square test we are interested in shows a probability of 0.276 that the Coldron and Boulton results arose by chance alone. This suggests that we would be wrong to reject the null hypothesis of no difference between boy and girl families. The logic is the same as in our made-up example about GPs. This re-analysis of existing figures shows that the opposite conclusion should have been drawn to that which is published. Unfortunately, this kind of error is common (see Gorard 1997b for further problems with this same study, and Gorard 2000b for further examples). Of course, we cannot go around re-analysing all of the results we read (and many writers do not give us sufficient detail to do so anyway). We are supposed to rely on peer-review and referees for this, so that the results published in journals are only the best and the most rigorous. Nevertheless it is instructive to do so occasionally, and the number of times you reach a different conclusion from that published may surprise you. If these published results really are the most rigorous, what must the rest be like? If they are not the most rigorous, then what are they? The most comfortable? The biggest names? The most acceptable to the editors?

Let us finish this section by considering three more technical terms, as used in the two reports from SPSS we have seen. The 'minimum expected count' is, as it sounds, the number in the smallest cell of the expected frequency table (the number of families of girls involved in choice, in this example). The importance of this was described in Chapter Four. In order to draw conclusions we need a good number of expected cases in each cell, otherwise the calculations are too sensitive to the 'movement' of one or two cases between cells. It is important, therefore, to make your sample as large as possible, and to consider the number of sub-groups you will use in the analysis when deciding on the scale of your research. Of course, you do not need to have any particular number of cases in each cell for your *observed* frequencies. You might find that all men and no women had visited GPs in the first example, giving you two completely empty cells, but this would not alter your null hypothesis, nor would it lead you to empty cells in your table of expected frequencies (try it out if you can't imagine it). The practical point is that if your minimum *expected* value is less than ten cases approximately, you may need to take remedial action (see Siegel 1956) or even abandon your analysis.

The 'alternative hypothesis' is, like the null hypothesis, a technical creation, which summarizes the basic situation if the null hypothesis is rejected. In the current example our alternative hypothesis might be that the families of boys and girls involve their children in choice differentially. As discussed above, we would need to go a lot further than this and explain what this means and why it occurs, but at an elementary level this alternative is like an understudy actor waiting to be used if the main actor (the null hypothesis) cannot perform on the night (i.e. if it is rejected). It can be argued that if the null hypothesis is rejected there are in fact an infinite number of alternatives that could be used instead (for example by taking a simple explanation and repeatedly adding redundant clauses to it – a problem known technically as the 'under-determination of theory by data'). This is part of the reason why we use the parsimonious approach of Ockham's razor (see above). Parsimony is a general criterion for choosing an appropriate alternate hypothesis, and it eliminates 'silly' explanations with redundant clauses in them. This is also part of the reason why rejecting the null hypothesis does not *prove* an alternative to be right. We may easily choose an incorrect alternative from the infinite number available, and anyway we would have rejected the null hypothesis on probability grounds only (so we could easily be wrong about that as well).

In our second example there appear to be three equally simple alternative hypotheses. If there is a difference, it could be expressed as a general difference (girls and boys will be different) or as a directed difference (girls will score more/less than boys). This is what the chi-square report above refers to as one-sided or two-sided (or more often one- or two-tailed). A two-tailed test of significance involves checking for an unspecified difference between two groups, such as 'The rates of GP visits will be different for men and women'. A one-tailed test involves checking for a directional difference, such as 'Women are more likely to visit GPs than men', or its inverse. All three possible explanations are equally simple, but the directional hypotheses are intrinsically more convincing because they set us a more difficult test. If we predict that men and women differ in their frequency of visiting we could be right if men visit more or if women visit more. We are, *a priori*, about twice as likely to find this as to find specifically that men visit more than women (or vice versa). We might therefore wish to adjust our significance level (5% in our first example) accordingly, by decreasing it to 2.5% for two-tailed tests perhaps, or by increasing it to 10% for one-tailed directional tests. This is part of the judgement that you, as researcher, must make and explain to your readers.

SUMMARY OF CHI-SQUARE – A SIMPLE TEST OF SIGNIFICANCE

These are the outline steps in carrying out a test of significance, using two groups (e.g. middle-class and working-class) and a categorical variable (e.g. have been a victim of crime or have not).

1. State the *null hypothesis* of no difference between the groups (e.g. the same proportion of middle- and working-class people in the population have been victims of crime).
2. State an alternate hypothesis, either *one-tailed* (e.g. proportionately more working-class people in the population have been victims of crime) or *two-tailed* (e.g. a different proportion of middle- and working-class people in the population have been victims of crime).
3. Decide on a *level of significance*. This is an estimate, based on assumption of no difference between groups in the population, of the acceptable probability that any apparent difference between groups in the achieved sample is due to chance. For example, using 5% would mean that the researcher is prepared to reject the null hypothesis if the probability of the null hypothesis's being true is less than 5%. Using a higher level of significance (e.g. 10%) increases the possibility of incorrectly rejecting the null hypothesis (a *Type I error*), and using a lower level (e.g. 1%) increases the possibility of incorrectly retaining the null hypothesis (a *Type II error*). See Chapter Nine for more on this.
4. Calculate the test statistic (e.g. chi-square) with appropriate *degrees of freedom* (or df). The degrees of freedom represent the number of values in the table of calculation that could be altered (that have the 'freedom' to be different) while the marginal totals remain the same. In a chi-square test, df = (number of rows-1)

times (number of columns-1). In Table 6.13, if the sample of 300 cases has 140 middle-class cases and 100 victims of crime, and any one of the four central cells is known then all others are known as well. If, for example, 60 middle-class people report being victims of crime, then 40 working-class people have been victims of crime, and 80 middle-class people have not been. Degrees of freedom are therefore one (two rows and two columns).

Table 6.13: Example of two-by-two cross-tabulation

	Crime victim	Not crime victim	Total
Middle-class	60	80	140
Working-class	40	120	160
Total	100	200	300

5. Calculate the probability of the test statistic assuming the null hypothesis. If the result is less than the pre-determined level of significance, then the null hypothesis is rejected and the alternate hypothesis used in its place. If the result is more than or equal to the pre-determined level of significance, the null hypothesis is retained.

It is clear that more middle-class people in the sample in Table 6.13 report having been victims of crime. The test of significance is used to help decide whether the results for the sample would also be true for the larger population from which they are drawn. Thus, the population to which the results could generalize must have been described before carrying out the test. 'Significance' is used here to refer to the technical decision about retaining or rejecting the null hypothesis. Statistically significant results can be rather ordinary in social science terms, whereas non-significant results can be surprising (e.g. finding no significant difference in attainment between those who had practised a skilled task and those who had never tried it). When carrying out a chi-square test in practice the actual steps are much simpler than those above. Putting the table in a statistical package and asking for a chi-square test leads to step 5 immediately.

All tests of significance have underlying assumptions that must be met before they can be used. Chi-square is perhaps the most tolerant of the standard tests and therefore the most widely applicable. It can be used to compare two (or more) categorical variables as long as the expected number of cases in each cell is a reasonable number (at least ten perhaps). Expected cases are calculated under the null hypothesis. In Table 6.13, if there was no difference in reporting crime between middle-class and working-class people in the population, one would expect around 47 middle-class people to be victims, i.e. $(100 \times 140)/300$. Since $df = 1$ one would therefore expect 53 working-class people to be victims (as there are 100 victims in total), etc. Chi-square is calculated from the difference between observed and expected values in each cell (Table 6.14).

Table 6.14: Expected values for Table 6.13

	Crime victim	Not crime victim	Total
Middle-class	47	93	140
Working-class	53	107	160
Total	100	200	300

Chi-square can be used for larger tables with more than two categories per variable, but becomes correspondingly harder to interpret. For example, it may tell you that there is a significant difference within a table of eight rows and seven columns but it cannot pinpoint where (see below).

Chi-square is not a very powerful test, where *power* is defined as the ability to guide you to genuine patterns in your data while minimizing the chance of Type I errors. Increased power can be attained by increasing the number of cases, looking for larger effect sizes, being more precise in the alternate hypothesis by adding a direction of difference, or using a more powerful test (see Chapter Ten). Of these, the simplest solution is to have a larger sample.

OTHER NON-PARAMETRIC TESTS

This chapter concentrates on the chi-square test for several reasons. My intention is to convey the logic and some of the technical vocabulary of significance testing. In the summary steps above you could replace the term chi-square with the name of a different statistic. It would make no practical difference to the overall steps.

Chi-square is also the most general test. It could conceivably be used for any analysis, including checking for reliability in the one-sample case. Siegel (1956) recommends chi-square for all designs involving variables with nominal characteristics (see Chapter Three for explanation of levels of measurement).

Nevertheless, there are many other tests (see Kanji 1999, for example). Which of these should you use and when? The proper answer is, whichever you need whenever it is appropriate. For the benefit of the novice several textbooks contain charts, tables or flow diagrams on their inside cover as a prompt to find the section of the book relevant to the test you need, but these also provide a useful reference for identifying which test that is. The charts generally refer to dimensions such as level of measurement, the number of sample groups, the relationship between the sample groups, and your purpose in using the test (for measuring associations or differences). Table 6.15 provides a simple example for all non-parametric designs (see Chapter Nine for parametric designs, and Reynolds 1977, Lee et al. 1989 and Gilbert 1993 for more on the analysis of tables). For any analyses using only nominal variables the chi-square test is appropriate, although this can lead to problems with large tables (see below). For analyses with ordinal variables mixed with nominal variables (e.g. level of qualification by ethnic group) more powerful tests (often named after their 'inventors') are available that take advantage of the ranked nature of at least one of the variables. In situations where chi-square would be appropriate you can also use Cramer's V (or Yule's Q, see Chapter Three) as a measure of the actual association between the two categorical variables.

Table 6.15: Which non-parametric test to use?

	one sample	two independent samples samples	k independent samples (where k is any number greater than 2)
Nominal	chi-square	chi-square	chi-square
Ordinal	Kolgorov-Smirnov	Mann-Whitney	Kruskal-Wallis

COMMON ERRORS WITH TABLES

This section contains common errors in the construction and presentation of tabular information. I understand their temptations well because I have probably made all of them at some stage.

- Making insufficient reference to tables in the text
- Over-description of tables in the text
- Publishing computer printout
- Uncritical use of the omnibus chi-square test
- Post hoc recoding of items/collapsing categories
- Violating the assumptions of a test

Making insufficient reference to tables in the text
Although it is important that tables are presented in a way that is comprehensible to the reader, it is still necessary to refer to them and explain their significance in the accompanying text. Tables, like graphs, are a way of illustrating or backing up a point made in your argument. If any tables are not relevant to your argument they should be deleted from the presentation. In the same way, tables should contain information relevant to that argument only and therefore often need to be pruned ruthlessly. All analysts are probably guilty of including unwanted information in their tables and at the same time providing insufficient explanation in the text. A cynic might say that statistics are being displayed in journal articles to help persuade a cursory reader of the validity of the conclusions, but in insufficient detail for the more pedantic reader to attempt to verify them.

An article by Cheung and Lewis (1998) on the expectations by employers of new graduates provides several examples of this problem. In what is essentially a long empirical paper of 14 pages they provide only one brief paragraph on the methods they used. Consequently most of their 'results' have to be taken on trust (not something I like to do too often). There is no description at all of the instrument used to collect their primary data (see Chapter Five for the possible importance of this). Therefore, when the authors present findings, such as the 12 skills rated as 'very important' by employers, we do not know the length of the list from which these 12 were selected. The responses were apparently obtained using a five-point Likert scale, but no account is taken in the report of four of the possible responses on that scale. Their Tables 2 and 3 show only the percentage of respondents reporting a skill as 'very important'. We have no idea therefore of the distribution of other responses. There may, for example, be skills that all employers rate as 'important' but without being 'very important', and others that a few rate as 'very important' but most rate as 'of no importance'. In the method adopted by Cheung and Lewis the second of these would be reported and the first would not – a gross distortion of the truth. As with many of the examples used in this book it would be fascinating to know how this paper was able to 'pass' the peer-review process before acceptance for publishing.

Over-description of tables in the text
An alternative but less serious problem arises where the tables are fully explained and described in the text to the extent that the tables themselves are not necessary. This is very common in student dissertations. Consider, for example, Table 6.16.

Table 6.16: Car ownership by sex of respondent

Sex	N	Owns car	%	Doesn't own car	%
Male	56	23	41%	33	59%
Female	61	37	61%	24	39%
Total	117	60	51%	57	49%

I have often seen tables like this presented in dissertations as descriptive treatments of research results. Their purpose may be to describe the findings of a survey and no more complex analysis is presented. In the text, Table 6.16 is described by the student as showing that 41% of males but 61% of females own cars. Assuming that the nature of the sample (size and sex breakdown) has already been described, the use of table here in addition is ponderous and wasteful. Novices may consider that it has rhetorical appeal, but the last two columns are totally superfluous and the others may be summarized in a sentence. In many examples, a simple description of frequencies is easier to understand and shorter than a table.

Publishing computer printout
Related to the above habit of presenting ponderous tables (and to the use of technical variable-names as descriptors, see Chapter Ten) is the habit of presenting undigested computer printouts in research reports. As you will have noted, computer packages for data analysis are notoriously profligate in their use of space for reports.

A full report even from a simple 2 × 2 chi-square test might look like this (Table 6.17):

Table 6.17: Undigested output from a chi-square test

Crosstabs

Case Processing Summary

Cases

	Valid		Missing		Total	
	N	Per cent	N	Per cent	N	Per cent
VAR00001*VAR0002	91	100.0%	0	.0%	91	100.0%

VAR00001*VAR0002 Crosstabulation

Count

		VAR00002		
		1.00	2.00	Total
VAR00001	1.00	22	15	37
	2.00	26	28	54
Total		48	43	91

Chi-Square Tests

	Value	df	Asymp. Sig. (2-sided)	Exact Sig. (2-sided)	Exact Sig. (1-sided)
Pearson Chi-Square	1.127[b]	1	.288		
Continuity Correction[a]	.719	1	.396		
Likelihood Ratio	1.132	1	.287		
Fisher's Exact Test				.393	.198
Linear-by-Linear Association	1.115	1	.291		
N of Valid Cases	91				

a. Computed only for a 2x2 table
b. 0 cells (.0%) have expected count less than 5. The minimum expected count is 17.48

This output contains much more detail and information than most readers would want. Decide which part of this report is important to you, and display only that part in your own writing. Do not reproduce the whole, either because you cannot be bothered to work out the key message, or as a flourish to show that you have done the test. Design your own table layout. Decide for yourself how to structure the report of your findings, how many decimal places to use, and so on.

Uncritical use of the omnibus chi-square test
In the case of a 2 × 2 table the results of a significant chi-square test are unambiguous. The direction of difference is always clear, since one of the two groups will have the higher value for the test variable. Where the table is more complex than this then a significant result shows that there is a pattern/difference in the table but not where it is (as also happens when there are more than two groups for Analysis of Variance, see Chapter Nine). Further analysis is needed to characterize the differences in the table. Despite this, I regularly see students who feel that this second stage is too much effort and that they can see the pattern easily anyway. Their approach is therefore similar to that of finding the outlines of animals in the stars in the night sky, but with the added appeal of a statistically significant omnibus chi-square test. In reality they are trying to answer hopelessly imprecise or even unthought-of research questions (Rosenthal 1991). For example, consider the cross-tabulation in Table 6.18.

Table 6.18: Large table analysis

area of residence	non-participant	delayed learner	transitional learner	lifelong learner	still in education	total
Bridgend	97	43	79	130	20	369
Blaenau Gwent	141	47	81	81	11	361
Neath Port Talbot	101	54	62	142	11	370
total	339	144	222	353	42	1100

This table results from the sample of patterns of adult participation in learning described in Chapter Five. The table has eight degrees of freedom, and the probability for the associated chi-square test is reported as 0.000. This means that there is a very small chance indeed that the pattern of learning experiences (columns) is the same in the three geographical areas (rows). We can safely reject the null hypothesis of no difference between the three groups. However, this does not help us identify what the significant difference is. Is it that more people in the area known as Blaenau Gwent (141/361) do not participate in adult education at all? Is it that more people in Neath Port Talbot (142/370) are lifelong learners? Is it that more people in Bridgend (20/369) are still in full-time initial education?

There is really only one way to answer these questions, and that is to consider each pairwise comparison separately in a specially constructed 2 × 2 version of the table. For example the first question could be answered by collapsing the table to the following form (Table 6.19).

Table 6.19: Recoding a large table

	non-participant	all other learners	total
Blaenau Gwent	141	220	361
Bridgend or Neath	198	541	739
total	339	761	1100

The cells for Bridgend and Neath Port Talbot have been added together, and the cells for all learning experiences except non-participants have been added together. A simpler chi-square test can now be conducted on this 2 × 2 table, and if the result is significant (which it is, incidentally) we can attribute it to a difference between areas. A potential problem with this approach is the number of tests that need to be carried out, leading to a greater danger of spurious findings. Each test carries a possibility of leading to an error, so conducting more tests means more chances of error (see Chapter Nine for a discussion of this 'shotgun' effect).

Post hoc recoding of items/collapsing categories
Although there are often good reasons why survey items need to be recoded or categories within variables collapsed after the data has been collected (as in the last example), I have a feeling that this approach is over-used. Considering the nature of the analysis during the design stage helps us to reduce the need for such recoding. It should therefore be necessary only when the actual frequencies reported are somewhat skewed or where the preliminary consideration of analysis has been deficient. An example of the first sort might be where a questionnaire used the Registrar-General's traditional seven-point scale for collecting occupational classifications, but the nature of an achieved sample of 660 random cases was such that 'unskilled manual' and 'semi-skilled manual' occupations were both very rare. In this case, the analyst may wish to collapse these two categories for some forms of analysis requiring robust numbers of cases in each cell of the table (creating one

category for 'less-skilled' occupations, for example). Providing the compromise is reported, this is a perfectly proper action. An example of the second sort might be where the same scale was used with a sample of 30 cases. Here, unlike the first example, it would be entirely predictable that some if not all of the seven occupational categories would be very sparsely represented. The 'fault' lies with the analyst for having too many sub-groups in relation to the sample size.

Violating the assumptions of a test
All tests of significance are based on underlying assumptions about the research design. If these are violated (i.e. if the test is used even when the assumptions are not true) then the results may be invalid (see Chapter Nine for more about this). It is therefore important at least to know what these assumptions are. Tests, such as chi-square, for nominal variables are very tolerant, having the fewest assumptions and making them usable in a wide variety of situations. Two problems that I have seen in beginners' work are as follows. Table 6.20 is an example of a problem already described above. The observed figures in themselves give no cause for analytical concern, appearing to suggest that the practice of brushing teeth daily is higher among children in local authority care than those living with a family. But the expected value (shown in brackets) for one cell is very small. Since so few children are in care (16) and so few overall do not brush their teeth (10), we *expect* only two cases of not brushing teeth among children in care, even if there is no real difference between the two groups of children (our null hypothesis). This figure is so small that any test might not be valid, so we should point out the problem in any publication, and remember to go for a larger sample next time.

Table 6.20: Small expected count

	Brush teeth	Not brush teeth	Total
Local authority care	15 (14)	1 (2)	16
Family care	60 (61)	9 (8)	69
Total	75	10	85

Table 6.21 shows a problem I have encountered only once, but which is typical of a certain type of novice quantitative 'analyst'

who feels a need to use a significance test but who does not follow the logic of testing with which this chapter started. The analysis compares the pass rates in an examination between fee-paying and female students. If female students could also be fee-paying students then we cannot complete this cross-tabulation and we cannot use chi-square. The categories in our cross-tabulation must be mutually exclusive. The example I saw was more complex than this and stemmed from a survey question that asked respondents to 'tick as many answers as apply' (see Chapter Six for more on the difficulties of such designs). I repeat: the categories must be mutually exclusive for this kind of analysis.

Table 6.21: Need for mutually exclusive cases

	Pass	Fail	Total
Fee-paying students	12	12	24
Female students	47	17	64
Total	??	??	??

This chapter has introduced the logic of statistical testing using the most common non-parametric approach. The next chapter is an introduction to the nature of the models used in statistical analysis, and the conclusions that can and cannot be drawn from them.

Research claims: modelling the social world

This chapter is somewhat different from all the others. It contains a brief discussion of some wider issues in research, such as what it is we are trying to model with numbers when we study social phenomena. The chapter is therefore a key introduction to the rest of the book, in which modelling of social processes is broached. Some readers will find it more difficult and less immediately practical than the other chapters in the book. I suggest that perhaps you read this chapter briskly, noting its contents and purpose, and then return to it at the end. At that stage, after consideration of experimental designs, multivariate analyses, combining methods, and something of the relationship between the natural and social sciences, you may see more clearly why this chapter is used as a preface.

It is intended as a stimulus to discussion on the relationship between research evidence (of the type we generate in our studies) and the conclusions we can validly draw from that evidence. There have been several examples of this relationship (including several poor examples) in this book so far. The chapter is more about the general principles of what are termed here the 'warrants' for our research conclusions. Key among these are the principles involved in modelling cause and effect relationships. We can never 'see' *cause:effect* directly, so that all and any claims about causes are inferences drawn from, but not explicit in, our evidence. We need to be able to consider the extent to which such claims are warranted. After a brief introduction to the idea of warrants, the chapter proceeds by considering three positions in relation to causal models — that they exist, that they do not exist, and that they exist alongside non-causal phenomena. It suggests that there is no logical or empirical reason to reject any of these positions, but that social science researchers, by the nature of their remit, are committed to the first.

WARRANTING CLAIMS FROM EVIDENCE

Research itself is quite easy. Everyone (even an infant) does it every day by gathering information to answer a question and so solve a problem (e.g. to plan a rail journey, Booth et al. 1995). In fact most of what we 'know' is research-based, but reliant on the research of others (such as the existence of Antarctica). Where we have no other choice we may rely on our judgement of the *source* of that information (an atlas may be more reliable than memory, the rail enquiries desk may be more reliable than last year's timetable). But where we have access to the research findings on which any conclusions are based we can also examine their quality and the warrant that connects the two. Similarly when we present our own research findings, we need to give some indication, via caveats, of the extent to which we would be prepared to bet on their being true, or the extent to which we would wish others to rely on their being true. This is part of our 'warrant'. Obviously, producing high-quality research is important but even high-quality work can lead to inappropriate conclusions.

Huck and Sandler (1979) remind readers of a silly example in order to make an important point about warrants. An experimental psychologist trains a flea to jump in response to hearing a noise. Every time the noise is made the flea jumps. They then cut the legs off the flea and discover that it no longer jumps when the noise is made. Conclusion: cutting off the legs has affected the flea's hearing. Of course, this is clearly nonsense but, as with the politicians' error in Chapter Three, it is likely that we have all been persuaded by similar conclusions. If a physiologist cuts out a piece of someone's brain and the person can no longer tell us about a memory (or perform a skilled action) that he was able to previously, then is this evidence that the specific memory or skill was 'stored' in that section of brain? Many such claims have been made, and early maps of brain function were based on just this approach. However, the same effect of inability to report recall of memory (or skill) could have been achieved by cutting out the person's tongue, or removing his heart. All three operations may prevent memory recall for different reasons without showing that the part of the body removed in each case is the *site* of the memory.

Brignell (2000) provides another example. The chemical industry routinely uses a chemical called 'dihydrogen monoxide'. While tremendously useful, this chemical often finds its way via spillages into our food supply. It is a major component of acid rain and a cause of soil erosion. As a vapour it is a major greenhouse gas. It is often fatal when inhaled, and is a primary cause of death in several UK accidents per year. It has been found in the tumours of terminally ill patients. What should we do about it? In a survey the clear majority of respondents believed that *water*, for that is what it is, should be either banned or severely regulated. All of those statements about water are basically 'true', yet clearly none of them means that water should be banned. Now replace water with another, less abundant chemical. How do you feel about banning it now? You have no obvious reason to change your mind. Yet you will probably have accepted just such evidence as we have about water to accept the banning of other chemicals. Do you see how difficult, but also how important, the warrants for research conclusions are? In both the flea and the water example the problem was not principally the research quality (or, put another way, the problem was separate from any reservations we may have about quality). The problem was that the conclusions drawn were not logically entailed by the research evidence itself.

The warrant of an argument can be considered to be its general principle – an assumption that links the evidence to the claim made from it (Booth et al. 1995). Claims must be substantive, specific and contestable. The evidence on which they are based ought to be precise, sufficient, representative, authoritative and clear to the reader (as far as possible). In logical terms, if we imagine that our simplified research evidence is that a specific phenomenon (A) has a certain characteristic (B), then our evidence is that A entails B. If we want to conclude from this that phenomenon A therefore also has the characteristic C, then the third component of our syllogism (the classic form of our argument) is missing or implying. This third component is that everything with characteristic B also has characteristic C. Thus, our complete syllogism is:

> This A is B
> All B are C
> Therefore, this A is also C.

While the first part (A is B) may be likened to the evidence in a research study (e.g. water can be fatal), and the third (A is C) is the conclusion (e.g. water should be banned), then the second (B is C) is like the warrant (e.g. everything that can be fatal should be banned). In research this step is often missed, as it is tacitly assumed by the author and the reader. However, where the research is intended to change the views of others it is necessary to make the warrant explicit. It can be challenged, but unlike a challenge to the evidence it is not about quality but rather about the *relevance* of the evidence to the conclusion. In the water example the warrant is clearly nonsense. Water can be fatal, but we cannot ban everything that *could* be fatal. But accepting that this warrant is nonsense also means that no evidence, however good, can be used with this precise format of argument to justify banning anything at all.

The warrant may be part of the research design but it is independent of any particular method of data collection (de Vaus 2001). Methods – whether quantitative or qualitative – cannot be judged in isolation from the questions they are intended to illuminate (National Research Council 2002). The results should be disclosed to critique, and the conclusions drawn based on an explicit coherent chain of reasoning that rules out all plausible counter-explanations and is intended to be persuasive to a sceptical reader (rather than playing to a gallery of existing 'converts', for example). The first question to be asked of any evidence presented in support of a model of a social process is, 'but what else might this mean?'. The ability to discern rival explanations, while varying considerably between individuals, probably grows with practice (Huck and Sandler 1979). It is a key skill for good research (but manifestly not a necessary one for 'success' in a research career). But, perhaps more importantly, it is a key skill for everyone to have as a consumer of research – so we won't get fooled again (see Chapter One). One way of improving this skill is to learn to recognize common forms of misleading argument. For example, the 'fallacy of affirming the consequent' is quite commonly encountered in social science. The fallacy argues that if A is true then B will follow. Then if B appears it is taken by some researchers to mean that A is true. While seductive there is no logic to this argument unless it starts more strongly with 'only if'. Otherwise exactly the same argument can be made with Z (or anything else) substituted for A.

The boxing off of plausible rival explanations is therefore generally at the heart of effective warrants. For any real system of variables there are nearly infinite models that could explain them (Glymour et al. 1987), just as an infinite number of equations can join any two points on a graph. Therefore, no one can consider all possible theories to explain any finding – so that in social science, as in natural science, every 'law' that is ever proposed is probably false. The purpose of the warrant is show readers that the proposed explanation is the best we have at this moment. As we have seen, a useful short-cut is to employ parsimony to eliminate many of the potential alternatives (cf. the canon attributed to Morgan 1903, p. 53: 'In no case may we interpret an action as the outcome of the exercise of a higher psychical faculty, if it can be interpreted as the outcome of one which stands lower in the psychological scale'). It is, for example, simpler and usually safer for a doctor to diagnose a complaint of headache, neck stiffness, fever and confusion as meningitis, rather than as a combination of brain tumour, whiplash, tuberculosis and acute porphyria. Of course, the latter could be correct, but parsimony encourages us to eliminate the more mundane and simplest explanations first. We therefore limit our potential explanations to those that employ the fewest (ideally none) assumptions for which we have no direct evidence.

CAUSAL MODELS

One thing that both the water and the flea examples have in common, at least implicitly, is that their conclusions are 'causal' in nature. They each represent a causal model – that cutting legs off fleas causes them to lose their hearing, and that water causes the many negative things associated with it. Of course, not all research is seeking to create or test a causal model. Some research is, and should be, solely descriptive. Descriptive work is anyway an essential first step to doing exploratory work, for 'before asking why we must be sure about the fact' (de Vaus 2001, p. 2). It is, in my opinion, far too common that researchers set out to explain and explore a phenomenon that does not actually exist. Recent examples that I have been involved with include attempts to explain: the school-mix effect (the supposed impact on one child's results of the results of his/her peers in the same class/school – does one improve simply by going to school with clever people?); the growing gender gap in attainment; and increasing socio-economic segregation in school compositions. The fact that we can create a plausible theory to explain imperfectly understood notions such as these is not evidence that they must exist (generating theories is easy). Such research should, rather, routinely start from a re-analysis of relevant existing datasets, and base the ensuing exploration on the patterns uncovered in the preliminary work.

Other than in purely descriptive work (e.g. '17% more of this type of crime was committed by men than women in 1999'), a research report that did not at least imply a causal model might look rather odd. Causes are central to our notion of understanding why things work as they do, and are just as central to the less sophisticated 'what works' approach (see Chapter Eleven). Yet despite this prevalence, social science research methods courses and textbooks tend to overlook the discussion of causal models completely or else prepare the novice researcher simply with the negative advice that a correlation is not the same as causation. If, over time, the income of the Archbishop of Canterbury tends to rise in line with the street price of cannabis this is not evidence that the Church of England makes money from drug-dealing. In these standard books, everyone is reminded therefore what is not a cause, and what a cause is not. In some methods books there is a section on the potential and limitations of experiments, which points to their unique selling point – the claim to be a direct test of cause and effect (Fisher 1935). But this is a scarce and recently revived phenomenon in social science outside psychology. In general, the concept remains untaught and undiscussed. Truly, it is a 'skeleton in the cupboard of philosophy' (Russell, in Ayer 1972). This makes it appropriate to consider here the nature of causal modelling in rather more detail than we usually do.

IS THERE SUCH A THING AS A CAUSE?

One possibility to be recognized and examined is that the concept of causation, on which the apparent pre-eminence of experimental methods rests, is an illusion. It is not possible to detect a cause empirically or prove that one exists philosophically. Effects cannot be deduced from observing causes, nor causes from observing effects (seeing a light bulb going off does not, by itself, allow the observer to deduce whether it has been switched, whether there is power failure or whether the bulb is broken, for example, Salmon 1998). It is even possible to imagine and describe social life and events more generally without reference to causes. Since this is so and we cannot see, smell, hear, measure or register causes directly, it may be unwise to assume that they exist. In fact, an argument could be advanced that this is the most parsimonious and therefore the most scientific explanation of our observations. We can never directly sense a cause. We merely induce its existence from our experience of the association of two or more events, and this is nothing more than a habit of mind – immutable though it appears (Hume 1962). A cause is therefore 'when the occurrence of one event is reason enough to expect the production of another' (Heise 1975). A very similar process is observed in both classical and operant conditioning, where the association of two things leads the conditioned subject to behave in the presence of one thing as though it implied the presence of the other.

A perfectly plausible alternative is one based purely on random events. A large table of pseudo-random numbers can contain arithmetic sequences and passages of repetition without our denying their essential randomness. The sequence '0 1 2 3 4 5 6 7 8 9' is as likely to be generated randomly as any other sequence of ten digits, such as '3 2 7 5 8 8 4 5 1 9'. Both are equally 'random' in the sense that we mean when describing such tables. In the same way, perhaps, the apparent regularities and repetitions that we observe more generally would be expected in a large (possibly infinitely large) universe. On this admittedly rather extreme view, all scientific propositions are like the behaviour of a pigeon in a Skinner box, repeating pointless actions in face of an accidental reinforcement schedule. However, this view, while intellectually coherent, means the end of scientific endeavour and, by definition, is not one that can be logically espoused by anyone engaged in publicly relevant research. Similarly, an economist believing that market indicators were actually following a 'random walk' could not earn a living as a predictor of these indicators, except as a charlatan.

Nevertheless, causes are seen by some respected commentators as pre-scientific. Pearson (in Goldthorpe 2001) as early as 1892 was calling the idea of causes a 'mere fetish', which was holding up the advance of correlational techniques in statistics. Russell (in McKim and Turner 1997) argued in 1968 that physics no longer seeks causes as they simply do not exist. According to him, causality is a relic of a bygone age, like the theory that infections were caused by demons invading the body. The best we can apparently hope for is the identification of 'relatively invariant functional relationships among measurable properties'. So Russell, like Pearson, would argue that scientific laws are idealized correlations. Mathematical statements or systems of equations can describe systems but they cannot express either intention or causality. If we drop a ball in a round bowl it will come to rest in the centre. We may predict this and say that it was 'caused' by gravity, but we can see neither the cause nor the gravity, and the cause itself could not be expressed mathematically. This becomes clearer if we drop two balls in the bowl. We can model the final resting places of both balls mathematically, but we cannot use this to decide which ball is 'causing' the other to be displaced from the centre of the bowl. The events are mutually determined and this system of mutual determination is what the equations express (Garrison 1993).

In economics as well as physics some commentators have tried to move away from causal explanations. Wages and interest rates might be inversely related over time, but rather than deciding that one causes the other it might be more realistic to describe them as mutually determining. Mathematics can be used to show that systems are or are not in equilibrium, and to predict the actual change in the value of one variable (or more) if another variable (or more) is changed. However, this prediction works both ways. If $y = f(x)$ then there will be a complementary function such that $x = g(y)$. Which variable is the dependent one (on the left-hand, predicted side) is purely arbitrary. Nothing in mathematics can overcome this. Non-causal mutuality (or concomitance) could be a perfectly reasonable and reasonably useful interpretation of many such sets of events.

WHAT IF CAUSE AND NON-CAUSE CO-EXIST?

Another position worthy of consideration in relation to the existence of causes is that they exist alongside non-caused events. One version of this stance was taken by those advancing the teleological argument for the existence of a god. Their argument was that everything has a cause, so it is possible to follow the causal chain back to the first cause, which was, for the want of a better term, god. Ignoring the simple counter-argument that the existence of a first cause actually refutes the first premise (i.e. that everything has a cause), it is clear that such advocates are allowing both causes and non-caused phenomena to exist in the same universe. The same approach is now followed by economists who present evidence for rational choices as a causing agent. These choices, such as those involved in human capital theory, do not appear to work for individuals but only at aggregated levels. One interpretation therefore is that individuals operate using idiosyncratic processes that only *appear* to be rational when grouped. More overtly, this position was adopted in the twentieth century by physicists and others believing that events at some levels are random (uncertain) while at higher levels of analysis they are patterned. In social science this belief appears in models, both quantitative and qualitative, in which the predictable components of behaviour are seen as causal in nature, and the unpredicted (and unpredictable) parts are seen as random error terms or individual whimsy (Pötter and Blossfeld 2001).

An alternative view is that all of these positions, while logically possible, are invalid for the practising social scientist. The number of potential explanations for any finite set of observations is actually infinite (created by simply adding more and more redundant clauses to a proposition, for example). We overcome this practical problem and foster cumulation by concentrating only on the simplest explanations available. These are the most parsimonious, seeking to explain the observations we make without using additional propositions for which there is not already evidence (see above). They are also the easiest to test and to falsify in the Popperian model. We have no direct evidence to decide between explanations based on causes or on random events (Arjas 2001), so to use either one of them in an explanation involves making an assumption. To explain a set of observations using both involves making *two* assumptions, and is therefore unparsimonious. We have enough trouble establishing whether causes exist or not. To allow them to exist alongside unrelated phenomena makes most social scientific propositions completely untestable (for the falsification of a purported cause can always be gainsaid by the 'whimsy' element). Perhaps this is why social science shows so little practical progress over time.

Uncertainty could also be merely unpredictability, and it would be arrogant to assume that if we cannot yet predict a set of events then there is no more predicting to be done. Chaos theory is clearly causal but it allows for unpredictability due to complications in computation from the initial states (Gleick 1988). This unpredictability could stem from our inability to predict causatory events or from our misunderstanding of the basic randomness of events. Both explanations are plausible, but currently untestable. Using both processes together is unnecessary, and trying to combine them into one description often leads to logical difficulties anyway. For example, if sub-atomic events are really random but have an effect on larger processes that are themselves causes, then following the causal chain argument, the larger 'causes' are themselves randomly determined and therefore random. And if 'random' events can have a cause then they are not random, by definition.

A more complex solution is to construct a model that involves both causation and other competing explanations of a non-determinist nature, such as intentionality through personal choice. Gambetta (1987) describes career decisions, for example, as a product of what is available to the individual, what the individual wants and, indirectly, the social conditions that shape the individual's intentions. However, explanations such as this are unparsimonious. The problem with causation is not that there are events that it cannot explain, but that it is itself impossible to observe. Therefore, there is no value in mixing it up with a model of intention, which is also perfectly capable of explaining decisions by itself but which is also not open to observation by social scientists. Given that there is no way of deciding between them empirically, either causation or intention can be adopted (it makes little practical difference which at this stage). There is no empirical justification for working with both at the same time (any more than there is for working with causation and randomness). Rather, in a causal explanation, an intention or an individual choice can be an outcome (of social or family background, for example) as well as a cause. The argument is actually about the nature of the cause (or effect), not about whether it is a cause. When psychologists argue the nature/nurture controversy, or sociologists debate the relative importance of structure and agency, for example, they are simply arguing about what the relevant causes are.

NOTIONS OF CAUSALITY

One way of viewing causation is as a stable association between two elements. Where one is present the other is also, and when one is absent the other is also. It is the constant conjunction that suggests that all possible futures will be like all pasts (Hume 1962). This view of causation has two main problems: we know that it opens us to superstition, and it does not allow for intermittent association. Skinner's accidental reinforcement schedule is a powerful reminder of the dangers of allowing causal models to be based only on association. Skinner's intermittent reinforcement schedule shows us how difficult it might be to shake such causal models once they have been accepted.

We can be easily fooled by association (hence the common caveats about correlations in standard textbooks), especially where these associations involve large numbers and are backed by expertise or apparent authority (Brighton 2000). This point was made recently by Johnson (2001) in relation to the false distinction in the US between 'causal-comparative' studies using analysis of variance techniques (see Chapter Nine) and 'correlational' studies (see Chapter Ten). Comparative models do not provide positive evidence of causation in non-experimental designs. It is, perhaps, simply their increasing complexity and the apparent authority of the statisticians who understand them that makes others prepared to accept this falsehood.

Despite all of these caveats, purported causal models based only on association appear throughout the research literature, sometimes dominating entire fields of endeavour. Where economists talk about causation they often mean something much weaker, like Granger-causation or temporal relationships, which takes the *post hoc ergo propter hoc* fallacy of logic and converts it via a little flourish and an empirical test of 'causality' to a seemingly respectable principle. Granger-causation in economics assumes that we are working with a universe of information. If a variable is eliminated from this universal model and this produces no change in a second variable, then the first variable cannot be the cause of the second (Hendry and Mizon 1999). Otherwise it can be said to 'Granger-cause' it. The practical problem with this empirical approach to causation is that a Granger-cause and a cause are not the same thing but they sound confusingly similar, and anyway no one actually works in the 'universe of information'. Economists use regression models very far from universal in nature, sometimes even bivariate, and still claim Granger-causation, which becomes, in essence, a fancy term for a correlation. A similar approach is sometimes used in partialling variance in school effectiveness work (see Chapter Ten). Here the argument is for robust dependence. According to this, a variable is not a cause if its influence (regression coefficient) is eliminated by the addition of new variables to the system. But the obverse is clearly nonsense (Goldthorpe 2001). A causal path analysis may show that education leads to a higher income but this is very far from showing that education *causes* income. Robust dependence is not enough. Only a prediction from theory or a test via intervention can take us any further than a purely descriptive mathematical relationship.

Given the difficulty of identifying causes, perhaps the best that can be hoped for is to identify only weak causes or 'determinants'. These could be the producers of the observed effects, or they could be simply the indicators, or signposts, of a future outcome. In fact, social scientists use many forms of determination that are not strictly causal, including historical and structural analyses (Pötter and Blossfeld 2001). We should also accept a causal model that is probabilistic rather than determinist in nature (Goldthorpe 2001), although we would be unable to decide whether this worked because the world is actually non-determinist, or because it is too complicated to explain fully and so we allow for error. Simple deterministic causation is rare in reality, where even physical 'laws' are actually generalizations from many differing observations, or *ceteris paribus* (Hammersley 2001). Water tends to boil at 100 degrees centigrade, but the precise temperature depends on the atmosphere and the purity of the water. Even such a simple law *appears* probabilistic.

'It can be said to be axiomatic to any notion of causality that it only acts forward, that is, a cause must precede its effects in time' (Arjas 2001, p. 60). In research, as in life, an easy assumption is sometimes made about the direction of causation that does not really stand up to scrutiny. This assumption is that one event can be considered a cause of another only if it occurs first, therefore if two variables are related then their temporal sequence defines which is the cause. The approach was summed up in one study thus: 'what we do now becomes what we are, and what we are in part determines what we do next' (Gershuny and Marsh 1994, p. 69). In their analysis of the determinants of unemployment, variables were entered into the model in the order that they occurred historically, from parents' occupational class through initial education to the work details. The 'effect' of the earlier episodes was assumed to be present throughout the analysis but was found to diminish over time. In this way, the past is seen as affecting the present while both can affect the future, but the future cannot affect the present and the present cannot affect the past.

However, in many respects this assumption of unidirectional causation is unrealistic (Berry 1984). Causality is merely assumed to be time-determined (Hume 1962). The relationships between data that are seemingly in a temporal sequence are often reciprocal (Hagenaars 1990). Mutual causation can be in the form of amplification, where A leads to B which leads to A, as in sales and advertising perhaps (Heise 1975). Or it can be in the form of control, where A leads to B which leads to NOT A, as in thermostatic coupling, for example. Or it can be instability, as when a microphone is too close to a speaker. In addition, the direction of the arrow of causation is not at all clear even in well-established links between variables. Rational choices might allow people to jump towards attractive options rather than being 'pushed from behind' (Gambetta 1987). Does greater investment in training lead to company growth or are richer companies more likely to spend money on training? When birds regularly gather in the park five minutes before the arrival of person who feeds them daily does this mean that the birds are causing the arrival of the person?

In evaluating whether a possible causal theory makes sense, de Vaus (2001) suggests that, in addition to explaining the co-variation and time sequence, and being plausible, the proposed dependent variable must be capable of change. While the sex of the student could affect the outcome of a job interview, the reverse could not be true. Sex would be unchanged by the interview. In fact, we can go further than saying the dependent variable must be capable of change. It must be able to be changed *by* the independent variable. If there is a relationship between the level of poverty among 16-year-olds and their examination results, then the only causal model that makes sense in the short term is one where poverty affects examination results.

A possible characteristic of a good causal model is an explanatory process or theory that takes these restrictions on plausibility into account. If causation is a generative process then something must be added to the statistical association between an intervention and an outcome for the model to be convincing. The cause must be tied to some process that generates the effect. The standard example is the clear relationship between smoking and lung cancer. The statistical conjunction and the observations from laboratory trials were elucidated by the isolation of carcinogens in the smoke, the pathological evidence from diseased lungs and so on. From this complex interplay of studies and datasets emerges an explanatory theory – the kind of theory that generates further testable propositions. This is the key role for theory-building in research.

This brings us back to the role of experiments. Another way of viewing causation is via the effect of an intervention. If causes are not susceptible to direct observation, but what they 'cause' is effects, then at least those effects must be observable. We should therefore probably follow the principle of 'no causation without manipulation'. This is the approach used by Pavlov in so far as classical conditioning involved a causal model of learning and extinction. Koch used a very similar approach of intervening and treatment removal to show causation in infections (Cox and Wermuth 2001). Unfortunately in a social science where the subject of study is people we cannot usually expose the same people both to the treatment and not, as might be possible by using two near-identical cases in physics, for example. We therefore use statistical approaches (including random allocation to groups) to overcome this limitation. And this, of course, may be why probabilistic models of causation emerge. They may reflect, not the reality of the study, but the practical limitation of our experimental designs when dealing with people. These same statistical procedures are now more widely used where an intervention is not even attempted, but there remains fundamental disagreement over the validity of these approaches (McKim and Turner 1997, and see Chapter Ten).

CONCLUSION

Causes are particularly relevant in a climate of evidence-informed policy-making and practice for at least two reasons. Causes are really only susceptible to *testing* by intervening and measuring, the technique of randomized controlled trials and related designs. In addition, in order to determine what works in any given situation the intervention must be proposed first (for there are an infinite number of potential interventions). While this creative phase of a study can be, and has been, inspired or serendipitous, the closest we have to a technique for generating such ideas is to try and understand why things work. This is the role of theory – not banner-waving grand theory, but attempts to provide simple explanations for observed phenomena in ways that are fruitful and actually testable. A useful causal theory would have the characteristics of all of the models proposed above. It would involve conjunction (relatively stable association between two things), a measurable effect from the intervention and at least a tentative theoretical explanation.

Having resolved this, in practical terms cause/effect is still difficult to isolate. Given the design bias and sampling and measurement errors in all our work, we may end up with estimates rather than simple, almost mechanical cause and effect models. While perhaps disappointing to some, this is actually inevitable. Our role as researchers is to minimize the bias and the sampling and measurement errors. Statistics, as popularly conceived, can help only with the least important of these – the sampling error. Overcoming the rest of the error, the bulk of it in any design, is to do with rigour. Rigour would transcend any specific approach or method. It is certainly not the prerogative of experiments (whose importance lies in the intervention only). The current paucity of experiments in social science is therefore not an excuse to evade the need for rigour, both in analysis and warranting. The same situation is faced in many fields such as archaeology, palaeontology and astronomy, and for more solidly practical reasons perhaps. Even cutting-edge sciences such as molecular genetics use relatively few genuine experimental designs (although the routine benchwork creates controls as a matter of course). The same situation applies in a range of scientific and quasi-scientific settings (Collins and Pinch 1993).

'Physics envy' among social scientists is misplaced, and there remain many useful strategies of a non-experimental nature that enable us to increase our confidence in perceived causal relationships (such as selection modelling, or longitudinal studies combined with triangulation of methods, see also Johnson 2001 and Chapter Eleven).

A final example
Consider this example of a warrant involving a causal model. Death rates due to cancer (of all types) increased over the course of the twentieth century in the UK, and they look set to continue to rise. One possible conclusion is that 'modern' lifestyle is to blame, including perhaps the food we eat and damage to our environment. The warrant here would be largely based on causation as correlation. Two sets of events, growth of cancer and lifestyle changes, are contemporaneous. Therefore, we assume that they are causally related and, of course, they may be. But we should also automatically start seeking alternative explanations, and see how these shape up. Another very plausible alternative is based on the fact of mortality. We all die. Therefore, a change in the probability of death by any one cause affects the probability of death by all other causes (put in the terms of Chapter Six – the degrees of freedom of our model are fixed). As death rates due to typhoid, smallpox and war have declined, so the death rates due to heart disease or cancer would be expected to rise. If we add some more evidence, that people in the UK now live longer, on average, than at the start of the twentieth century, then the lifestyle theory becomes a much poorer explanation for the rise in cancer than the simple reduction of other avoidable causes of death. The latter explanation makes fewer assumptions for which we do not have direct evidence, and is therefore currently more 'scientific'.

The next chapter describes some simple experimental designs for testing causal models.

Experimental approaches: a return to the gold standard?

WHY USE EXPERIMENTS?

In many ways the experiment is seen as the 'flagship' or gold standard of research designs. The basic advantage of this approach over any other is its more convincing claim to be testing for cause and effect, via the manipulation of otherwise identical groups, rather than simply observing an unspecified relationship between two variables. In addition, some experiments will allow the size of any effect to be measured. It has been argued that only experiments are thus able to produce secure and uncontested knowledge about the truth of propositions. Their design is flexible, allowing for any number of different groups and variables, and the outcome measures taken can be of any kind (including qualitative observations), although they are normally converted to a coded numeric form. The design is actually so powerful that it requires smaller numbers of participants as a minimum than would be normal in a survey, for example. The analysis of the results is also generally easier than when using other designs.

Social science research has, for too long, relied on fancy statistical manipulation of poor datasets, rather than well-designed studies (Fitz-Gibbon 1996, 2001). When subjected to a definitive trial by experiment, many common interventions and treatments actually show no effect, identifying resources wasted on policies and practices. Perhaps that is also partly why there is considerable resistance to the idea of the use of experimental evidence. Social work was one of the areas where natural experiments were pioneered but, when these seldom showed any positive impact from social work policies, social workers rejected the method itself rather than the ineffective practices (Torgerson and Torgerson 2001). Those with vested interests in other current social science beliefs and theories may, similarly, consider they have little to gain from definitive trials (although this is, of course, not a genuine reason for not using them).

As should become clear in this chapter, the experimental method can be extremely useful to all researchers even if they do not carry out a real experiment. How is this possible? Knowing the format and power of experiments gives us a yardstick against which to measure what we do instead, and even helps us to design what we do better. An obvious example of this occurs in a 'thought experiment', in which we can freely consider how to gain secure and uncontested knowledge about the truth of our propositions without any concern about practical or ethical considerations. This becomes our ideal, and it helps us to recognize the practical limitations of our actual approach. Another example is a natural experiment where we design an 'experiment' without intervention, using the same design as a standard experiment but making use of a naturally occurring phenomenon.

EXPERIMENTAL DESIGN

This section outlines the basic experimental design for two groups. In this design, the researcher creates two (or more) 'populations' by using different treatments with two samples drawn randomly from a parent population (or by dividing one sample into two at random). Each sample becomes a treatment group. As with all research, the quality and usefulness of the findings depend heavily on the care used in sampling (see Chapter Four). The treatment is known as the 'independent' variable, and the researcher selects a post-treatment test (or measure) known as the 'dependent' variable. Usually one group will receive the treatment and be termed the experimental group, and another will not receive the treatment and be termed the control group (see Table 8.1).

The researcher then specifies a null hypothesis (that there will be no difference in the dependent variable between the treatment

Table 8.1: The simple experimental design

	Allocation	Pre-test	Intervention	Post-test
Experimental	random	measurement	treatment	measurement
Control	random	measurement	–	measurement

groups) and an experimental hypothesis (the simplest explanation of any observed difference in the dependent variable between groups). The experimental hypothesis can predict the direction of any observed difference between the groups (a one-tailed hypothesis) or not (a two-tailed hypothesis). Only then does the experimenter obtain the scores on the dependent variable and analyse them. If there is a significant difference between the two groups, it can be said to be caused by the treatment.

A one-tailed prediction is intrinsically more convincing and thus permits a higher threshold for the significance level used. There are always apparent patterns in data. The experimental design tries to maximize the probability that any pattern uncovered is significant, generalizable and replicable. Merely rejecting the null hypothesis as too improbable to explain a set of observations does not make a poorly crafted experimental hypothesis right. There are, in principle, an infinite number of equally logical explanations for any result. The most useful explanation is therefore that which can be most easily tested by further research. It must be the simplest explanation, usually leading to a further testable prediction.

There are in summary six steps in the basic experiment:

- formulate a hypothesis (which is confirmatory/disconfirmatory rather than exploratory)
- randomly assign cases to the intervention or control groups (so that any non-experimental differences are due solely to chance)
- measure the dependent variable (as a pre-test, but note that this step is not always used)
- introduce the treatment or independent variable
- measure the dependent variable again (as a post-test)
- calculate the significance of the differences between the groups (or the effect size, see Chapter Nine).

A simple example might involve testing the efficacy of a new lecture plan for teaching a particular aspect of mathematics. A large sample is randomly divided into two groups. Both groups sit a test of their understanding of the mathematical concept, giving the researcher a pre-test score. One group is given a lecture (or lectures) on the relevant topic in the usual way. This is the control group. Another group is given a lecture using the new lecture plan. This is the experimental treatment group. Both groups sit a further test of their understanding of the mathematical concept, giving the researcher a post-test score. The difference between the pre- and post-test scores for each student yields a gain score. The null hypothesis will be that both groups will show the same average gain score. The alternate hypothesis could be that the treatment group will show a higher average gain score than the control group. These hypotheses can be tested using a t-test for unrelated samples (see Chapter Nine). If the null hypothesis is rejected, and if the two groups do not otherwise differ in any systematic way, then the researcher can reasonably claim that the new lecture plan *caused* the improvement gain scores. The next stage is to assess the size of the improvement, at least partly in relation to the cost of the treatment.

CHALLENGES FOR VALIDITY

The logic of an experiment like the example above relies on the criterion that the only difference between the groups is due to the treatment. Under these conditions, the experiment is said to lead to valid results. There are several threats to this validity in experiments. Some of these are obvious, some less so. An often cited, but still useful summary of many of these potential threats comes from Campbell and Stanley (1963) and Cook and Campbell (1979). These are conveniently grouped under eight headings, discussed briefly here.

History   Some people taking part in experiments may have other experiences during the course of the study that affect their recorded measurement but which are not under experimental control. An example could be a fire alarm going off during the exposure to one of the treatments (e.g. during the maths lecture for one of the groups above). Thus, an 'infection' or confounding variable enters the system and provides a possible part of the explanation for any observed differences between the experimental groups.

Maturation   By design, the post-treatment measure (or post-test) is taken at some time after the start of the experiment or, put more simply, experiments require the passage of time. It is possible therefore that some of the differences noted stem from confounding factors related to this. These could include ageing (in extreme cases), boredom and practice effects. Time is important in other ways. If, for example, we are studying the effect of smoking prevention literature among 15-year-olds, when is the pay-off? Are we concerned only with immediate cessation or would we call the treatment a success if it lowered the students' chances of smoking as adults? To consider such long-term outcomes is expensive and not attractive to political sponsors (who usually want quick fixes). A danger for all social policy research is therefore a focus on short-term changes, making the studies trivial rather than transformative (Scott and Usher 1999). Even where the focus is genuinely on the short term, some effects can be significant in size but insignificant in fact because they are so short-lived. Returning to the smoking example, would we call the treatment a success if it lowered the amount of smoking at school for the next day only?

Experimenters need to watch for what has been termed a 'Hawthorne' effect. A study of productivity in a factory (called Hawthorne) in the 1920s tried to boost worker activity by using brighter lighting (and a range of other treatments). This treatment was a success. Factory output increased, but only for a week or so before returning to its previous level. As there was apparently no long-term benefit for the factory owners, the lighting level was reduced to the *status ante*. Surprisingly, this again produced a similar short-term increase in productivity. This suggests that participants in experiments may be sensitive to almost any variation in treatment (either more or less lighting) for a short time. The simple fact of being in an experiment can affect participants' behaviour. If so, this is a huge problem for the validity of almost all experiments and is very difficult to control for in a snapshot design. It can be seen as a particular problem for school-based research, where students might react strongly to any change in routine regardless of its intrinsic pedagogical value (and the same issue arises with changes of routine in prisons and hospitals). Of course, the Hawthorne effect could be looked at in another way (e.g. Brown 1992). If you were not interested in generating knowledge in your research, but literally only concerned with what works, then adopting Hawthorne-type techniques deliberately could be seen as a rational approach. Since production increased both when lighting levels were increased and when they were decreased, some of the factory owners were naturally delighted with the results (although this part of the story is seldom told in methods textbooks).

Testing The very act of conducting a test or taking a measure can produce a confounding effect. People taking part may come to get used to being tested (showing less nervousness perhaps). Where the design is longitudinal they may wish to appear consistent in their answers when re-tested later, even where their 'genuine' response has changed. A related problem can arise from the demand characteristics of the experimenter who can unwittingly (we hope) indicate to participants his or her own expectations or otherwise influence the results in favour of a particular finding. Such effects have been termed 'experimenter effects' and they are some of the most pernicious dangers to validity. In addition, apparently random errors in recording and analysing results have actually been found to favour the experimental hypothesis predominantly (Adair 1973). If the researcher knows which group is which and what is 'expected' of each group by the experimental hypothesis then his or her behaviour can give cues to this.

Traditionally, this effect has been illustrated by the history of a horse that could count (Clever Hans). Observers asked Hans a simple sum (such as $3 + 5$), and the horse tapped its hoof that number of times (8). This worked whether the observers were believers or sceptics. It was eventually discovered that it did not work only if the observers did not know the answer (i.e. they were 'blind', see below). What appeared to be happening was that the horse was tapping its hoof in response to the question, and after tapping the right number of times it was able to recognize the sense of expectancy or frisson of excitement that ran through the observers waiting to see whether it would tap again. The horse presumably learnt that, however many times it tapped, if it stopped when that moment came it would then receive praise and a sugar lump. Social science experiments generally involve people both as researchers and as participants. The opportunities for just such an experimenter effect (misconstruing trying to please the experimenter as a real result) are therefore very great. If we add to these problems the other impacts of the person of the researcher (stemming from clothes, sex, accent, age, etc.) it is clear that the experimenter effect is a key issue for any design (see below for more on this).

Instrumentation 'Contamination' can also enter an experimental design through changes in the nature of the measurements taken at different points. Clearly we would set out to control for (or equalize) the researcher used for each group in the design, and the environment and time of day at which the experiment takes place. However, even where both groups appear to be treated equally the nature of the instrument used can be a confounding variable. If the instrument used, the measurement taken or the characteristics of the experimenter change during the experiment this could have differential impact on each group. For example, if one group contains more females and another more males and the researcher taking the first measure is male and the researcher taking the second measure is female then at least some of the difference between the groups could be attributable to the nature of same- and different-sex interactions. Note that this is so even though both groups had the same researcher on each occasion (i.e. they appeared to be treated equally at first sight).

Regression   In most experiments the researcher is not concerned with individuals but with aggregate or overall scores (such as the mean score for each group). When such aggregate scores are near to an extreme value they tend to regress towards the mean score of all groups over time, almost irrespective of the treatment given to each individual, simply because extreme scores have nowhere else to go. In the same way perhaps that the children of very tall people tend to be shorter than their parents, so groups who average zero on a test will tend to improve their score next time, and groups who score 100% will tend towards a lower score. They will regress towards the mean irrespective of other factors (and this is related to the saturation effect discussed in Chapter Three). If they show any changes over time these are the only ones possible, so random fluctuations produce 'regression'. This is a potential problem with designs involving one or more extreme groups.

Selection   As with any design, biased results are obtained via experiments in which the participants have been selected in some non-random way. Whenever a subjective value judgement is made about selection of cases, or where there is a test that participants must 'pass' before joining in, there is a possible source of contamination. This problem is overcome to a large extent by the use of randomization both in selecting cases for the study and in allocating them to the various treatment and control groups, but note the practical difficulties of achieving this (see Chapter Four).

Mortality   A specific problem arising from the extended nature of some experiments is drop-out among participants, often referred to by the rather grim term 'subject mortality'. Even where a high-quality sample is achieved at the start of the experiment this may become biased by some participants not continuing to the end. As with non-response bias, it is clearly possible that those people less likely to continue with an experiment are systematically different from the rest (perhaps in terms of motivation, leisure time, geographic mobility and so on). Alternatively, it is possible that the nature of the treatment may make one group more likely to drop out than another (this is similar to the issue of drop-out in the longitudinal studies discussed in Chapter Five).

Diffusion   Perhaps the biggest specific threat to experiments in social science research today comes from potential diffusion of the treatments between groups. In a large-scale study using a field setting it is very difficult to restrict the treatments to each experimental group, and it is therefore all too easy to end up with an 'infected' control group. Imagine the situation where new curriculum materials for Key Stage 2 Geography teaching are being tested out in schools with one experimental group of students and their results compared to a control group using more traditional curriculum material. If any school contains students from both groups it is almost impossible to prevent children helping one another with homework by showing them their 'wonderful' new books. Even where the children are in different schools this infection is still possible through friendship or family relationships. In my experience of such studies in Singapore the most cross-infection in these circumstances actually comes from the teachers themselves, who tend to be collaborative and collegial and very keen to send their friends photocopies of the super lesson plans that they have just been given by the Ministry of Education. For these teachers, teaching the next lesson is understandably more important than taking part in a national trial. On the other hand, if the experimental groups are isolated from each other, by using students in different countries, for example, then we are introducing greater doubt that the two groups are comparable anyway. Similar problems arise in other fields, perhaps most notably the sharing of drugs and other treatments in medical trials.

As you can imagine, given these and other potential limitations of experimental evidence, the ideal, the flagship of social science research, is far from realizable for most of us. There will always be some room for doubt about the findings even from a properly conducted experiment. It is important, however, to note two points. First: there are some things we can do with our basic design to counter any possible contamination (see next section). Second: the experiment remains the most completely theorized and understood method in social science. With its familiarity comes our increased awareness of its limitations, but other and newer approaches will have as many and more problems. Worse, other designs will have dangers and limitations that we are not even aware of yet.

CONTROLLING CONTAMINATION

The basic experimental design (see Table 8.1 above) takes care of several possible threats to validity. The random allocation of participants to groups reduces selection bias, so that the only systematic difference between the groups is the treatment, and the control group gives us an estimate of the differences between pre- and post-test regardless of the intervention.

Designs usually get more complex to control for any further threats to internal validity. In psychology in particular some very large and sometimes rather unwieldy approaches are used. A 'factorial design' uses one group for each combination of all the independent variables, of which there may be several. So for an experiment involving three two-way independent variables there would be eight conditions plus at least one control group. The effects of these variables would be broken down into the 'main effects' (of each variable in isolation) and the 'interaction effects' (of two or more variables in combination).

As you may imagine the analysis of such advanced designs becomes accordingly more complex also, and is therefore largely beyond the scope of this book (but see Chapters Nine and Ten). For despite the fact that undergraduates are routinely taught these designs, they do not always, in my experience, either appreciate or understand them. And they even more rarely use them properly. I recently came across an entire student cohort of psychologists who were 'sharing' the syntax instructions (i.e. a computer program) to run a multi-variate analyis of variance with their dissertation data. The syntax was given to them by a member of staff who appeared to believe that it could be used without explanation, and for all and any experimental designs. None of the students I spoke to had the faintest idea what the numbers generated by this program meant.

Factorial designs are anyway sometimes used in situations when they are not necessary (perhaps only because 'we have the technology'). When faced with considerable complexity in the topic of an investigation I feel that a more helpful response is to seek greater simplicity of approach rather than greater sophistication. For example, it is clear that the pre-test phase in an experiment can sensitize people for their subsequent post-test (an experience/ instrumentation effect). So we *could* use at least four groups and alternate both the treatment and whether there is a pre-test or not. A simpler variant with the same advantage is the post-test-only design (Table 8.2). If the sample is large enough it is possible to do away with the pre-test and assume that the randomly allocated groups would have had equivalent mean scores before treatment. As this is even simpler than the basic design we can be even more confident that it is only the intervention that causes any difference between groups. Problems are quite often solved in this way, via *simplification* of the process. This brief discussion therefore rehearses several of the key themes in this book – use a large sample (if population figures are not available), plan the detailed analysis as part of the initial research design, don't over-complicate things (the social world is already tricky enough to research) and collect high-quality data that is easy to analyse. These and other themes are summarized in Chapter Eleven as some of the 'new rules' for social science research.

Table 8.2: The post-test-only experimental design

	Allocation	Pre-test	Intervention	Post-test
Group A	random	–	treatment	measurement
Group B	random	–	–	measurement

Since the researcher can have a social impact on the outcomes of an experiment, this needs to be controlled for in the design, if possible, and made visible in the reporting of results. There are various standard techniques to overcome the experimenter effect, though it is doubtful that all would be available for use in a small-scale student project. To start with, it is important that the participants are 'blind' in that they do not know the precise nature of the experiment until it is complete (see below for a discussion of the ethical considerations relating to this). Ideally the experimenter should also be 'blind' in not knowing to which group any participant belongs (and this is also some protection against the ethical quandary of running a real-life experiment when you already believe, but have no publishable evidence, that one treatment is better than another). This double-blind situation is sometimes maintained by means of a *placebo* (the name deriving from drug trials) in which everyone appears to undergo the same treatment even though some of the treatment is phoney or empty (equivalent to a sugar pill rather than a drug). Finally, if practical, it is better to have a 'triple blind' situation in which the person coding and analysing the data does not know until later which is the experimental group.

  Another way of achieving the same end is to automate the experiment and thereby minimize social contact (often not possible of course). Another is to sub-contract the experiment to someone else who does not know the details. You could, for example, offer to conduct an experiment for a colleague in return for their conducting yours. Other ways of minimizing experimenter bias include getting more than one account of any observation, by using several people as observers and looking at the inter-rater reliability of all measurements taken, or by a triangulation of methods wherein the experimental findings are checked against evidence from other sources. All of these are good, and many can be used in combination.

THE SEVEN SAMURAI

So, guard against the possible limitations to your experiment as far as possible. However, problems such as diffusion or the Hawthorne effect are almost impossible to eliminate as possibilities. Therefore consider them and report them in your explanations in the same way as I have advised you to do for any other limitations, such as those in your achieved sample.

Although I have not seen the classic film *The Seven Samurai* for many years now, I recall the scene when the Samurai arrive at the village, and begin to arrange for it to be fortified against the bandits. They ask the villagers to build a wall/barrier all around the village, but to leave one large gap. The headman queries this and suggests that the fortification should be made continuous. One of the warriors replies that 'every good fort has a defect', and therefore the most important thing is to know where that defect is. If you were attacking the village, you would focus on the gap in the wall, and that is where the defenders (only seven in number, remember) will be strongest.

Now I am not suggesting that you leave a gaping hole in your PhD method chapter so that you will know what to discuss in your *viva voce* examination! Rather, the point is that, like a fort, every good research design has defects. Your job as researcher is both to minimize the defects and, equally importantly, to recognize where the remaining defects are. Self-criticism is your best defence against the criticism of others, and using the ideal of an experiment (or at least a fantasy experiment) can help you identify the defects and so make relevant criticisms (see below).

CHALLENGES FOR ETHICS

The biggest challenge facing any increased use of experimental designs in social science research is, however, an ethical and not a technical one. Of course, ethical issues do not apply to experiments only and many of the issues discussed here also apply to all other forms of research. While perhaps overplayed in importance by some writers, there will be at least some ethical considerations in any piece of research (see for example Walford 2001). Consider this example. NHS Direct is a telephone helpline set up to relieve pressure on other UK National Health Service activities. Callers can ask for help and advice or reduce their anxiety about minor injuries or repetitive illness, without going to their General Practitioner or to hospital out-patients. Research reported by Carter (2000) found serious shortcomings in this new service. The evidence was collected by making a large number of fake calls to test the consistency, quality and speed of the advice given. In ethical terms, is this OK?

One argument against this study is that it has misused a procedure intended to relieve pressure on an already pressurized and potentially life-saving public service. By conducting the research via bogus calls, it is at least possible that individuals have suffered harm as a consequence. One argument for the study would be that realistic (and therefore 'blind', see above) evaluations are an essential part of improving public services, and that the longer-term objective of the study was to produce an amelioration of any shortcomings discovered. If, for the sake of argument, NHS Direct was actually a waste of public funds it would be important to find this out at an early stage and redirect its funding to other approaches. This, in a nutshell, is the major issue facing ethics and research. Researchers will not want to cause damage knowingly, but is it worth their risking possible harm to some individuals for a greater overall gain? As with most decisions I am faced with, I do not have a definite answer to this one. Or rather, my definite answer is, 'it depends'.

It depends, of course, on the quality of the research being conducted. Most observers would agree with this on reflection, but it is seldom made explicit in any discussion of ethics. It would, for example, be entirely reasonable to come to opposite conclusions about the example above dependent on the quality of the study. If calling the helpline for research purposes runs a risk of replacing other genuine callers, then it has to be considered whether the value of the research is worth that risk. The risk can only be judged against the purpose and rigour of the research. If, for example, the study found that the line was working well, then no more research is needed (and the study has served its evaluative purpose). If the study found problems and as a result these could be ameliorated (although it is clearly not the full responsibility of the researcher if they are not), then the study could claim to be worthwhile. The one outcome that would be of no use to anyone is where the research is of insufficient quality to reach a safe and believable conclusion either way. In this case, all the risk has been run for no reason and no gain. From this it would not be too much of a stretch to say that, in general, poor research leading to indefinite answers tends to be unethical in nature, while good trustworthy research tends to be more ethical.

In many fields in which we wish to research, our influence over ethical situations is marginal. One may have to 'befriend' convicted serial killers, however repugnant the task, in order to find out about their motivations (if we feel it is important to know this). Our control over the quality of our work is generally much greater than our control over ethical factors. Thus, ethically, the first responsibility of all research should be to quality and rigour. If it is decided that the best answer to a specific research question is likely to be obtained via an experimental design, for example, then this is at least part of the justification in ethical terms for its use. In this case, an experiment may be the *most* ethical approach even where it runs a slightly greater risk of 'endangering' participants than another less appropriate design. Pointless research, on the other hand, remains pointless however 'ethically' it appears to be conducted. Good intentions do not guarantee good outcomes. Such a conclusion may be unpalatable to some readers, but where the research is potentially worthwhile and the 'danger' (such as the danger of wasting people's time) is small relative to the worth, my conclusion is logically entailed in the considerations above. I am, of course, ruling out entirely all actions, such as violence or abuse, that we would all agree are indefensible in *any* research situation.

Reinforcement for this conclusion comes from a consideration of the nature of funding for research. Whether financed by charitable donations or public taxation, research must attempt to justify the use of such public funds by producing high-quality results. If the best method to use to generate safe conclusions to a specific question is an experiment (for example), then there should be considerable ethical pressure on the researcher to use an experiment.

The application of experimental designs from clinical research to educational practice does, however, highlight specific ethical issues (Hakuta 2000). In a simple experiment with two groups, the most common complaint is that the design is discriminatory. If the control group is being denied a treatment in order for researchers to gain greater knowledge about it, this could be deemed unethical. Fitz-Gibbon (1996) counters that this approach is unethical only if we know which group is to be disadvantaged. In most designs, of course, the whole purpose is to decide which treatment is better (or worse). We need evidence of what works before the denial of what works to one group can be deemed discriminatory. In our current state of relative ignorance about public policy and human behaviour, it is as likely that a treatment will serve some less well as doing nothing, so as to find out what works, will damage the chances of others. An analogy for our present state of affairs might be the development of powered flight. All aeroplanes and flying machines designed around 1900 were based on the same Newtonian aerodynamics in theory. In testing, some of them flew and some crashed, despite the belief of *all* designers that their own machine would work. It was only the testing that sorted one group from the other. To strain the analogy a little, one could hardly argue that it would be more ethical for us all to fly in planes that had not been tested. For some reason, most discussions of ethical considerations in research focus on possible harm to the research participants, to the exclusion of the possible harm done to future users of the evidence that research generates. They almost never consider the wasted resources and worse consequences in implementing treatments and policies that do not work (see Torgerson and Torgerson 2001). In the UK it is illegal to market a new powder for athlete's foot without testing it, but we spend billions of pounds on public policies for crime, housing, transport and education that affect millions of people without any real idea of whether they will work. How ethical is that?

On the other hand, is it fair to society (rather than just the control group) to use an intervention without knowing what its impact will be? Would it be reasonable, for example, to try not jailing people sentenced for violent crimes simply to see if this led to less re-offending (de Leon et al. 1995)? Again the answer would have to be 'it depends'. What we have to take into account is not simply what is efficient or expedient but what is right or wrong. This judgement depends on values, and values are liable to change over time. In fact, doing the work of research can itself transform our views of what is right and wrong. If an alternative punishment to prison led to less violent crime, who would object (afterwards)? Would we have oxygen treatments for neonates or drugs for heart diseases if we were dominated by short-term ethical considerations? Ideally, we should test all public and social interventions before using them more widely. The problems above are also shared with disciplines like history (archaeology, palaeontology, astronomy, etc.), but the difference here is that these disciplines are *constrained* to be non-experimental and is, in effect, making the best of what is possible. Social science research has no such general constraint about experiments (although it applies to *some* research questions).

Is deception of the participants in an experiment OK? Should we always tell the truth? Should we encourage others to behave in ways they may not otherwise (by making racist statements, for example)? What is the risk to the participants? Can we assure confidentiality? Moral judgements such as these require deliberation of several factors, and there is seldom a clear-cut, context-free principle to apply. Even the widely accepted notion that it is always more ethical not to identify our research participants can be contested (see Grinyer 2002). There are two main contradictory principles in play here: respect for the welfare of participants and finding the truth. The right to 'know' is an important moral, after all, even where the consequences might hurt some individuals (such as those with a commercial interest in our ignorance). We can never fully ignore the consequences of our study and we need to be tentative in our claims, as even experiments lead only to possible knowledge. Nevertheless, we also need virtues such as honesty to behave as researchers, to publish results even when they are painful or surprising (and the question, 'could you be surprised by what you find?' is for me one criterion of demarcation between research and pseudo-research) and the courage to proceed even if this approach is unpopular.

For further discussion of the role of ethical considerations see Pring (2000). If in doubt whether a method you propose is defensible check the ethical guidelines for your professional society (BSA, BPS, BERA, etc.). Each society publishes a list of essentially very similar 'rules' about honesty, sensitivity and responsibility in conducting research. Your institution probably also has an ethics board to whom you can apply for informed consent. You should, of course, also check your ideas with your supervisor/mentor, who should have a clear idea of the norms and standards applied to your field. The most unethical thing I have done was to ask a friend to call a number of fee-paying schools, posing as a prospective parent, and request promotional literature to be mailed to him. My justification is that I wanted not just the literature but notes on the telephone manner, promptness and so on of each school. Although I could therefore be accused of wasting the money and time of the schools, the situation is not as serious as with the NHS (see above), and I was able to give the schools feedback about their presentation, which was generally well received (Gorard 1997b).

FIELD AND FANTASY TRIALS

Without wishing the exaggerate the difficulties, it is true that experimental designs are not always possible – for practical and ethical reasons, because of the nature of the research questions, or because the dataset to be considered already exists. Of course, debates about the value of experiments are not new (Shipman 1981). Much of what we know is not experimental, and what we want to know cannot be (Glymour et al. 1987). Trials by themselves (although never intended to be used in isolation, see Gorard 2002c) are also unlikely to lead to an understanding of detailed causal mechanisms (Morrison 2001). Their simplicity, which is part of their appeal, might lead us to concentrate on one 'effect' but not pick up multiple side-effects (including possibly deleterious ones). What are the alternatives?

The biggest problem in using experiments comes from their chief source of strength: the level of control of the research situation possible in a laboratory. Traditionally experiments, following a natural science model, have been conducted in laboratory conditions. A laboratory allows the experimenter to control extraneous conditions more closely, and so to claim with more conviction that the only difference between the two groups in an experiment is the presence or absence of the treatment variable. This level of control often leads to an unrealistic setting and rather trivial research questions. It has been said that a series of experiments allows us to be more and more certain about less and less. In fact, although it may be desirable in research terms, this level of experimental control is usually absent when confronting research in real-life situations. For example, it is not possible to allocate people randomly to groups in order to investigate war, disease, marriage, employment or imprisonment. Yet these might be seen as some of the most interesting areas for social science research. In addition, it is actually the control of the experiment by the researcher that can lead to self-fulfilment (delusion) or selective bias in observation. There can also be ethical problems in deceiving participants since, even where the treatment is non-harmful, it is usually necessary for the participants to be ignorant of the purpose of the experiment.

A more common (though currently still far from popular) form of experiment in social science research is the field trial. The most obvious way in which field trials differ from laboratory ones is that they tend to use existing groups as the basis for treatment (Hakim 1992). These 'quasi-experiments' therefore do not use random selection or allocation to groups but often recognize natural clusters in the population (see Chapter Four). It is just about impossible to allocate patients to doctors or students to teaching processes (such as schools or classrooms) at random. What is possible is to use existing doctor practices or teaching groups and vary the treatments between them, using statistical procedures to try and iron out any differences in the results due to pre-existing group differences. This approach gives the experiment a lower general level of internal validity but, because the setting is more realistic than a laboratory, the external validity (relevance to real life) is probably greater.

Bernard (2000) draws a useful distinction between a naturalistic field experiment that is most similar to the laboratory set-up, since the experimenter intervenes with a treatment, and a natural field experiment in which the researcher merely identifies an existing quasi-experimental situation and monitors it. Selecting twenty classes in different schools across England and Wales, and teaching half of them arithmetic with a calculator and half without, in order to test the impact of calculator use on an eventual test score, would be a naturalistic experiment. The researcher has intervened to produce two different treatment groups (and of course the experiment has considerable difficulties in terms of the diffusive effects of calculator use at home).

The alternatives to laboratory and naturalistic experiments are based on what Fitz-Gibbon (2000) calls essentially 'passive' approaches to research. The key difference is that in the former the researcher introduces a change into an environment and monitors subsequent events for the potential impact of that change. In the latter design the researcher simply monitors events and attempts to track back to a 'cause' *post hoc* – a much more difficult task both conceptually and technically (in terms of compensatory statistical analysis, for example). Ironically, it is not always easier to judge with the benefit of hindsight.

Nevertheless, the model of an experiment can still be of assistance, even in passive designs. One way is to use the natural experiment model. A passive approach can include the recognition that there are naturally occurring interventions going on around us all of the time when interventions occur as part of the policy process. The subsequent monitoring phase can be attached to an intervention that is not controlled by the researcher, but using the same analytical methods as for an experiment, sometimes long after the intervention (e.g. Gorard and Taylor 2002b). If one local health authority changes its practice in some way then this authority can be construed as the experimental group, with the remaining authorities as controls, in a natural experiment. In fact, much social science research is of this type – retrospectively trying to explain differences between two groups such as those in Table 8.2. All of these designs are inferior in terms of validity to a true experimental design but much more practical. Knowing how an experiment works is important because it enables us to see how far a natural experiment is from that 'ideal'. But it also alerts us to the need for things like comparison or control groups, and it is alarming how often passive researchers attempt to make comparisons over time and place on the basis of *one* set of observations (and even more alarmingly are believed and cited favourably by others). It also alerts us to the need for a transparent written protocol, so that our findings can be replicated just like those of a real experiment (Moses 2001).

For me, a true laboratory experiment is therefore akin to an ideal. It is how we would like to conduct research to get clear answers about the implications of our actions. Therefore, even if you never conduct a true experiment, knowing what it would have been is an important yardstick to help evaluate what you do. Everything that has been said about the problem of internal validity in experiments applies with even greater force to all other designs. If an experimenter, while trying to be neutral, unwittingly conveys demands to participants in fairly meaningless laboratory tasks, imagine the likely effect of an interviewer in personal communication with a interviewee, for example. If an experimenter unwittingly makes favourable mistakes in noting or adding up a simple data collection form, imagine the level of bias possible in interpreting the findings from a focus group discussion. In this way, if we consider the ways in which our actual designs are like or unlike a true experiment it allows us a glimpse of their considerable imperfections and keeps us appropriately humble. It also helps with future research synthesis by giving us a common standard against which to compare all studies.

Another way in which experimental models retain relevance in passive research is via the invaluable 'thought experiment' now widely used in science. Thought, or fantasy, experiments are quick and cheap and have no ethical problems (since we have no intention of carrying them out). Our imagination is free to wander, unbounded by practical considerations. We can think the unthinkable by imagining what a true experiment would be like for our area of investigation, and then compare the actual and ideal designs to help show up the defects in our actual design. Knowing the format and power of experiments gives us a template against which to measure what we do instead, and even helps us to design what we do better.

A third way in which experimental designs can contribute passively is via 'mental experiments' (Miles and Shevlin 2001). A mental experiment is a technical term from structural equation modelling referring to the precise prediction of the role of terms within the equation before analysis. Mental experiments are used in statistical modelling (often erroneously referred to as causal modelling) to help determine plausible directions of causation in our explanations. Structural equation modelling allows models based on non-experimental evidence to be rejected as inconsistent or to be tentatively retained as an explanation (Maruyama 1998). Such approaches cannot make up for poor design/data, and the models they generate should not be based on statistical criteria alone (Kline 1998). This is why the mental experiment is valuable, allowing the researcher to specify a model or models in advance of analysis. In the model the 'causal' paths are specified in advance in order to avoid the charge of dredging (simply looking for anything 'significant' *post hoc*) or of both building and testing a model on the same dataset, adopting statistics as a pseudo-science (Glymour et al. 1987). Of course, the dataset can never confirm the model, so the key issue here is to consider (and presumably eliminate) all plausible rival explanations and to work towards the most parsimonious version of the model. The same applies to all other forms of statistical modelling, whatever they are called, since despite differences in classification there is no real difference between all forms of analysis of non-experimental work (Johnson 2001, Gorard 2002d).

CONCLUSION

The danger of the rhetorical power of an experiment may be glimpsed in the way in which a small study by Woolford and McDougall (1998) was built by the UK media into a panacea for boys' under-achievement at school requiring immediate changes in policy (Western Mail 1998, TES 1998). In fact, their 'study' consisted of comparing the end-of-year assessments of two primary classes in the same school, one of which had a male teacher and the other a female teacher. The results of boys in the male class were better than those in the female class, and the researchers concluded therefore that having more male teachers is the answer to the apparent under-achievement of boys. This study has the form of a natural experiment (the two groups were already formed and the treatment was 'accidental'), but has many clear problems. It is a very small study. One of the boy groups was likely to perform better, and *a priori* there is a 50% chance of its being the one taught by the male teacher. There was no attempt to match the ability of the groups. There are no prior attainment scores (pre-test), no comparison of the skills and experience of the two teachers, the classes were taught in different rooms, and so on. I do not imply that the conclusion is not true, merely that this study provides no decent evidence for it.

As we have seen, a true experiment with a large representative sample is complex, costly and therefore rare. Laboratory experiments by themselves often answer apparently trivial or feeble questions with very limited samples, so quasi-experimental designs such as field trials are more common in social sciences. These designs may exhibit less rigour, with no control group or else using self-selecting clusters from the population. To be convincing they therefore require very clear logic in the evaluation of their results and in the consideration of alternative explanations. The triangulation of different methods can help, so there should be no suggestion that experiments are the only research design of any consequence (indeed, complex experiments would be impossible without multiple forms of data collection). However, it is important to remember that all of the problems facing experiments apply with equal or even greater force to all other research designs. The experiment is currently the most theoretically based and considered design available, and it has led to considerable research cumulation in many fields of endeavour of the kind that other, perhaps weaker designs have yet to achieve.

Good experimental designs testing quite narrowly defined hypotheses (to minimize confounding variables) have considerable power, especially as part of a larger cumulative programme of research via replication, expansion and verification of the findings. Above all, they can help us overcome the equivalent of the potted-plant theory, which is distressingly common in much research, policy-making and practice. For example, this theory suggests that if efficient hospitals have a potted plant in the foyer, then putting a potted plant in the foyer of other, less successful hospitals will lead to an improvement in their quality. Sounds ludicrous? I bet that much of the research evidence you have read recently is just as ludicrous in nature, once you think about it carefully. Unless we intervene or rigorously monitor the effect of natural interventions we can never be clear whether our observations of patterns and apparent relationships are real or whether they are superstitions similar to the potted-plant theory.

The power of the experiment comes not from the design alone but from the power of the questions to which experiments *can* be addressed. Such designs should therefore be additional to, not replacements for, other recognized modes such as detailed case studies and secondary analysis (and it should be noted that multiple perspectives and approaches are used relatively unproblematically in natural sciences). My message in this chapter would be that experiments can be powerful but they are not 'magic bullets'. Research is not high-quality just because it is experimental. If it is high-quality *and* experimental then it is probably as good as we are ever going to achieve in social science research. The next chapter looks at some the prominent issues and techniques of data analysis associated with the simple experimental designs discussed here.

Elementary parametric tests: what do they signify?

Chapter Three describes methods for analysing results using relatively simple arithmetic techniques, while Chapter Six introduces the notion of null hypothesis testing for statistical significance using non-parametric techniques. This chapter expands on this theme by describing some simple 'parametric' tests. These are slightly more difficult to use and more likely to be misused than the others because, in general, they make several assumptions about the form and distribution of your data (its 'parameters', in other words). However, they are worth using for two main reasons. Parametric tests are generally more powerful than non-parametric ones, making them more likely to distinguish between chance occurrences and actual patterns in the data. Using a parametric test is therefore directly equivalent to an increase in your sample size or in the effect size you are measuring, or to a decrease in the variability of your measurements (see Chapter Four). In addition, there is a wide range of parametric tests and associated statistical models available (some of these are described in Chapter Ten).

STATISTICAL POWER AND ERRORS

Before introducing the tests, let us consider further the general issue of using a statistical test to help make a decision about the significance of our findings. We say that results are 'significant' if we can reject the null hypothesis of no difference between two groups (see Chapter Six). In traditional null hypothesis testing this decision is based on a probability (the significance level). If there is a low probability that that null hypothesis is correct on the basis of what we have observed then we reject it. In doing so we *could* be wrong. If we set our significance level high then we are increasing our chance of obtaining a significant result but also increasing our chance of rejecting the null hypothesis incorrectly (what is unimaginatively called a 'Type I error' in statistics). If we set our significance level lower then we are decreasing the chance of a Type I error, but we are increasing our chance of retaining our null hypothesis when it is actually incorrect (a 'Type II error', where we are being too stringent). The reason the parametric tests described in this chapter are more powerful is because they are better than tests like chi-square at detecting a pattern or difference in the data without producing a Type I error. They are better at discriminating between useful patterns and what engineers call 'noise' in the system. This is their analytic power.

A SIMPLE PARAMETRIC TEST

The stages of creating the null and alternate hypotheses, selecting a significance level, calculating a test statistic with the appropriate degrees of freedom, avoiding Type I and II errors, and so on are generally the same for parametric tests as for the simple chi-square test in Chapter Six. There are three key differences. First: the test statistic is different for each test ('t' or 'F', for example, as opposed to chi-square), but since this calculation is handled by a computer it is of little practical importance to us. The associated probability means pretty much the same whatever test we use. Second: the tests are more powerful than non-parametric tests, and so are more likely to detect patterns in the data (see above). Third: the tests generally have more important underlying assumptions that have to be met before they can be used (see below).

Perhaps the simplest and most widely used parametric test in social science is the t-test for independent samples. The t-test is used to compare the mean scores of two groups. It is therefore ideal for dealing with the results of a simple experimental design (see Chapter Eight) using a treatment group and a control group. Table 9.1 presents some imaginary scores for a simple experiment with 22 participants (or subjects). We can see that there is some difference in the scores between the two groups, since the mean score for the control group is larger. How likely is it that these two groups actually represent sub-samples from the same population such that the experimental treatment to the first group has made no difference to their scores (our null hypothesis of no difference)? Can we reject this null hypothesis and suggest, on the other hand, that the experimental treatment has made these two sub-samples have different scores? This is what a t-test for independent samples can be used to help with.

Table 9.1: Scores in a simple experiment

Case	Treatment group	Control group
1	1	1
2	1	2
3	2	2
4	2	3
5	2	3
6	2	4
7	3	4
8	3	4
9	4	5
10	4	5
11	5	–
12	5	–
Mean score per group	2.83	3.30
Standard deviation	1.27	1.34

The samples are 'independent' because the individual cases in each group are different people, so that it is possible, as in this example, for there to be a different number of cases in each group (12 in the treatment group, and 10 in the control here). The degrees of freedom, calculated by the computer package in any case, would be 20 or the sum of the number of cases minus the number of groups. As with the chi-square test, the computer calculates a test statistic from the scores. In this case the statistic is called 't', but as with the chi-square test the precise meaning of this value need not concern the novice researcher. What is of more concern is the associated probability that the two means were actually taken from samples of the same population – or rather that the difference between the means is due only to sampling error. In this example the values might be reported as follows (Table 9.2).

This report shows a probability of .411 (or around 41%) for the null hypothesis, which is considerably larger than any level of

Table 9.2: Results of an independent t-test

	t	df	Sig. (2-tailed)
Score (equal variances assumed)	–.839	20	.411

significance that we might conceivably wish to use. Therefore, we have no evidence on the basis of these figures to suggest that our experimental treatment has had any impact on the scores. Although it may be that there actually is an effect but that the sample is too small, the null hypothesis of no effect still remains preferable as being the most parsimonious explanation of the observed scores so far.

UNDERLYING ASSUMPTIONS

When can we use the t-test? The chi-square test is used with two variables when both are categorical (and nominal). Chapter Ten describes bivariate analyses to use when both of the variables involved are real numbers. The t-test and the other tests discussed in this chapter are used with one nominal/categorical grouping variable and one real number score (either interval or ratio in form). The t-test is used to compare the groups formed by two different values of the nominal variable in terms of their scores on the real number. Thus, the t-test could be used to compare the height of respondents (real number) by their sex (nominal with two categories). Or it could be used with a test score (real) in terms of being either in the experimental or the control group (nominal with two categories). To compare more than two groups at once see 'analysis of variance' (below).

The power of the t-test derives from the known mathematical properties of the t distribution, but this power comes at a price. The calculations involved make several assumptions about the nature of the data used, and the more assumptions a test makes the more likely it is that it is abused. This is one of the best things about the non-parametric approach described in Chapter Six. It is very tolerant of the hiccups in your research design.

One of the assumptions for the use of the t-test (that the measurement used for one of the two variables must be at least interval in nature, i.e. a real number) has already been described. This test is also assumed to be based on two sets of scores that are approximately normally distributed (i.e. they have the standard symmetrical bell-curve pattern when plotted on a graph). The two sets of scores should also have approximately equal variances (the 'variance' is the square of the standard deviation, described in Chapter Three), or else the ratio of the two variances should be known. The variables should have been measured without error. Finally, as described in Chapter Four, the test assumes that the sample for each group has been selected at random and that each case is independent of every other.

According to traditional statistical theory, where even one of these five assumptions is not valid the t-test should not be used as it is liable to give biased results. In a sense all decisions based on all significance tests carry the proviso that, 'if the statistical model used was correct and the measurement requirement satisfied, then ...' (Siegel 1956). In practice, all five of the assumptions are commonly flouted, sometimes in combination, and a debate continues about the merits of this approach. I take a fairly middle-of-the-road stance on this issue, but it is up to each researcher when using parametric techniques to face up to these practical problems and resolve them to his or her own satisfaction. Many statistical users ignore the assumptions underlying the tests they want to use, particularly those concerning the nature and distribution of their data. In itself, this action may not be a great problem and many good findings may have come using methods that a purist mathematician might mock (Achen 1982). It is almost impossible to imagine a social science study in which there was *no* measurement error. It is, however, important to be aware of which assumptions are overlooked, in order to assess the value and applicability of any findings (Berry and Feldman 1985). This section therefore continues with a general discussion of these 'assumption' issues, which have a bearing on the remainder of this chapter and on the whole of Chapter Ten.

The underlying assumption of all statistical testing, which is that samples have been selected at random from a known population, is probably the most commonly flouted. Where care has been exercised in the creation of a high-quality, *probability*-type sample and the sample size for each sub-group is large, then this provides a good defence of the use of non-random sampling. In fact, to a great extent, the use of a large, quality sample is the best defence for the violation of any of the following assumptions. If you are intending to use a parametric test, re-read the logic of Chapter Four, use as large and as high-quality a sample as possible and then don't worry overmuch about this particular assumption.

Perhaps the next most commonly ignored assumption is that concerning the use of real numbers. The types of numbers used in social science research are discussed in Chapter Three. The practice of imagining that ordinal values are actually interval in nature is so widespread that it even has a name. Ignoring the nature of the data thus, in order to be able to use a more powerful parametric test, is known as the 'parametric strategy'. It has become almost standard practice in some fields of social science such as psychology. Aside from the other practical problems that such research often also entails (see below for the problems of indexing attitude scores, for example), I question the use of the strategy on several grounds. It is true that if the assumptions of a test are flouted the result can still be valid, and that Monte-Carlo (repeated random number) simulations of ordinal data analysed using both parametric and non-parametric techniques give very similar results. Nevertheless, not meeting the assumptions presumably leads to a loss of power in the test used (Siegel 1956), and therefore defeats the primary purpose of the strategy. If a parametric test is required for its power, the same effect without even a hint of dubious practice can be achieved by simply increasing the size of the sample. I am therefore surprised that this simple expedient is not more commonly advocated (but perhaps it is part of a wider statistical 'culture' that seeks complex ways of overcoming the deficiencies in data during analysis rather than simply collecting better data from the outset, see Chapter Ten). It is also true that the range and flexibility of non-parametric techniques have been considerably developed since the parametric strategy became popular. Therefore, if the strategy is pursued not so much for its power as for the range of statistical models that are available, then the recent considerable development of multivariate nonparametric approaches such as log-linear modelling or logistic regression should have made the strategy less attractive.

Despite all of these arguments, researchers will presumably continue as they have always done, and treat ordinal values as interval in nature when it is convenient to them. My advice therefore would be, again, have a good sample. Also design your data collection instruments so that the respondent/experimenter is clear that the numbers (s)he is recording are supposed to be interval in nature. For example, when using a five-point Likert scale from 1 (strongly agree) to 5 (strongly disagree), it is hard to argue that the interval or difference in agreement between 'strongly agree' and 'slightly agree' is identical to that between 'slightly agree' and 'neither agree nor disagree'. A three-point scale, on the other hand, is much easier to defend as being equal interval in nature, since the only two intervals are between 'agree' and 'neutral' and 'neutral' and 'disagree'. Alternatively, instead of using a written scale at all, you could ask respondents to score or rate their agreement out of a fixed total (which might be seen to imply that the scale of values has equal intervals). There are no right answers. Again, the decision is yours. Be prepared to defend it.

Finally, the assumptions about the distribution and shape of the data are often ignored because they are perhaps the least important or because their application is not as clearcut. The key to appreciating this lies in your understanding of the word 'approximately'. What does it mean for a set of figures to be approximately normally distributed or for two sets to have approximately equal variances? This judgement is another one to be made and defended by the researcher. My suggestions for this decision will be familiar to anyone who has read the book through to this point. Do not gloss over the decision. Plot the datasets on a graph (a bar chart of the frequencies is a useful method) and look at the pattern. Does it look like a normal curve? Similarly, calculate the standard deviations (or square root of the variances) for each group. Are they similar, bearing in mind their order of magnitude and that of the scores themselves? If your answer to both questions is 'yes' then you have no problems in using the test, as long as your sample is good and you are prepared to publicize and defend your decision (in a *viva voce* examination for a PhD student, perhaps). Bear in mind the principle above. A large sample cuts a substantial number of the ties from the underlying assumptions. A skewed or flattened distribution for 12 cases might not be considered even approximately normal, but the same distribution of 1,200 cases probably only needs to look vaguely symmetrical, with a denser cluster of values around the mean and many fewer extreme scores, to be considered good enough for the test to be used.

A RANGE OF TESTS

The t-test for related samples

Another test, also confusingly called a t-test, uses the same theoretical distribution (t) as that above. The t-test for related samples is indeed very similar, with mostly the same assumptions as the t-test for independent (or unrelated or unmatched) samples. The chief advantage of the related t-test is that, correctly used, it is even more powerful in enabling you to reject correctly an untrue null hypothesis. The test is appropriate when each individual in the two groups you wish to compare is related in an important way to a paired individual in the other group. Since in this design we wish to match each score in one group with a specific score in the other group this means, of course, that the two groups must be the same size.

A typical example of the use of the related samples t-test occurs in an experiment with a pre-test and post-test (see Chapter Eight). Here the two 'groups' are actually the same individuals but with two scores, from before and after the experiment respectively. We may wish to find out if their two scores differ, and therefore decide if our experimental treatment has had any effect. Another common situation occurs where the cases in each group are different individuals who have been matched in terms of key characteristics (such as sex, age, occupation, prior score, etc.). In an extreme example of this matching, the two groups may each be composed of one of a pair of identical twins.

Other than this 'restriction' about matched individuals the test is the same as that for independent samples. The degrees of freedom are one less than the number of pairs and this, coupled with the use of pairs, affects the calculation of t (by the computer). However, as far as we are concerned, the probability that emerges means the same as in both tests we have met so far. The test estimates the chance that both groups are really from the same population. Has our treatment/experiment created a separate population from the one we started with? Consider Table 9.3. The scores in each column are for the same individual in a repeated measures design. The score for each individual in the test that takes place after the experimental treatment is generally higher than his or her earlier score. Are these differences large enough and consistent enough for us to reject the null hypothesis?

Table 9.3: Scores in a repeated measures design

Case	Pre-test score	Post-test score
1	25	31
2	26	32
3	27	30
4	26	34
5	21	32
6	27	31
7	24	29
8	23	26
9	25	30
10	25	31
Mean score per group	24.90	30.60
Standard Deviation	1.85	2.12

The answer appears in a report of the kind generated by a related samples t-test (Table 9.4). The value of t is reported. Degrees of freedom are one less than the number of people in the study, since both groups are the same size. The probability associated with our observations is very low – less than 0.0005 in fact. This means we can safely reject the null hypothesis of no difference – and conclude that the scores for the two groups are significantly different. Whether we can now argue that the difference is attributable to the experimental treatment or whether there are confounding variables depends upon the quality of our experimental design (see Chapter Eight). As ever, this is where the fun starts.

Table 9.4: Results of a related t-test

	t	df	Sig. (2-tailed)
Post-test – Pre-test	–7.492	9	.000

One-way analysis of variance
If you are interested in looking at the differences between more than two groups, you could look at each of the paired comparisons separately, using the appropriate version of the t-test. For example, if you wish to compare groups A, B and C, you can run a t-test for each of A and B, A and C, and B and C. This approach is similar to that described in Chapter Six using the chi-square test for multiple comparisons. In the same way, however, this approach increases the number of tests carried out individually and so increases the chances of a Type I error (see below for a discussion of the 'shotgun' effect).

A better solution is provided by a technique from a group known collectively as 'analysis of variance', or sometimes just 'ANOVA'. Here I intend to describe only the simplest version, termed one-way analysis of variance (or just 'one-way'). Apart from the calculation of a value from a different theoretical distribution (called 'F' in all ANOVA), the assumptions for this test are mostly the same as for the independent samples t-test. It provides the flexibility of handling more than two groups at once, while not requiring a series of separate tests. Imagine that we are looking at the mean ages of 1,100 respondents living in three different local authorities (Table 9.5). Do we have any evidence that the samples in each group come from populations with differing ages?

Table 9.5: Mean age in three areas

Area of residence	Blaenau Gwent	Bridgend	Neath Port Talbot
Mean age of resident	50.75	51.30	51.76
Standard deviation	13.22	12.97	2.53
Number of cases	361	369	370

The stages of selecting a level of significance and using a null hypothesis of no difference between the groups are the same as for other tests. Our computer output might look something like Table 9.6. The probability (labelled 'Sig.') for our null hypothesis is high (57%), and therefore we have no reason to reject it. This is just as well for me since the data is actually from the systematic sample described at the end of Chapter Four, which was intended to be stratified by age. The figures are used here simply as an example of a non-significant ANOVA (and the result tells us nothing about the actual populations of the three areas).

Table 9.6: Results of one-way analysis of variance (I)

	Sums of squares	df	Mean square	F	Sig.
Between groups	187.20	2	93.60	.562	.571
Within groups	182,859.43	1,097	166.69		
Total	183,046.64	1,099			

On the other hand, the data from the same study (Gorard and Rees 2002) reported in Tables 9.7 and 9.8 do show a significant difference between the three areas. These represent an analysis of the figures for the same three areas as above, but in relation to the number of episodes of education or training reported by each respondent since leaving school. In the Blaenau Gwent area of residence, for example, the 361 respondents with an average age of 51 reported on average only a quarter of an episode each. Put another way, in this ex-coal-mining valley, no more than one in every four people took part in any further education or training once reaching school-leaving age. In Bridgend the figure is twice as high. Therefore, it is perhaps no surprise to find such a low probability associated with it in Table 9.8.

Table 9.7: Mean education episodes in three areas

Area of residence	Blaenau Gwent	Bridgend	Neath Port Talbot
Number of episodes	0.26	0.52	0.38
Standard deviation	0.54	0.79	0.72
Number of cases	361	369	370

Table 9.8: Results of one-way analysis of variance (II)

	Sums of squares	df	Mean square	F	Sig.
Between groups	12.34	2	6.17	12.883	.000
Within groups	524.98	1,096	.479		
Total	537.32	1,098			

One-way analysis of variance has therefore answered our first question. We can reject the null hypothesis, and conclude that the number of post-compulsory education episodes reported in the three areas shows a significant difference. We can assume, given this, that the difference between Bridgend (with the highest mean score of 0.52) and Blaenau Gwent (with the lowest mean score of 0.26) is also significant. This would be the minimum difference required to produce the overall result in Table 9.8. We are not able at this stage to tell whether the other two possible comparisons also lead to significantly different results. We must therefore conduct a range test to determine which of the three possible differences are significant. This is not difficult since the one-way ANOVA incorporates a choice of different range tests, so that, using a computer package, the range test you choose can run automatically after a significant result at the overall level. When you come to try this, do not be confused by the choice of so many range tests. All of them do pretty much the same thing. I tend to use Tukey's Honestly Significant Difference (which I think sounds a bit like a real ale). For the figures in Table 9.7, the results of Tukey's test are as in Table 9.9.

Table 9.9: Tukey's Range Test

	Bridgend	Blaenau Gwent	Neath/Port Talbot
Bridgend	–	.000	.021
Blaenau Gwent	.000	–	.040
Neath/Port Talbot	.021	.040	–

The figures in Table 9.9 are the probabilities for the null hypotheses of no difference in each two-way comparison as provided by the range test. All of these values would suggest a significant difference between respective pairs at the 5% level, and we could conclude that area of residence is therefore a general predictor, or possibly a determinant, of patterns of post-compulsory education and training. This could be an interesting finding, worthy of further investigation since Blaenau Gwent is the area of South Wales with the highest levels of unemployment and economic inactivity. Bridgend, on the other hand, has attracted a lot of inward investment. Is there, therefore, a relationship between economic activity and patterns of lifelong learning? As with much research, making progress often means finding new questions to answer.

One-way analysis of variance is so called because it involves one independent variable, but with any number of categories. If you wish to use two independent variables at the same time, then you would use two-way ANOVA. If you wish to have more than one, but related, dependent variables then you would use multivariate anova (MANOVA).

DO WE REALLY NEED STATISTICAL TESTS?

Statistical testing has many historical roots, although many of the tests in common use today, such as those attributable to Fisher, were derived from agricultural studies (Porter 1986). They were developed for one-off use, in situations where the measurement error was negligible, in order to allow researchers to estimate the probability that two random samples drawn from the same population would have divergent measurements. In a roundabout way, this probability was then used to help decide whether the two samples actually come from two different populations. For example, vegetative reproduction could be used to create two colonies of what is effectively the same plant. One colony could be given an agricultural treatment, and the results (in terms of survival rates, for example) compared between the two colonies. Statistics would help us estimate the probability that a sample of scores from each colony would diverge by the amount we actually observe, assuming that the treatment given to one colony was ineffective. If this probability is very small, therefore, we might conclude that the treatment appeared to have an effect. As we have seen, that in a nutshell is what significance tests are and what they can do for us.

In light of current practice, it is important to emphasize what significance tests are *not* and what they cannot do for us. Most simply, they cannot make a decision for us. The probabilities they generate are only estimates, and they are, after all, only probabilities. Standard limits for retaining or rejecting our null hypothesis of no difference between the two colonies, such as 5%, have no mathematical or empirical relevance. They are only arbitrary. A host of factors might affect our confidence in the probability estimate or the dangers of deciding wrongly in one way or another. Therefore there can and should be no universal standard. Each case must be judged on its merits. However, it is also often the case that we do not need a significance test to help us decide this. In the agricultural example, if all of the treated plants died and all the others survived (or vice versa) then we do not need a significance test to tell us that the probability is very low (and precisely how low depends on the number of plants involved) that the treatment had no effect. If there were 1,000 plants in the sample for each colony, and one survived in the treated group and one died in the other group, then again a significance test would be superfluous (and so on). All that the test is doing is formalizing the estimates of relative probability that we make anyway in everyday situations. They are really only needed when the decision is not clear-cut (for example where 600/1,000 survived in the treated group but only 550/1,000 survived in the control), and since they do not make the decision for us, they are of limited practical use even then. Above all, significance tests give no idea about the real importance of the difference we observe. A large enough sample can be used to reject almost any null hypothesis on the basis of a very small 'effect' (see below).

It is also important to re-emphasize that the probabilities generated by significance tests are based on random samples. If the researcher does not use a random sample then inferential statistics are of little use since the probabilities become meaningless. Researchers using significance tests with convenience, quota or snowball samples, for example, are making a key category mistake. Similarly, researchers using significance tests on populations (from official statistics, perhaps) are generating meaningless probabilities. It is possible that a trawl of educational, psychology or sociology research journals would reveal very few technically correct uses of significance tests. Added to this is the problem that social scientists are not generally dealing with variables, such as plant survival rates, with minimal measurement error. In fact, many studies are based on latent variables, such as attitudes, of whose existence we cannot even be certain, let alone how to measure them. Further, there are problems of non-response and participant drop-out in social investigations that also do not occur in agricultural applications. All of this means that the variation in observed measurements due to the chance factor of sampling (which is all that significance tests take into account) is generally far less than the potential variance due to other factors. The probability from a test contains the unwritten proviso that the sample is random with full response, no drop-out and no measurement error. The number of social science studies meeting this proviso is very small indeed. To this must be added the caution that probabilities interact, and that most analyses in the IT age are no longer one-off. Most analysts start each probability calculation as though nothing prior is known, whereas it may be more realistic and cumulative to build the results of previous work into new calculations (see Chapter Eleven).

Therefore, while it is important for novice social scientists to be taught about the use of significance tests, it is equally important that they are taught about the limitations as well (and alerted to possible alternatives, such as confidence intervals, effect sizes and graphical approaches). Significance tests have a specific valuable role to play in a limited range of research situations. Statistics cannot be used *post hoc* to overcome design problems or deficiencies in datasets. If all of the treated plants in our example were placed on the lighter side of the greenhouse, with the control group on the other side, then the most sophisticated statistical analysis in the world could not overcome that bias. It is worth stating this because of the current push for more complex methods of probability-based analysis, when a more fruitful avenue for long-term progress would be the generation of better data, open to inspection through simpler and more transparent methods of accounting. Without adequate empirical information 'to attempt to calculate chances is to convert mere ignorance into dangerous error by clothing it in the garb of knowledge' (Mills 1843, in Porter 1986, pp. 82–83). Significance tests may even be a hindrance to scientific progress (Harlow et al. 1997).

Statistics is not, nor should it be, reduced to a set of mechanical dichotomous decisions around a 'sacred' value such as 5%. Suggested alternatives to reporting significance tests have been the use of effect sizes (Fitz-Gibbon 1985), meta-analyses, parameter estimation (Howard et al. 2000) or standard confidence intervals for results instead, or the use of more subjective judgements of the worth of results, and even more non-sampled work (an area where the UK psychological, rather than sociological, tradition has been weak). In the USA there has been a debate over whether the reporting of significance tests should be banned from journals to encourage the growth of these alternatives (Thompson 2002). Both the American Psychological Society and the American Psycho-logical Association have recommended reporting effect sizes and confidence intervals, and the greater use of graphical approaches to examine data. An effect size is an estimate of the scale of divergence from the null hypothesis (such as R-squared, see Chapter Ten). The larger the effect size, the more important the result. A confidence interval is defined by a high and low limit between which we can be 95% confident (for example) that the 'true' value of our estimate lies (see Chapter Four). The smaller the confidence interval the better quality the estimate is (for more on this, see de Vaus 2002).

Of course, several of the proposed replacements, such as confidence intervals, are based on the same sort of probability calculations as significance tests. Therefore, they are still inappropriate for use with populations and non-random samples, and like significance tests they do nothing to overcome design bias or non-response. Most of the alternatives require considerable subjective judgement in interpretation anyway. For example, a standard effect size from a simple experiment might be calculated as the difference between the mean scores of the treatment and control groups (see Chapter Eight) proportional to the variance (or the standard deviation) for that score among the population. This sounds fine in principle, but in practice we will not know the population variance. If we had population figures then we would not need to be doing this kind of calculation anyway (see Chapter Three). We could *estimate* the population variance in some way from the figures for the two groups, but this introduces a new source of error, and the cost may therefore override the benefit on many occasions. There is at present no clear agreement, other than the need for the continued use of intelligent judgement.

Recent UK initiatives, perhaps most prominently the new funding arrangements for ESRC PhD students, have been designed to encourage a wider awareness of statistical techniques among social scientists. While these moves are welcome, the lack of agreement about the alternatives, the absence of textbooks dealing with them (Curtis and Araki 2002) and their need for greater skill and judgement mean there is a consequent danger of simply re-visiting all of the debates about statistics that have taken place in other disciplines since at least 1994 (Howard et al. 2000). Although there are suggestions to replace p-values with standard errors or confidence intervals (e.g. Altman et al. 2000), many of the same problems would continue to apply. It is not clear why we should use standard errors anyway. They are not used in business reports or examination grades, for example, where they might be just as appropriate. In real life the best estimate is our current score for any measurement (while we should treat all such scores with caution).

Part of what this section tries to do is show that standard approaches to significance testing, currently the cornerstone of many 'quantitative' methods courses, should no longer have automatic pride of place. There is a pressing need for more general awareness of the relatively simple role of numbers in those common social scientific situations for which sampling probabilities are not relevant. The importance of this ongoing debate about tests is that it suggests, as I hope this book confirms, that we need to move away from a formulaic approach to research. However, we need to replace empty formulae for reporting results, not with an 'anything goes' philosophy, but with 'almost anything goes as long as it can be described, justified and replicated'. Above all, we need to remember that statistical analysis is not our final objective, but the starting point of the more interesting social science that follows. A 'significant' result is worth very little in real terms and will certainly not enable you to generalize safely beyond a poor sample (see Chapter Four). The key issue in research is not significance but the quality of the research design.

COMMON PROBLEMS IN STATISTICAL TESTING

This section considers a range of other problems that can arise in the statistical analysis of results.

- Obsession with indexing
- The shotgun approach
- Inappropriate level of aggregation

Obsession with indexing
In some forms of psychology especially there has been almost an obsession with the use of composite indicators (or indexes). These

indexes often appear in attitude questionnaires where the respondent is faced with a battery of questions, all of which are used to assess what is basically the same underlying variable. In essence, the same or very similar questions are asked repeatedly and the answers are used in combination to create an overall attitude score. There may be times when this approach is necessary, and I confess to maybe not appreciating all of the arguments for it, but it is quite clear that indexing has several methodological shortcomings.

First and foremost, the notion that several questions or indicators can be combined to produce a better answer than just one is premised on sampling theory (Anderson and Zelditch 1968). It assumes that the variability of each indicator is equal to every other and that this variance is due solely to random error. If either assumption is false (and in most actual examples I have seen both are almost certainly false) then using one indicator is probably at least as reliable as many. At the very least, therefore, it is wasteful and time-consuming to ask respondents many questions whose correlation with each other is no greater than the correlation of any one of them with the latent underlying variable you are trying to measure (see Chapter Ten for a description of correlation). On the other hand, if the correlation between all indicators is very high you have to ask why only one of them would not do anyway, since all of them are so nearly measuring the same thing. Another problem arises in the scoring system (and this is in addition to any doubts about whether the respondents' answers are interval in nature). In a typical index the value of each question is assumed to be the same, and the score for each is totalled and then averaged. I have never seen an argument explaining why, for each test, this is considered appropriate and how we know that the answer to each question is precisely equivalent in importance to all others.

I do not recommend that students never use indexes, but that they should have a good reason for doing so, and that they should be careful about the potential flaws and artificialities in the process. As suggested in Chapter Five, surveys are better at collecting 'factual' information like date of birth than 'theoretical' data such as attitudes to car ownership.

THE SHOTGUN APPROACH

Making a predictive alternate hypothesis, especially a one-tailed one, deciding on a theoretically suitable level of significance in advance, and then carrying out one test of significance is what the mathematics for each test are based on (originating from an era before computers and hand calculators). However, it is now possible for us to enter a large number of variables into a package like SPSS, run a series of chi-square tests or analyses of variance, pick out those results with probabilities less than a *post hoc* level of significance, work out alternate hypotheses for only these 'significant' tables and results, and then publicize these hypotheses as our findings. This is what has been termed the 'shotgun' or 'dredging' approach to analysis. The results of such over-use of a test designed for one-off calculation should be seen as far from convincing (Stevens 1992), and it is therefore important to report it if this is what you have done.

For example, using a 5% level of significance means that the researcher accepts a 1 in 20 chance of making a Type I error. Probabilities such as these are multiplied (just like the probability of rolling a six with more than one throw of a die). Thus, using the 5% level on two successive tests means that the likelihood that no Type I error will occur on either test drops to $19/20 \times 19/20$ (or 0.9). On ten successive tests the likelihood that no error will occur drops to $19/20^{10}$ (or 0.6). After 100 tests, the probability of at least one error rises to over 99%. Therefore, the more tests you do, the less confident you can be that your results do not include a spurious finding emanating from chance alone. Carrying out every combination of one test of bivariate analysis involving as few as 20 variables (and bearing in mind that many student questionnaires have over 100 variables) means that you will perform 495 tests. The chance of at least one Type I error would therefore be more than 99.999999999%.

There are four key defences to this problem. First of all, even a scatter approach to analysis does not have to be *completely* mindless. You will know that there are relationships between some variables that you are simply not interested in. Exclude these. In addition, you can lower your threshold for significance (to 1% for example), increasing the chance of Type II errors but making your 'significant' results more convincing. You can also often replace multiple bivariate analyses with a more appropriate and one-off multivariate test (see Chapter Ten). But above all these technical solutions, you need to consider your purpose in conducting the analysis. Significance test results can lead to interesting ideas for further investigation, but never to any kind of proof or certainty. Therefore with shotgun results, as with any other, you should treat them as very tentative findings until they can be confirmed by a different methodological approach (triangulation) and until you have worked out a plausible explanation for them. In summary, be a little cavalier in your investigation by all means, but then be more conservative in your explanations. Remember that statistical significance and social science significance are not the same thing at all.

Consider the following as an example of why this might matter. Twenty social scientists, unknown to each other, all conduct a test of the same hypothesis. Assuming that the 'true' result is a non-significant one, on average 19 of the researchers will reach the correct conclusion using a significance test with a 5% (1 in 20) threshold. The 20th researcher finds a spurious 'significant' result. Most of the 19 researchers decide not to try and publish their results, because the non-significant finding is not very interesting. The rest of the 19 have their papers rejected by the journals they submit the findings to, for the same reason. Therefore, the only result eventually published is the one 'significant' result. All future reviews of this field of work will find only the published spurious result!

Inappropriate level of aggregation
The best-known example of this problem has been termed an 'ecological fallacy', in which data collected at one level of aggregation is used to draw conclusions about phenomena at another level. This can occur in considering school effects. Suppose we have summary measures of examination outcomes (e.g. pass rate at GCSE) and socio-economic composition (e.g. percentage of pupils from poor families) in a number of schools, we may be able to draw conclusions about the nature of the relationship between these variables. For example, we might conclude that schools with high levels of pupil poverty tend to have lower pass rates. This would be perfectly proper. What we cannot do is draw sensible conclusions about individuals (lower level of aggregation) or national systems (higher level of aggregation). We would have no reason from this aggregated data to assume that it is simply the individual pupils from poor families who obtain weaker results (or vice versa).

A clearer, but less well-known example leads to a kind of 'paradox' (attributed to Simpson 1951, but probably much older). Suppose a health authority monitors 2,000 patients in terms of the treatment they are given for a specific medical condition. Of these, 1,000 are given an experimental treatment, perhaps a drug or therapy. The other 1,000 are treated using traditional methods for this diagnosis. In a post-test 600 of Group A (experimental) survive, while 500 of Group B (control) survive. If the design of the experiment is adequate, then this is *prime facie* evidence that the new treatment leads to better results. Suppose the researcher then considers survival rates in terms of patient background character- istics such as sex. The survival rate was higher for female cases (67%) than for male (43%). This in itself is interesting but when disaggregated by sex and group the results are paradoxical (Table 9.10).

Table 9.10: Survival rates by sex of patient and experimental group

sex/group	A	B	Overall
Female	520/800 (65%)	150/200 (75%)	670/1,000 (67%)
Male	80/200 (40%)	350/800 (44%)	430/1,000 (43%)
Overall	600/1,000 (60%)	500/1,000 (50%)	1,100/2,000 (55%)

The survival rate for Group A (60%) is higher than for Group B (50%), yet females in Group B (75%) do better than females in Group A (65%) while males in Group B (44%) also do better than males in Group A (40%). This is enough to make you doubt what is going on in the universe. 'X Files' or what? I shall leave the reader to ponder this. The message from both examples is that problems can be introduced when changing the level of aggregation of your data. This does not mean you should never do it, but do take care when you do.

This chapter has introduced some common parametric approaches to analysis, which are especially relevant to simple experimental designs. There are a very large number of other tests available to the analyst (see Kanji 1999 for a description of 100 tests). For more on specific experimental designs and their analysis see Edwards (1972), Everitt and Hay (1992), Hinton (1995), Howell (1989), Kalton (1966), Maxwell (1958), McIlveen et al. (1992), Peers (1996) or Shaughnessy and Zechmeister (1994). The next chapter looks at the correlational approach to analysis as an introduction to more complex methods involving more than two variables.

Progress via regression: introducing correlations

This chapter introduces the idea of a correlation, in which two or more variables tend to change values in step with each other. Using this kind of relationship it is possible to predict (or explain) the value of one variable from the value of another. This approach is known as regression, and it forms the basis for several more advanced statistical techniques, some of which are discussed here. An understanding of correlation is therefore a useful door into the fascinating world of statistical modelling of social events.

INTRODUCING CORRELATIONS

The relationship between two variables known as a correlation is perhaps easiest understood graphically. Figure 10.1 shows the percentage of the 15-year-old cohort of students in each local education authority in England obtaining five or more GCSE qualifications at grade C or above (the government GCSE benchmark). These scores are plotted against the proportion of children in each area eligible for free schools meals (thus coming from families officially defined as in poverty). The two sets of scores are clearly related, such that areas with high poverty (x-axis) have lower GCSE results overall (y-axis), and areas with less poverty generally have higher GCSE results. This kind of relationship is called a correlation – in this example a negative correlation since the two values are negatively related (i.e. as one increases the other tends to decrease).

Key assumptions underlying this relationship are that the two variables must be real numbers (see Chapter Three), and they must cross-plot to form an approximately straight line. How close to a straight line this has to be is a matter of judgement, and it is always possible to transform one or more of the scores to try and make the

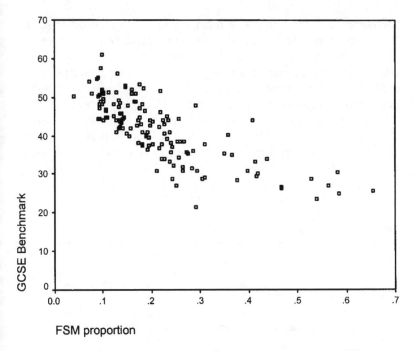

FSM proportion

Figure 10.1: Scatterplot for each Local Authority: GCSE benchmark 1998 against percentage of children eligible for free school meals

linear fit better. For example, a simple curved relationship can often be altered to a straight line by converting the scores to logarithms (Figure 10.1 might be improved by doing this, see Gorard 2000b). Since the analysis of correlations is based on deviations from the best-fitting straight line, setting out to use the techniques described here with data exhibiting curvilinear relationships (or worse) is unlikely to be effective. Alternative correlational techniques are available for curved relationships (Norusis 2000) and for categorical variables (Siegel 1956).

Where the two variables do appear approximately linearly related it is possible to conduct a significance test for the null hypothesis that they are actually unrelated. The most common of these uses the correlation coefficient known as Pearson's R, with an associated probability for the null hypothesis (see Chapter Six). If this probability is very small (below 5%, for example) there is clearly some evidence of a correlation, and the null hypothesis can be quite safely rejected. In addition (and unlike the values such as chi-square, t and F introduced so far), the value of R gives us an indication of the nature and strength of the relationship (it is, or rather its square R^2 is, an 'effect size' using the concept introduced at the end of Chapter Nine). R has a value between −1 and +1. A value of 0 shows no relationship at all (appearing as random scatter when cross-plotted on a graph). A value of +1 shows a perfect positive correlation between the two variables, meaning that they both increase or decrease in step with each other. A value of −1 shows a perfect negative correlation between the two variables, meaning that as one increases the other decreases in step with it. The scores in Figure 10.1 yield a value of −0.77, showing a fairly strong negative correlation, with an associated probability for the null hypothesis of less than 0.0005 (Table 10.1).

Table 10.1: Correlation between GCSE benchmark and levels of free school meals

		GCSE	FSM
GCSE	Pearson correlation	1.000	−.773**
	Sig.	−	.000
	N	140	140
FSM	Pearson correlation	−.773**	1.000
	Sig.	.000	−
	N	140	140

** Correlation is significant at the 0.01 level (2-tailed).

A computer-based correlation analysis will lead to a report like that in Table 10.1. By this stage of the book you should be aware of the meaning of the terms involved. The report is symmetrical since the same relationship holds between free school meals (FSM) and examination results (GCSE) as between GCSE and FSM. It is, after all, a *co*rrelation. The correlation between each variable and itself is 1, by definition. The 'significance' is the probability that the null hypothesis (that there is no correlation) is true. N is the number of observations − in this example the number of Local Education Authorities (140). The correlation coefficient of −.773 provides an estimate of the strength of the relationship. The amount of variation in one variable that can be predicted (or explained) by knowing the value for the other is the square of .773 (or 60%). Put another way, if you tell me the amount of poverty in the schools in one authority then I can tell you their GCSE results with around 60% accuracy (or more strictly I can account for 60% of the variance in the results). This is the basis of value-added approaches to performance measurement, such as studies of school effectiveness. The technique is called regression, and is the focus of the next section.

To summarize here: Pearson's correlation coefficient (R) is used to measure the common variation in two sets of scores. Whereas a chi-square test compares two categorical variables (Chapter Six) and the t-test compares one interval and one categorical (grouping) variable (Chapter Nine), this kind of correlation requires two interval variables. The other main requirement is that the two variables are approximately linearly related (i.e. they cross-plot to form a straight line). It is sometimes possible to transform the variables (e.g. by conversion to logarithms) to make a better line, although using logarithmic transformations to overcome non-linearity might introduce further problems (Harwell and Gatti 2001). The probability resulting from the test is used as normal to help decide whether the two variables are related or not (but bear in mind that a non-significant result suggests not that they are unrelated, but only that they are not *linearly* related).

The test also provides the researcher with an estimate of the variance common to the two variables. The correlation coefficient is 0 if the two items are completely unrelated, 1 if the two items are 'identical', and −1 if they are the exact opposites. The square of this coefficient shows how much of the variance is common. For example, if two variables have a correlation of .5, then 25% of their variance is common (and may measure the same underlying social scientific phenomenon). Correlation is also the basis for regression analysis, where values in one variable are used to 'predict' values in another. The standard caution given about the interpretation of correlation is that it gives no indication of the real relationship between the two variables (see Chapter Seven). There may be a clear correlation in Denmark between the number of children in any house and the number of storks nesting in its roof. Is this evidence that the activities of storks are involved in childbirth or that larger houses tend to have both more roof space and more residents? Children with bigger feet also tend to spell better (because they are older?).

A correlation is the start, not the end, of an investigation, and its explanation is likely to involve theoretical considerations and the triangulation of knowledge from other data sources. Even then, the proposed explanation can be only a tentative one. This basic fact is important to note before we consider more complex designs. There is a danger that novices confuse complexity with rigour, whereas the more complex designs mentioned in this chapter suffer from the same flaws and limitations as the simplest correlation, as well as introducing their own problems. In my experience complexity and rigour are often negatively 'correlated', in the same way that complexity and reliability are in engineering. This is true, however extravagantly their results are described.

LINEAR REGRESSION

Simple regression

Where two variables are linearly related (as they are in Figure 10.1), there is a line of best fit. This is usually seen as the line on the graph that minimizes the mean deviation of all points (note that the issue of whether to include or exclude extreme scores, or 'outliers', is discussed in Chapter Three). Once this line has been calculated, it is possible to use it to read off the values of one variable (the dependent variable) from the values of the other (the independent variable). Any such reading will not be totally accurate unless the correlation is perfect, and it will therefore contain a substantial error component. Which of the two variables is termed the 'dependent' is a matter for the researcher to decide, and is not derived from the nature of their statistical inter-relationship (see Chapter Seven). In Figure 10.1 it might make more sense to use GCSE as the dependent value because I can see a way in which poverty could affect examination performance, but no way in which the reverse could hold (at least over the short term). However, it is a fallacy to imagine that simply calling one variable 'dependent' actually makes it so – the model you create in doing so is theoretical and tentative.

Table 10.2 shows the results of a simple linear regression analysis, based on the scores in Figure 10.1. The dependent (predicted) variable is the GCSE benchmark for each area, and the independent (predictor) variable is the proportion of children in poverty. In SPSS, the 'Analyse' menu offers a choice entitled 'Regression' and the regression sub-menu offers a choice entitled 'Linear'.

Table 10.2: Regression analysis, predicting GCSE from FSM

Model	Component	B	Std. Error	Beta	t	Sig.
1	Constant	53.01	0.91		58.23	.000
	FSM propn.	−53.32	3.72	−.773	−14.33	.000

This result leads us to a theoretical function, or equation, relating the two variables:

GCSE score $= b_0 +$ *(b_1 times FSM score)* $+$ *error component*

In this equation, b_0 is the constant (53.01), and b_1 is the coefficient (−53.32) acting as a multiplier for the FSM score. If we ignore the error component (since we know nothing about it, including how large it is), we can estimate the GCSE score for any Authority. We can therefore use our equation to predict the scores for Authorities not involved in the calculation (such as those in Wales) or to decide which Authorities are scoring higher or lower than we expect. For example the proportion of school children eligible for free school meals in Cardiff (Wales) in 1998 was .23. Our equation suggests that Cardiff should appear on the line in Figure 10.1 at y = 40.75, since 40.75 is 53.01–(53.32 times .23). In fact the GCSE benchmark for Cardiff in that year was 43%, slightly higher than expected. The dot for Cardiff would therefore appear just above the line of best fit. However, the level of poverty is not the only factor relating school compositions to school outcomes. There are many other contributory factors, apart from the omitted error component, and combining these could make our predictions more accurate. Which leads us on to multiple linear regression.

Multiple regression
As with any estimate, the one above could probably be improved by considering further variables. It is likely that location, types of school, gender mix, ethnic mix, parental education, prior attainment and a host of other factors are also related to the GCSE results at a Local Authority level. A practical problem is that many of these further variables will themselves be interrelated. We cannot therefore simply total the correlations of each variable with the GCSE scores. For example, if the proportion of ethnic minority pupils is negatively correlated with GCSE results, we cannot simply add this correlation to that for poverty. This is so for two main reasons. First, poverty and ethnicity are likely to have some correlation between themselves (with poverty more prevalent among some ethnic goups), so using both together means we end up using their *common* variance twice. The real multiple correlation between ethnicity and poverty on the one hand and GCSE score on the other is likely to be less than the sum of the two correlations. Second, the real multiple correlation between ethnicity and poverty on the one hand and GCSE score on the other could be greater than

the sum of the two correlations. This would mean that there is an 'interaction' effect between ethnicity and poverty, whereby the one reinforces the impact of the other (Pedhazur 1982). One technique in common use to overcome both of these problems is multiple linear regression. This takes into account the correlations between multiple independent variables when combining them to predict/explain the variance in the dependent variable.

I used this technique to examine patterns of differential attainment between schools and sectors of schools in the study represented by Gorard (1998b, 1998c, 2000c, and 2000d). The relationship between poverty and school examination outcomes holds at the school level as well as the Local Authority. Schools with more than their fair share of children from poor families generally have a larger number of children who obtain no qualifications at all at age 16. Figure 10.2 represents scores for every secondary school in Wales in 1999. Schools with few children in poverty (zero on the x-axis) also tend to have few children leaving with no qualification (100 on the y-axis).

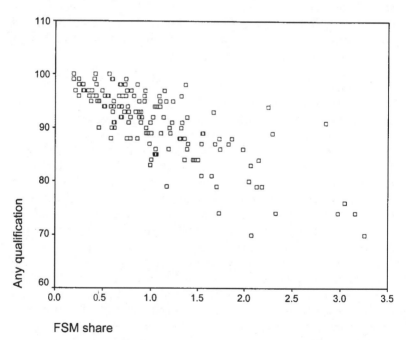

Figure 10.2: Scatterplot for each school: proportion of students attaining any qualification 1999 against school share of students eligible for free school meals

A similar relationship exists between qualifications and the proportion of children per school with a statement of special educational need (SEN), and between qualifications and levels of unauthorized absence ('truancy'). Schools in which most children obtain at least one GCSE at grade G or above tend to have fewer SENs and less truancy. These three independent variables were the most powerful predictors of qualification rates at the school level available to me. When all three are used simultaneously in a multiple regression analysis with qualification as the dependent variable, part of the output appears as in Tables 10.3 and 10.4. Tables such as these are obtained via SPSS in the same way as for simple linear regression (but you would enter more than one independent variable in the appropriate dialog box).

Table 10.3 shows the value of R (+ .815), which means the same as it does in simple regression, except that it now expresses the multiple correlation between qualifications, on the one hand, and all three independent variables in combination, on the other. The probability (.000) is again the same as in a simpler test of significance, and would show the likelihood of there being no linear relationship between the two groups of variables (but in this example it is meaningless since the figures do not come from a random sample).

Table 10.3: Multiple regression analysis

Model	R	R Square	Adjusted R Square	Std. Error of the Estimate
3	.815	.665	.656	3.79

Predictors: Constant, Segregation, Special Needs, Truancy
Prob. .000

Table 10.4 shows the coefficients (b_0 to b_3) for the resulting multiple regression equation of the form:

Qualification rate = 100 − (6.49 times FSM share) − (.38 times SEN)− (.74 times Truancy) + error component

Given the values in Table 10.4, you can therefore calculate (or use the computer to calculate) expected scores for any school, as long as you know its share of free school meals, etc. In part of my study I used an equation based on all of the schools in one sector to predict the scores for schools in another sector. In this way, I showed that once the variation due to poverty and SEN is taken into account there was no evidence of differential effectiveness of different types or sectors of school. There is, therefore, no need for comprehensive schools to look at other types of school as models of improvement in terms of these scores. No sector appears to be doing any better than any other with *equivalent* pupils.

Table 10.4: Coefficients for multiple regression analysis

Value	B	Std. Error.	Beta	t	Sig.
Constant	100.20	.78		128.69	.000
FSM share	−6.49	.83	−.63	−7.75	.000
Special Needs	−.38	.12	−.17	−3.10	.002
Truancy	−.74	.33	−.19	−2.27	.025

The underlying assumptions for this analysis are basically the same as for correlation. All values must be real numbers, linearly related to the dependent variable, and meeting strict assumptions about the distribution of the error terms (Maxwell 1977, Achen 1982, Menard 1995). In any real research project involving multiple regression, some of the assumptions underlying it are likely to be violated (Berry and Feldman 1985). This, in itself, may not be not fatal to the validity of the work, and even where the regression is flawed it is sometimes only the intercept (the constant b_0 in our first equation) that is affected, and the derived coefficients may still be used with care. On the other hand, some commentators insist that regression analysis makes sense only when the variables are precisely measured (Guidry 2002), otherwise the coefficients (column B in Table 10.4) and significance values will be misleading. As with almost any technique, the best defence against any such problems is a large, high-quality sample.

Since the technique is so useful, it is frequently used in modelling situations for which it was not intended. Chief among these are the very common situations where some of the independent variables are categorical in nature. Standard regression does not work well with categorical independent variables having more than two values (Hagenaars 1990), but if a variable (such as sex) has only two possible values it can be treated as an equal interval variable (since there is only one interval). Further, even variables with more than two categories can be used by converting them to a series of dummy variables. A social class scale with three categories, for example, could be treated as two dummy variables. The first dummy is a yes/no variable representing being in the 'Service' class or not, and the second dummy represents being in the 'Intermediate' class or not. 'Working' class is therefore defined as being not Service and not Intermediate class. Some writers have argued that this treatment is a distortion and not really appropriate, especially now that newer methods have been developed specifically to deal with categorical variables (see later section on logistic regression). Since it is assumed in regression that the variables are normally distributed (Lee et al. 1989), and dummy variables cannot have such a distribution, then simply converting a categorical variable into a set of dummies is not the solution. Dummy variables add to the measurement error (Blalock 1964). For more on this and other potential flaws in regression analysis, such as omitted variable bias, heteroskedasticity and multicollinearity, see Maddala (1992). I am not saying you should not use dummy variables, merely that you should be aware of the downside and be prepared to defend your decision either way.

The remainder of this section raises two less well-known problems in regression as commonly used in social science research: the level of data aggregation and the order of entering variables into the model. For example, it is generally assumed, although without much independent evidence, that where we are analysing school outcomes it is better to use data relating to the individual student rather than aggregated figures relating to classes, groups or schools. This is certainly the path followed in standard school effectiveness studies. However, we should all be aware that there is a considerable error component in the allocation of school outcomes. Whatever the system of moderation used, public examinations are inaccurate, so much so that they are estimated to be accurate only to within a grade or two (Nuttall 1987, Gorard 2001b). In a large aggregate analysis (e.g. at school level), we can assume that these 'random' errors are largely cancelled out, but this is not so when the analysis focuses on individuals. Raudenbush (2002) concludes that randomized studies of school reform should use the school as the unit of allocation, treatment and analysis (presumably).

For any study, the regression model explaining the greatest variance in the dependent variable (e.g. exam score) will use all available independent variables. This is the model you get if you simply enter all the variables at once. However, it is possible to create simpler models containing fewer variables but still explaining a large proportion of the variance. These models are easier to use and understand, and so more practical. It may be that ethnicity and first language, as variables, are measuring much the same thing in terms of school outcomes. The same may be true of social class and indicators of poverty. In such cases, we are better off picking the best single indicator from a group of related measures, and using that one only. We could pick the best indicator on theoretical grounds or in terms of availability. Both of these approaches are fine. However, the most common ground for selection of variables is the proportion of variance that they explain. If language and ethnicity are related and language is a better predictor of examination scores then we might omit ethnicity from our analysis.

In several forms of multivariate analysis, the order in which independent variables are entered into the explanatory model can also make a very substantial difference to the results obtained (and see below for more on this). Different explanations of social phenomena can be derived using the same technique but with only minor variations in the order of entering variables. Since many well-known and influential theories are based on precisely such models, the importance of bearing this principle in mind is difficult to exaggerate. Put simply, in the absence of greater detail about the order in which variables are considered, some of these theories may be less secure than previously imagined (Gorard and Rees 2002).

MORE ON UNDERLYING ASSUMPTIONS

In standard multivariate linear regression techniques (multiple regression), the analyst attempts to 'explain' the variation in a dependent variable (the outcome) in terms of independent variables (the inputs). For example, a model may be constructed in which pupil examination scores are explained in terms of prior examination scores for the same pupils, and their sex. Which of these three variables is used as the outcome is a matter of choice, and the solution could be recast statistically to show prior attainment, or even sex, as the outcome or dependent variable. The choice of dependent variable depends on the causal model you adopt (see Chapter Seven). In this example, we might argue that two of the variables are determined prior to the final examination and that the arrow of causation can run only one way (one cannot change sex through performance in an examination, for example). At least implicitly, therefore, all regression adopts a path analysis approach to testing the feasibility of a previously determined causal path (and it might be better for this path to be made explicit via structural equation modelling, Maruyama 1998). Regression cannot, of course, prove that the independent variables *determine* the variation in the dependent variable, but it can show whether that is possible. Whatever you do with regression, and this includes the techniques discussed below, cannot overcome this limitation.

The full set of assumptions underlying regression techniques is quite large and therefore can be rather terrifying. It is also the subject of some dispute, both over what the assumptions really are and over the implications for running an analysis that does not meet them (e.g. Menard 1995, Miles and Shevlin 2001, de Vaus 2002). I present here 13 separate assumptions, although some of these are clearly related.

- The measurements are from a random sample (or at least a probability-based one)
- All variables used should be real numbers (or at least the dependent variable must be, see above)
- There are no extreme outliers
- All variables are measured without error (but when is this possible?)
- There is an approximate linear relationship between the dependent variable and the independent variables (both individually and grouped)
- The dependent variable is approximately normally distributed (or at least the next assumption is true)
- The residuals for the dependent variable (the differences between calculated and observed scores) are approximately normally distributed
- The variance of each variable is consistent across the range of values for all other variables (or at least the next assumption is true)
- The residuals for the dependent variable at each value of the independent variables have equal and constant variance
- The residuals are not correlated with the independent variables
- The residuals for the dependent variable at each value of the independent variables have a mean of zero (or they are approximately linearly related to the dependent variable)
- No independent variable is a perfect linear combination of another (not perfect 'multicollinearity')
- For any two cases the correlation between the residuals should be zero (each case is independent of the others).

In general, if these are not true for any analysis, the impact is to reduce the apparent size of any relationship uncovered. Therefore, and in general, if you obtain a significant result it is still relatively safe even when some of these assumptions are not met. I have listed the assumptions in full here so that the last one – the independence of cases in the analysis – can be seen in context.

OVERCOMING 'AUTO-CORRELATION' VIA MULTI-LEVEL MODELLING

This last assumption is the key one for a more complex variation of regression called 'multi-level modelling' (MLM), and it is this that determines whether MLM is particularly appropriate for your analysis. MLM is actually the name for a range of techniques, including both fixed and random effects, developed from 'hierarchical' approaches to analysis in fields such as agriculture. It emerged particularly in the classic paper by Aitkin and Longford (1986) and in writing by Raedenbush and Bryk (1986) and Goldstein (1987). It is based on a recognition that in the social world much of the data we wish to analyse has an inherent structure that we may be foolish to ignore. This means that the measurements we take may routinely flout the last assumption of regression techniques. Cases are *not* independent of each other. We might expect people in one family to be more like each other than like a person in another family. We might expect the health problems of all girls to be more similar in some respects to each other than to those of boys. We might expect pupils in one school to perform more like each other than like a pupil in another school. Technically, such cases are said to be 'auto-correlated'. MLM advocates argue that since this is the case, we are better off building these similarities into our analytical methods. MLM is therefore simply regression that allows the analyst to use both individuals and groups of individuals in the same model to avoid flouting the last assumption (of independent cases), since the standard error of any results can be affected by the clustered nature of the data. However, some authorities argue that auto-correlation only leads to loss of power (Raudenbush 2002) and, as we have already seen, this can be righted simply by increasing the sample size rather than changing our methods of analysis.

Paterson and Goldstein (1991) use a hypothetical example based on 5,000 pupils in 100 schools to make the point about auto-correlation. If we wish to explain an examination outcome using standard regression, then we would treat the 5,000 cases separately and calculate a regression equation that maximized the accuracy of our predicted examination scores using the independent variables (such as sex or prior attainment). The equation would be of the form:

pupil score = constant + error term +
(coefficient1 times variable1) + (coefficient2 times variable2) ...

or in more formal terms for pupil i:

$$y_i = b_0 + e_i + b_1 X_{1i} + b_2 X_{2i} ...$$

The constant (b_0) is the 'intercept', the suggested value of the pupil score when the value of the predictor variable(s) is zero. If we allow this constant to differ between schools, since the predicted test score may also depend on the school attended by each pupil, then we are effectively adding a 'school term' to create an equation of the form:

pupil/school score = constant + error term + school term
+ (coefficient1 times variable1) + (coefficient2 times variable2) ...

or in more formal terms for pupil i in school j:

$$y_{ij} = b_0 + e_i + u_j + b_1 X_{1ij} + b_2 X_{2ij} ...$$

This is the simplest form of a multi-level model. The term for the constant plus school ($b_0 + u_j$) is now the intercept value for each school (in the same way as above, but where it is calculated per school rather than for the whole dataset). The model can be extended to allow more variables, more levels (pupils within schools within school districts, for example), and to allow the coefficients to vary between schools. It can be used in a variety of settings, perhaps most notably in repeated measures designs, where the individuals (cases) are measured more than once. We may assume that the scores for any individual are more alike than the scores of different individuals (in repeated measures the person is taking the place of the school, and the repeated scores are taking the place of the pupils). Variants of MLM have long been used in other fields, and analogues appear in techniques such as logistic regression and ANCOVA (analysis of covariance). The major change in the last 15 years has not been so much a statistical breakthrough, but rather an advance in the specialist software available.

As in most techniques we do not need to know a lot more about the calculations involved, since they will be performed for us by a computer anyway (see Plewis 1997, for example, for more on how to conduct MLM). Rather, we need to understand what the technique is about. Clearly the MLM approach is better than simply using the mean score for each school to look for differences between schools, since there would then be only 100 cases in the example above, which would make for less reliable findings, and may miss interesting variations at the pupil level. To what extent is the MLM approach genuinely better than, or even different from, doing two separate analyses – one with the school means, and one with the pupil scores in our example?

LIMITATIONS OF MULTI-LEVEL MODELLING

If the first assumption for the use of regression techniques – that measurements are taken from a random sample – is met then MLM is not needed (by definition). Any apparent auto-correlation that exists in the sample will also be random (accidental) rather than the result of social structures. For example, if the population is the Year Seven pupils in all schools in England, then a random sample will have a national 'spread'. There may be more than one pupil from the same school, just as there will almost certainly be more than one with the same sex, prior attainment, and class and ethnic background. It may be important that all of these variables, and more, are taken into account in the regression. But this is very different from the argument for MLM that is based on a very different kind of sampling – at best cluster-random and at worst cluster-convenience. MLM is, like all regression, based on probability theory, and the p-values generated in conducting an analysis are predicated on a random sample. But if the sample is truly random then MLM is not needed. Therefore the first 'intrinsic' problem is the lack of a clear area of application for MLM.

The chief argument for MLM based on auto-correlation applies only if the sample is a cluster-random one. Note that this is not the same as any 'sample' of cooperating institutions used as a cluster-convenience or cluster-opportunity sample. Nor is it the same as a sample where cases are chosen randomly within convenience/opportunity clusters. The argument for MLM clearly requires a defined population of clusters from which a sample is selected at random (with no replacement, no non-response and no drop-out). If this condition does not exist then the claimed increase in accuracy from using MLM is likely to be more than is lost by the design bias (Torgerson and Torgerson 2001). Therefore, many examples of MLM in actual use are inappropriate (e.g. Lauder et al. 1999). In fact, it now becomes unclear whether MLM could *ever* be appropriate. Statistical techniques are becoming more and more complex largely to overcome deficiencies in the datasets involved. Where experimental designs based on random samples are used, then the analysis of the results is largely straightforward (e.g. is the group A score larger than the group B score?). Where we attempt to make statistical adjustments for deficiencies in this design, then we often do not know which variables to adjust for, or do not have the necessary data at the appropriate level of aggregation, or do not have the techniques to adjust appropriately (Moses 2001). Is MLM such a technique?

My answer, on balance, would be 'no'. It is important that the unit of randomization is also the unit of treatment for results purposes (Moses 2001). For cluster samples this means that the cluster is the unit of analysis, not the individuals within them (and the ecological fallacy and other contra-indications suggest why). Of course, individuals are important, but to conduct a statistical analysis for individuals generally requires the collection of data from a random sample of *individuals*. A good cluster-random sample mimics a true random sample (as does a systematic or stratified one) and, insofar as it does, it then allows an individual-level analysis without concern for auto-correlation at the cluster level. Put simply, auto-correlation is a deficiency of sampling, not of analysis, and the appropriate solution is therefore better sampling, not more complex analyses.

It is important to recall that all of the limitations and assumptions of regression apply equally to MLM. There is a danger, otherwise, that MLM is seen as a kind of 'magic bullet', uncovering causation, overcoming poor design and allowing researchers to draw robust conclusions from poor datasets. It is nothing of the sort (Coe and Fitz-Gibbon 1998). It is simply a useful technique for specific situations. Fielding (2000) has argued that MLM is best used where experiments are not possible (perhaps for ethical reasons) in order to make up for defects in the data (see below). In practice, however, MLM is often simply used as a replacement for experiments (Fitz-Gibbon 2000), and leads to a pretence that this essentially passive approach can uncover causal mechanisms (in Goldthorpe 2001).

The approach allows for nested hierarchies, but neither considers how high or low to aggregate these hierarchies, nor gives clear guidance on what to do in the usual situation where hierarchies are competing rather than nesting. What is done about the auto-correlation also caused by sex, social class, ethnicity, days of the week for testing, time of day for testing, etc.? The hierarchies created by these clusters do not nest, so in practice they are ignored. Sex, for example, is used as a simple explanatory variable at one or more levels in school effectiveness research while the school is used as a cluster for analytic purposes. There seems no clear *a priori* reason for this.

Paterson and Goldstein (1991) claim that 'the key technical advance of multi-level modelling is to assume that the u_j vary randomly across schools' (p. 388). This constant determines the intercept for each school, and is an important part of the predicted score for each pupil. It is routinely calculated for each school, using observed differences between pupils in those schools. The reliability and scientific safety of any school term depends therefore not on the overall sample size, nor the number of schools, but on the size and nature of the sample in each school. In their example, having rejected using the sample of 5,000 individuals because of auto-correlation caused by the clustered nature of the sample, and rejected using the aggregate scores for 100 schools as too few to be safe, Paterson and Goldstein (1991) instead advocate using the 50 cases in each school to calculate 100 versions of u_j, and relying on these to help assess a school effect. The ensuing bias is likely to be far greater than that involved in simply using 5,000 cases and warning readers of the possible impact of auto-correlation. The medicine may be more harmful than the disease.

MLM was introduced to try and overcome what is only one of around 13 statistical assumptions underlying the use of standard regression techniques, and even that line of argument is based on accepting a deficiency of either research design or sample quality, or both. MLM involving ordinal and dummy variables, for example, might manoeuvre round the assumption of independence of cases but flout several other assumptions in doing so. What we gain from using MLM may be more usefully attained by better design or greater use of genuine random samples, and is anyway liable to be lost among the errors and complexity involved. It remains the case that anything that can be done with MLM can also be achieved by other means – perhaps most simply by conducting an analysis for each level with aggregated scores where necessary. This latter approach also has the advantage of allowing the levels to be non-nesting (such as sex and school), a major limitation for standard MLM approaches. MLM 'is technically an improvement over the traditional multiple regression model ... but there are simpler ways, ways that do not need more than one iteration' (Kreft, p. 14). When five large datasets were analysed using both standard regression and MLM the two sets of results from each correlated at around .99 (Fitz-Gibbon 2001). In this case, results using MLM are less accessible to a wider readership for no apparent reason. They are not as parsimonious as traditional regression (requiring more parameters to be estimated), they are less generalizable (i.e. more specific to the dataset they are fitted to), need a larger dataset and are more complex to estimate. Therefore, 'after 15 years of promotion of these models, some disappointment has set in' (Kreft 1996, p. 1). Perhaps 'we don't need more complex analytic techniques, we need better data collection' (Brighton 2000, p. 135).

LOGISTIC REGRESSION

Linear regression, whether multi-level or not, is both inelegant to use with categorical independent variables and impossible to use with a categorical dependent variable (Achen 1982). It is useless when the system to be analysed is non-linear, as most systems are in real life (Brignell 2000), the commonest pattern being an S-shape. The S-shape has a threshold value below which an increase on the x-axis produces little change on the y-axis, an active part where the relationship may be linear or curved, and a saturation value beyond which an increase on the x-axis again produces little change on the y-axis. However, several regression-type techniques are available that can deal with both of the first two problems while still coping with real-number independent variables, and with the added advantage that the variables need not be linearly related. Perhaps because logistic regression allows for more realistic non-linear relationships it routinely explains more of the variance (by around 12%, according to King 2002) than linear regression models or even discriminant function analysis using the same dataset. A simple binomial (two-category) 'logistic regression' is briefly described here as an example of the type (see Allison 1984, Mare and Winship 1985, Main and Shelly 1990, Whitfield and Bourlakis 1991 for descriptions of others, such as probit and logit loglinear models). Note that there are also more complex procedures for multinomial logistic regression (where the dependent variable has more than two categories).

Logistic regression uses predictor variables (of any sort) to compute a score on an underlying latent variable. If this score is above a specified critical value the dependent variable is set to one category, else it is set to the other. In other words, the procedure is used to 'predict' which of two categories each individual case will manifest, and in doing so creates a model based on the predictor variables. How this works, how variables are selected for inclusion and how to understand the resulting coefficients are all beyond the scope of this book. For further details see (Gambetta 1987, Greenhalgh and Stewart 1987, Gilbert 1993, Lehtonen and Pahkinen 1995, Gorard et al. 1997). The example here is taken from Gorard et al. (1999b), using the sample described at the end of Chapter Two.

One of the things I was trying to explain was the changing nature of extended initial education. Over the past 50 years, UK compulsory schooling has been extended from age 14 to age 16, and staying-on rates for further and higher education have increased considerably. Using a sample of 1,100 households representing nearly 4,000 people aged 16-65, logistic regression was able to predict/explain whether these people had stayed on after compulsory schooling with 80% success. This result is much better than could be achieved by chance, since only around 50% of the cases had stayed on. In order to achieve this prediction the model used a number of predictor variables of which the most important were personal characteristics, such as sex, which were known when each individual was born. This leads to the quite depressing thought that we can predict with nearly 80% success who is going to stay on at school or not from birth (despite the historical changes over 50 years). I do not mean this statement to sound determinist, merely to make the point that in the period in question family and social background was a key influence in educational careers.

The regression analysis calculates a coefficient for each predictor. For real variables these coefficients are similar to those in linear regression. Thus, my model gives a coefficient of .96 for age in years. The probability that an individual stayed on at school is 1, multiplied by .96 for every year of his/her age (as older people in the sample are much less likely to have stayed on). For categorical variables, a coefficient is calculated for each category compared to another one. Thus, my model gives a coefficient of 2.15 for male cases in comparison to female. This means that men are over twice as likely as women to have stayed on at school.

When the sample is divided into two equal-sized age cohorts, some of these coefficients remain the same for both groups (age is an example). Some coefficients, however, change dramatically in their impact over the 50 years represented by this study. Among the older cohort men are actually over three times as likely as women to have stayed on at school, but in the younger cohort men and women are equally likely to have stayed on. Conversely, in the younger cohort those who have not moved (i.e. whose families have always lived in the area they were born) are nearly one third as likely to stay on as those who have been geographically mobile. In the older cohort, geographical mobility does not make a significant difference. Over time, factors such as social class, parental education, ethnicity and first language have become less important as predictors of post-compulsory participation. This is, presumably, good news. These factors have been replaced in the regression model by early childhood experiences, which are therefore becoming increasingly key determinants of later patterns of education. Whether this is good news is still far from clear.

The point, made above, about the importance of the order in which variables are entered into a model can be illustrated by this work. The dependent variable in a logistic regression analysis was a four-category 'trajectory' or pattern of participation (ranging from no post-school participation to lifelong). Independent 'explanatory' variables such as the sex, age and initial schooling of each person remained robust in both appearance and the size of their standardized coefficients, whatever model I used for calculation. However, some other variables were extremely sensitive to the precise nature of the model. If I entered the variables in life order, calculating in turn the variance explained by factors known at birth, during early childhood and so on, then the results were quite different from when I entered all variables at once, or used a 'stepwise' method, or entered them in reverse life order (from adulthood to birth). In life order, variables such as parental education and religion were important precursors. In reverse life order, variables such as area of residence and geographic mobility were significant markers. Neither analysis threw up both sets of variables. I chose to publish the life order version for obvious reasons – based on path analysis of the likely direction of causation. I use the example here to make the point that the order of levels/stages and the order of entry of variables within each level/stage makes a fundamental difference to the results (and therefore to the warrant of the conclusions). Coefficients are not existential constants. They vary with the number of variables in the model, their order of calculation and the nature of the sample.

COMMON PROBLEMS WITH MULTIVARIATE ANALYSIS

Because multivariate analysis is rather complex and often rather specialist as well, it is possible for readers to be easily misled about the nature and value of findings so derived. There may be a tendency for readers to assume that anything so 'clever' must be OK, but the reality is, of course, that there are errors in multivariate analyses just as in any other. In fact, owing to the relative complexity of the techniques and the lack of independent peer-reviewers with sufficient technical knowledge, errors are probably more common in the published results of multivariate techniques than in those from any other. Here are just three examples of potential problems.

- Superfluity of technical information
- Representational errors
- Over-complicating things

Superfluity of technical information
This is probably the biggest catch-all problem area in statistical reporting today. Readers are given both too much *and* too little information about the methods used in multivariate analyses. This has become a commonplace in work using multi-level modelling. The nature of the techniques used means that there are very few people outside what has become a kind of cult or club, in fields such as school effectiveness, who can follow this kind of work, and it sometimes seems that writers work to keep it that way. A clear example is the tradition of using technical variable names to report findings. It is now standard practice to present findings in terms of brief acronymic names rather than descriptions. At the next level of absurdity writers then try to explain the meaning of their variable names. Why? Why not just use the description? I do not care what the variables were called.

For example, in their main chapter about the relationship between school choice and school performance – the empirical guts of their book – Lauder et al. (1999) present these less than fascinating facts: 'in the Year 11 School Certificate Study we included a Level 1 variable called FAMSTR which was not included in the Year 10 skills study' (p. 116), and 'at Level 1 the variable name was MAPTITUDE' (p. 117). In fact their Table 7.1, which looks at first sight like a set of results, is actually just a summary of their variable names. Why should I want to know this? I would not report a t-test and point out that when entering some numbers into SPSS I referred to them as 'X' or 'VAR00001'. This is not what my readers would need to know.

The reason I refer to this technical mumbo-jumbo as a 'superfluity' is that it is usually presented instead of, rather than in addition to, information that I do actually need. Lauder et al. (1999) present the chief results in their Table 7.4, which contains only variable names and associated alpha levels. We are not told what the units of measurement are for each variable, so when shown the coefficients from their regression analysis we can have no idea what these values mean (see above). The coefficients by themselves are useless information for us, and like the variable names therefore simply become rhetorical noise. Again, they do not report for their multi-level (actually two-level) model the order in which the variance for each level is calculated. Are both levels calculated at once or did the researchers start with an individual level analysis and move to a school level, or vice versa? For each level, were all of the appropriate variables entered at once into the model or were they selected somehow, and if so how? The order of entering variables into the model can make a big difference to the conclusions drawn. I need to know these things before I can give any credence to their claims. But, to repeat, I do not need to know what they chose as variable names when entering data into a computer.

Representational errors
Statistical analysis by computer involves very many calculations of which most of us are usually only dimly aware, and one of the dangers of this is that we cannot therefore make a reliable estimate of the 'propagation' of our measurement errors. It is a standard assumption in social science that any measurements we make are in error. I do not mean completely wrong, but not totally accurate. We can also introduce further small errors by restricting our working to a certain number of decimal places or significant figures. We simply do our best to take accurate readings, and include an error component in our subsequent modelling of society to represent these general flaws. To a large extent we behave as though the error component in our analysis remains constant, so if we start with figures at a certain level of accuracy, we will end up with results at approximately the same level of accuracy. In some cases this behaviour may be appropriate but in others, known in extreme form as 'ill-conditioned' problems, it is not so. If we assume that all of our measurements are in error (and with most

social science measures this is a safe assumption), then adding two figures also involves adding their error components. The error components may partly cancel each other out, or they may increase each other. More formally, imagine two numbers whose true value is A and B, for which our measurements a and b are only approximations, such that:

$$a = (A + E_a)$$
$$b = (B + E_b),$$

where E_a is the error in our measurement of A, and E_b is the error in our measurement of B. If we add our estimates of A and B we actually reach the sum $A + B + E_a + E_b$. This is unlikely to be a major problem since the relative error $(E_a + E_b)/(A + B)$ is probably not much larger than either E_a/A or E_b/B (the relative errors with which we started). Since we do not know whether E_a and E_b are positive or negative the same result occurs when we subtract A and B. If we multiply a by b we obtain $(A + E_a).(B + E_b)$ which equals $A.B + B.E_a + A.E_b + E_a.E_b$. The error terms $A.E_b$ and $B.E_a$ could be large if A or B is very large, and in this way the original error in our measurements could propagate with every calculation we make, being added to and multiplied in turn.

Unless we track the potential propagation of these errors it is possible for our answer effectively to 'cancel out' the estimates we started with, and so contain a much larger proportion of error component than we started with.

Consider the simultaneous equations:

$$400 = 200x + 200y$$
$$201 = 101x + 100y$$

Their solution is that $x = 1$ and $y = 1$. If a measurement in the second equation is incorrect by less than half a per cent, then the true value of the first figure could be 200 (rather than 201), making the equations:

$$400 = 200x + 200y$$
$$200 = 101x + 100y$$

The solution now is that $x = 0$ and $y = 2$. This is a totally different solution 'caused' by a small proportionate error in one term. Imagine the practical implications if x and y were the hypothesized components of an effective public service. For some problems the introduction of an error component makes a large difference, and for some problems the error makes *all* of the difference. For all problems this issue seems more important than not meeting the minor assumptions of regression.

Over-complicating things
As statistical techniques evolve over time, generally becoming more sophisticated, they provide a wider choice of modelling strategies and therefore the opportunity for more realistic (i.e. 'lifelike') analyses in social science. The potential downside is twofold. By increasing the number of decisions to be made by the analyst, the newer techniques introduce new sources of bias, and by becoming more complicated they reduce the number of readers prepared to check all of the caveats in the methodology. There is therefore a danger that method 'messiahs' can peddle their own solutions, mistakenly thinking that these can be judged apart from the problems that they are used for (in Snow 2001), and being respected for it simply because their technique is complex. This leads to mono-methodic researchers (and even entire fields), who use one technique like MLM again and again. Presumably the only logical way that this behaviour could be explained is that these researchers deliberately seek out problems suitable for their one technique and deliberately ignore problems that would require that they learn a new one. And there are many examples of 'sub-optimal' use of such complex techniques (Marayama 1998, p. 275), some bordering on statistical fantasy.

Where statistical techniques are involved in research there is often little general understanding of their strengths and limitations (Field and Wilkinson 2001). The least-squares model of regression in common use faces technical deficiencies and has had limited success. It has never predicted anything like an eclipse or even a thunderstorm (unlike fluid dynamics, for example, which takes existing known interactions into account, Brighton 2000). In addition to incompre-hensibility, the move towards more and more complex forms of multivariate analysis is increasing the schism noted in Chapter One, and leaves 'bread-and-butter' issues, such how to measure differences between things, unresolved (where only primary-school arithmetic but advanced-level logic are needed). There is also a danger that the same people who might argue that a correlation is not the same as causation have paradoxically seen complex models based on correlation as being causal models. This is a real danger of complexity, along with the reviewing problems that it entails.

This chapter has considered a range of multivariate approaches to analysis and modelling that emerge from the concept of correlations. There are many other statistical techniques available, for multiple analyses of variance or covariance (Hinton 1995), to explore the complexity of systems via simulation techniques (Gilbert and Troitzsch 1999), cluster analysis to examine the relationships between cases rather than between variables (Everitt 1980) or multi-dimensional scaling where the 'distance' between variables is plotted on a multi-dimensional map according to their inter-correlations (Kruskal and Wish 1978). There is also the set of techniques, heavily over-used, in my opinion, known as factor analysis (Marradi 1981, Cureton and D'Agostino 1983, Kline 1994, Gorard 1997b).

Combining approaches: a 'compleat' researcher

This brief concluding chapter, arguing as it does for a greater use of 'qualitative' approaches, might be considered by some as a peculiar way to finish a book on the use of numbers in research. However, such a view would be based on the notion of a state of war between the various research methods. Instead, my contention here is that all methods have relative advantages, making them more or less appropriate for answering different research questions. Putting them together increases our research power (Bryman 2001, Nash 2002). The combination of methods or of data derived from several methods is now a key topic for many disciplines such as psychology (Debats et al. 1995), sociology (Rogers and Nicolaas 1998) and medicine (Murray 2001). In most fields the question is no longer whether it is acceptable to combine findings from different approaches but, more crucially, how (National Institute of Health 1999). The 'compleat' researcher should presumably be prepared to find, use and critique *all* evidence relevant to his or her quest, regardless of its form (Gorard 2002c).

RESEARCH SYNTHESES

There are various standard approaches to combining methods, including design studies, new political arithmetic and complex interventions. There is sufficient space to discuss only one example of combining methods here. This arises when the *findings* of more than one study are systematically combined in synthesis, review or meta-analysis. This is the basis for establishing 'evidence-based' practice where medical, pedagogical and other decisions are guided by nationally agreed 'protocols' (e.g. Department of Health 1997). Syntheses of high-quality studies are used to produce the findings, which are then 'engineered' into practice. The assumption is therefore not that good evidence has not been provided by previous work, but that it is difficult to see its pattern without systematic evaluation, and impossible for it to have an impact on policy and practice with re-engineering. Simply publishing results is not enough. For example, in a review of administering albumin to humans, Roberts (2000) concludes that it 'provides a strong argument for preparing scientifically defensible syntheses of the evidence from randomized controlled trials in medicine, as well as in other important areas of social policy, such as education' (p. 235). The significance of this is that if albumin administration had ceased in the UK when doubts were first raised, according to this synthesis, around 10,000 patients who died may have been saved. Relying on theory and craft knowledge, rather than heeding the warnings from trials, led to needless loss of life.

However, while plausible, this approach does face technical difficulties that are not always highlighted by its advocates. Steering research in the direction of experimental trials (Evans and Benefield 2001) means that 'qualitative' evidence is largely ignored, which is particularly wasteful (Levacic and Glatter 2001), and this is in addition to the majority of studies that are anyway rejected because of poor design or lack of published details (a recent synthesis of evidence in the UK for the use of ICT in teaching found only one study meeting the criteria – not much of a synthesis there!). Systematic reviews can therefore be misleading by hiding details and privileging trials even where considerable evidence of other forms contradicts them. This has led to false conclusions that are just as important, in reverse, as those claimed for the evidence-based approach (Speller et al. 1997). Even in medicine, which receives a lot more funding than educational research, the approach is therefore being criticized (Hammersley 1997). Meta-analysis, or synthesis, of experimental evidence may show what works but it cannot uncover detailed causal mechanisms (Morrison 2001). 'It is unclear how an RCT [randomised controlled trial] can untangle this' (p. 74), nor how it can pick up multiple (side) effects. Other practical limitations of the research synthesis approach are discussed in Gorard (2001c). More detailed data collected in conjunction with the trials may, however, be able to remedy these deficits. But how can we combine these two forms of data within a research synthesis?

The standard ('frequentist') view of probability used in this book so far (and in nearly all statistics you will encounter) is based on several premises, at least two of which can be challenged. First, probabilities are assumed to be susceptible to objective measure-ment, and they are calculated from scratch for each new problem. An alternative ('Bayesian') approach to probability is based on an acceptance that all 'knowledge' is subjective and that all judgements of probability are therefore made on the basis of prior belief *and* new evidence combined (Roberts 2002). The decision to play in the UK National Lottery, for example, is not based on the odds of winning alone (1 in 14 million), but also on the more qualitative nature of the consequences (transforming your life). Similar factors affect the decision to give a child an MMR (measles/mumps/rubella) injection or not (Matthews 2002). Bayesian probability is about how a person should decide or bet (Hartigan 1983). It is therefore subjective – the value of a bet is subject to market forces, for example – but it is not 'anything goes'.

Second, evidence about a phenomenon does not exist in a vacuum and its likely impact on an observer will depend to some extent on that observer's prior beliefs about the topic (West and Harrison 1997). Put another way, any observer will have prior knowledge of the probability/uncertainty about any phenomenon. New evidence about a phenomenon provides a new likelihood that will modify, rather than completely override that prior probability. Therefore, the same evidence does not lead to precisely the same posterior probability/uncertainty for all observers. When all observers agree, whatever their prior position, this shows the convincing power of the new evidence. What advances in computing have now made feasible is a method for calculating the posterior distribution, making it proportional to the new likelihood multiplied by the prior probability (French and Smith 1997). Bayes's theorem for this calculation offers us a prescription of how to learn, collectively, from evidence (Bernado and Smith 1994). One way forward, therefore, is to use qualitative evidence to help create the prior probability for a Bayesian model, which can then be adjusted via Bayes's theorem using the quantitative evidence in an otherwise normal synthesis. In fact, the prior probability can also be based on theory, expert knowledge (the notion that some people intuitively know 'what works' under certain conditions) and on the results of prior meta-analyses. Successful syntheses *have* been conducted using this approach (Roberts et al. 2002). Whether they have a future in helping to heal the wasteful schism between 'quantitative' and 'qualitative' methods remains to be seen.

CONCLUSION

As advocated and illustrated throughout this book, some 'new rules' for social science research can be summarized as follows. Of course, these are neither new nor are they rules. For some readers they will seem obvious and old-hat, and for others they will be contentious. Why that is so would have to be the subject of another book.

- 'Taking sides' can influence your choice of what to research, but not what you find.
- The research question(s) determines the methods used.
- All disciplines have something to offer.
- Secondary data is used wherever possible.
- Population figures, or a large sample, are preferred for datasets.
- Using mixed methods is both feasible and powerful.
- Planning analysis comes before collecting data.
- The quality of the data and design are more important than the complexity of the analysis.
- Only *testable* theories are of any use.
- Warrants, relating findings to conclusion, should be explicit and based on common ground.
- Assumptions should be examined and arguments simplified.
- Simplification encourages testability, utility, replication, rigour and dissemination.

No short book can possibly hope to look at all techniques for 'quantitative' design, data gathering and analysis. What I have tried to do here is summarize some of the most fruitful basic approaches and suggest some general principles for all social science research. I hope you have found it of some help, both as a novice researcher and as a consumer of the research of others. As I stated at the outset, I firmly believe that no one method or type of method is intrinsically superior to any other (and the range of methods used in my own work displays my support for this). Rather, different methods are differentially suitable for answering specific kinds of questions. Therefore don't always rule out simple methods in favour of more complex ones, and don't rule out working with numbers. The two underlying pillars of social science research are curiosity and surprise. For me, these are the criteria that distinguish research from anything else: are you genuinely curious about the questions you are asking?, and is it possible for your results totally to surprise you? If you already think you know the answers and it is not possible for your data collection and analysis to upset those beliefs, then you are not doing research. If, on the other hand, you are really trying to find out something, then you will use all and any means available to you – and these will naturally involve numeric information.

Glossary of selected terms

Achievement gap – The measure of differences in attainment between groups (such as boys and girls) used by the Equal Opportunities Commission (Arnot et al. 1997) is called an achievement gap. It is identical to the segregation index (S) for a 2×2 table. An achievement gap between girls and boys would be calculated as the score (number attaining a certain examination level) for girls minus the score for boys all divided by the sum of the scores for boys and girls. If the total number of girls and boys taking the examination is not even, an entry gap is subtracted from the achievement gap. The entry gap is the number of girls taking the examination minus the number of boys taking the examination all divided by the total number taking the examination. More formally: $A = (gp\text{-}bp)/(gp + bp) - (ge\text{-}be)/(ge + be)$.

ANOVA – An abbreviation of analysis of variance, which is a test of differences between groups in terms of an interval measure. One-way analysis is used to test one dependent variable in terms of one independent variable (examination scores by social class for example). Factorial ANOVA deals with many independent variables. MANOVA deals with multiple dependent variables.

Bias – Any research design contains at least two sources of error: the random variation due to sampling and systematic bias. Bias may arise from a variety of sources including non-response and design error. Traditional statistical analysis can evaluate the random error but leaves the bias untouched, which is a shame since the bias is likely to be much larger in impact. Bias needs to be overcome directly by the common sense of the researcher, for example by dealing with non-response and curing design flaws. There is no magic bullet.

Box and whisker plot (also known as a **boxplot**) – A diagram used by some analysts to express the distribution of a set of values. A line (whisker) is drawn from the smallest to largest values that are not outliers, and a box is drawn in the middle of the line covering the median and the middle 50% of the values.

Cronbach's alpha – A measure of reliability. It assesses the extent to which a group of questions are asking for the same basic underlying information. A value of zero means the questions are all completely different, whereas a value of 1 means that they are effectively identical. Precisely what use this is remains unclear. A high value for alpha implies that a questionnaire is wasting the respondents' time by repeating the same question, yet a high value is what most textbooks tell readers to look for.

Degrees of freedom – The number of scores that are free to vary in any analysis. When analysing data we tend to use summary information such as the total of all scores. The degrees of freedom is the number of scores we need to know before we can calculate the rest. If the total of two numbers is 37 and we know that one number is 20, then we can calculate that the other must be 17, so the degrees of freedom would be one. This value is used to help estimate the impact of random variation in null hypothesis significance testing.

Finite population correction – Where your sample is large in comparison to the size of the population (typically more than 5%), you can apply a correction when calculating the required size of your sample for any given level of confidence using the standard error. This allows you to use a smaller sample.

Flesch index of readability – Grammar checkers on many popular word processors will produce an estimated reading level for a piece of text. One such measure is the Flesch index between 0 'very difficult' and 100 'very easy'. The measure can also be converted into school grade or reading age scores.

Interval measure – A score or value based on a real number. Technically it means that each value on the scale of measurement is an equal interval from the next value (the difference between 15 and 16 degrees centigrade is the same as between 115 and 116 degrees). In reality very few social science measures are interval without also being ratio in nature.

Likert-type scale – Is used to try to assess attitudes and related concepts (multidimensional underlying variables). Respondents are asked to read a statement or question and then rate their response on a scale of agreement (agree/disagree) or quality (good/bad). The scales usually have five or seven points, sometimes three or an even number. While clearly ordinal in nature, these scales are often treated as equal-interval and used with parametric techniques.

Mann-Whitney test – A null hypothesis significance test for differences between two or more groups. This difference is measured in terms of an ordinal measure. As such, Mann-Whitney does much the same thing as a t-test or one-way analysis of variance but for ordinal, rather than interval values.

Mean – The most popular form of average, giving the reader an idea of the central or most representative value of a set of measurements. It is the sum of a set of measurements divided by the number of measurements, and can be used only with data of interval or ratio level.

Median – A form of average, giving the reader an idea of the central or most representative value of a set of measurements. If the measurements are placed in order of size, the median is the value in the middle (with an equal number of values higher and lower than it). It can be used only with data of ordinal, interval or ratio level.

Minimum expected count – In a tables of scores the expected values for each cell are calculated assuming that each category (row and column) is proportionately represented. If the minimum (smallest) expected value is below a reasonable number (10 perhaps) then standard analytical techniques are inappropriate.

Mode – A form of average, giving the reader an idea of the central or most representative value of a set of measurements. If the measurements are grouped into frequencies, the mode is the most frequently occurring value. It can be used with data at any level of measurement (even nominal).

Nominal measure – A score or value from a scale that is not based on real numbers and in which the order is a matter of convention only. Examples would include binary variables such as male/female and categorical variables such as industrial classifications.

Normal curve – A bell-shaped symmetrical frequency distribution that underlies many social and psychological phenomena (such as population height or scores on an IQ test). 50% of the area under the curve is above and below the mean respectively, 68% is within one standard deviation of the mean.

One-tailed test – A calculation based on a prediction that two samples (or sub-groups within your achieved sample) will differ significantly in terms of their scores, making clear before collecting data which set of scores will be the larger. This is a stronger prediction, and therefore intrinsically more convincing if confirmed, than in a two-tailed test.

Ordinal measure – A score or value from a scale in which an order is clear, but which is not based on real numbers. A common example would be a Likert-type scale.

Outlier – A score in your results that is clearly outside the range of normal frequencies. It may be the result of an error in recording or transcription, or it may simply be a fluke result. A few such scores can have a disproportionate impact on your analysis (producing a mean score very different from the median, for example). Whatever you do about outliers, they must be handled with care and transparency.

Parsimony – A principle used to decide between competing explanations. The most parsimonious would be the simplest explanation. Technically this means the one that makes the fewest assumptions for which we have no direct evidence. The practical advantage of parsimony is that simple explanations are easier to test, so encouraging cumulative social scientific progress. Not using this principle would allow a researcher to produce an untestable explanation for his/her results (akin to a superstition).

Pearson's chi-square – A statistic calculated to test for differences in frequencies between categories. Named 'Pearson' after its developer, and chi-square for the Greek symbol 'χ'.

Population – The group (usually of individuals) to whom you wish your research results to generalize (be relevant to). Any and only individuals with a chance of being selected for your sample form the population you are researching.

Ratio measure – A score or value based on a real number, with equal intervals on the scale of measurement and a real value of zero. Technically this means that all points on the scale are in direct ratio to each other, for example 40 centimetres is exactly twice as much as 20. Note that for interval and other measures this is not so, since 40 degrees is not twice as hot as 20 degrees.

Reliability – Assessment of the extent to which a question, instrument or measure gives safe results (e.g. that it gives the same result on different occasions). See Cronbach's alpha.

Residual – In regression-type analyses, a predicted score for the dependent variable is based on the value of the independent variable(s). Because of measurement and sampling error and omission of key predictor variables, there will be a discrepancy between the observed and predicted score for each case. This is called the residual.

Standard deviation – The square root of the variance. It is a summary of the average difference between each score in your set of results and the overall mean. It therefore measures how spread out (how variable) your results are.

Standard error – The standard deviation of the distribution of sample statistics. Using the mean as an example, the standard error of the mean is a summary of the average difference between any sample mean and the overall mean of all means taken from equivalent samples. It therefore measures how closely your achieved mean matches the best estimate of the population mean.

Stem and leaf plot – Similar to a histogram. Scores are divided into intervals (between 30 and 39, for example), and the diagram has a row for each interval. The length of the row represents the number of cases with scores in that interval (how many scores in the 30s etc.). Each row is labelled with the 'stem' (the common or leading digits) of all scores in that interval (three for scores 30–39), and the actual entries in each row are the 'leaves' denoted by the remaining digits for each score. Thus the scores 31, 31, 31 and 32 would be represented as: 3 * 1112.

Two-tailed test – A calculation based on a prediction that two samples (or sub-groups within your achieved sample) will differ significantly in terms of their scores, but without a prediction of which set of scores will be larger. This is a weaker prediction, and therefore intrinsically less convincing if confirmed, than in a one-tailed test.

Weight – A value used to correct for deficiency in the sample. If a particular sub-group is disproportionately respresented in the achieved sample (too many males, for example), then the scores for this group can be multiplied by a weight to achieve a more balanced result (e.g. in which the scores for females are given due prominence).

References

Achen, C. (1982) *Interpreting and Using Regression*, London: Sage.

Adair, J. (1973) *The Human Subject*, Boston: Little, Brown and Co.

Aitkin, M. and Longford, N. (1986) Statistical modelling in school effectiveness studies, *Journal of the Royal Statistical Society Series A*, 149, 3, 1–43.

Allison, P. (1984) *Event History Analysis: Regression for Longitudinal Event Data*, London: Sage.

Altman, D., Machin, D., Bryant, T. and Gardiner, M. (2000) *Statistics with Confidence*, London: BMJ Books.

Anderson, T. and Zelditch, M. (1968) *A Basic Course in Statistics, with Sociological Applications*, London: Holt, Rinehart and Winston.

Arjas, E. (2001) Causal analysis and statistics: a social sciences perspective, *European Sociological Review*, 17, 1, 59–64.

Ayer, A. (1972) *Russell*, London: Fontana.

Badger, D., Nursten, J., Williams, P. and Woodward, M. (2000) Should all literature reviews be systematic?, *Evaluation and Research in Education*, 14, 3 & 4, 220–230

Banks, M., Bates, I., Breakwell, G., Bynner, J. and Emler, N. (1992) *Careers and Identities*, Milton Keynes: Open University Press.

Basic Skills Agency (1997) *Literacy and Numeracy Skills in Wales*, London: The Basic Skills Agency.

Beinart, S. and Smith, P. (1998) *National Adult Learning Survey 1997*, Sudbury: DfEE Publications.

Berliner, D. and Biddle, B. (1995) *The Manufactured Crisis: Myths, Fraud and the Attack on America's Public Schools*, Boston: Addison-Wesley.

Bernado, J. and Smith, A. (1994) *Bayesian Theory*, Chichester: John Wiley.

Bernard, R. (2000) *Social Research Methods: Qualitative and Quantitative Approaches*, London: Sage.

Berry, W. (1984) *Nonrecursive Causal Models*, London: Sage.

Berry, W. and Feldman, S. (1985) *Multiple Regression in Practice*, London: Sage.

Birbil, M. (2000) Translating from one language to another, *Social Research Update*, 31, 1–4.

Blalock, H. (1964) *Causal Inferences in Nonexperimental Research*, Chapel Hill: University of North Carolina Press.

Booth, W., Colomb, G. and Williams, J. (1995) *The Craft of Research*, Chicago: University of Chicago Press.

Boudon, R. (1974) *The Logic of Sociological Explanation*, Harmondsworth: Penguin.

Brighton, M. (2000) Making our measurements count, *Evaluation and Research in Education*, 14, 3 & 4, 124–135.

Brignell, J. (2000) *Sorry, Wrong number! The Abuse of Measurement*, London: European Science and Environment Forum.

Brown, A. (1992) Design experiments: theoretical and methodological challenges in creating complex interventions in classroom settings, *The Journal of the Learning Sciences*, 2, 2, 141–178.

Brown, A. and Dowling, P. (1998) *Doing Research/Reading Research: A Mode of Interrogation for Education*, London: Falmer.

Bryman, A. (2001) *Social Research Methods*, Oxford: Oxford University Press.

Bulmer, M. (1980) Why don't sociologists make more use of official statistics?, *Sociology*, 14, 4, 505–523.

Campbell, D. and Stanley, J. (1963) *Experimental and Quasi-experimental Designs for Research*, Boston: Houghton Mifflin.

Carter, H. (2000) NHS helpline offers bad advice, survey claims, *The Guardian*, 8/8/00.

CERI (1997) *Education Policy Analysis 1997*, Paris: OECD.

CERI (1998) *Education at a Glance: OECD Indicators*, Paris: OECD.

Cheung, C. and Lewis, D. (1998) Expectations of employers of High School leavers in Hong Kong, *Journal of Vocational Education and Training*, 50, 1, 97–111.

Clarke, A. (1999) *Evaluation Research*, London: Sage.

Clegg, F. (1992) *Simple Statistics: A Course Book for the Social Sciences*, Cambridge: Cambridge University Press.

Coe, R. and Fitz-Gibbon, C. (1998) School effectiveness research: criticisms and recommendations, *Oxford Review of Education*, 24, 4, 421–438.

Cohen, L. and Manion, L. (2000) *Research Methods in Education*, London: Routledge.

Coldron, J. and Boulton, P. (1991) 'Happiness' as a criterion of parents' choice of school, *Journal of Education Policy*, 6, 2, 169–178.

Collins, H. and Pinch, T. (1993) *The Golem: What You Should Know About Science*, Cambridge: Cambridge University Press.

Cook, T. and Campbell, D. (1979) *Quasi-experimentation: Design and Analysis Issues for Field Settings*, Chicago: Rand McNally.

Cooper, H. (1998) *Synthesizing Research: A Guide for Literature Reviews*, London: Sage.

Cox, D. and Wermuth, N. (2001) Some statistical aspects of causality, *European Sociological Review*, 17, 1, 65–74.

Creighton, T. (2001) *Schools and Data: The Educator's Guide for Using Data to Improve Decision Making*, Thousand Oaks: Corwin Press.

Crouchley, R. (1987) *Longitudinal Data Analysis. Surrey Conferences on Sociological Theory and Method 4*, Aldershot: Avebury.

Cureton, E. and D'Agostino, R. (1983) *Factor Analysis: An Applied Approach*, London: Lawrence Erlbaum.

Curtis, D. and Araki, C. (2002) 'Effect Size Statistics: An Analysis of Statistics Textbooks', presentation at AERA, New Orleans, April 2002.

Czaja, R. and Blair, J. (1996) *Designing Surveys: A Guide to Decisions and Procedures*, Thousand Oaks: Pine Forge Press.

Dale, A., Arber, S. and Proctor, M. (1988) *Doing Secondary Analysis*, London: Unwin.

Dale, A., Fieldhouse, E. and Holdsworth, C. (2000) *Analyzing Census Microdata*, London: Edward Arnold.

Dawes, R. (2001) *Everyday Irrationality*, Oxford: Westview Press.

de Leon, G., Inciardi, J. and Martin, S. (1995) Residential drug abuse treatment research: are conventional control designs appropriate for assessing treatment effectiveness?, *Journal of Psychoactive Drugs*, 27, 85–91.

de Vaus, D. (2001) *Research Design in Social Science*, London: Sage.

de Vaus, D. (2002) *Analyzing Social Science Data: 50 Key Problems in Data Analysis*, London: Sage.

Dean, H. (2000) 'What's the Evidence for 'Evidence-based' Social Policy? Welfare Reform, Low-income Families and the Role of Social Science', presented at fifth ESRC seminar on Measuring Success: What Counts Is What Works, Cardiff, September 2000.

Debats, D., Drost, J. and Hansen, P. (1995) Experiences of meaning in life: a combined qualitative and quantitative approach, *British Journal of Psychology*, 86, 3, 359–375.

Deloitte, Haskins and Sells (1989) *Training in Britain. A Study of Funding, Activity and Attitudes. Employers Attitudes*, London: HMSO.

Dennison, W. (1995) 'Researching the Competitive Edge: Detractors and Attractors in School Marketing', paper presented at ESRC/CEPAM Invitation Seminar, Milton Keynes, 1995.

Department of Health (1997) *Research and Development: Towards an Evidence-based Health Service*, London: Department of Health.

DfEE (1994a) *Statistics of Education. Public Examinations GCSE and GCE in England 1994*, London: HMSO.

DfEE (1994b) *Statistics of Education. Schools in England 1994*, London: HMSO.

Diamond, I. (2002) Towards a Quantitative Europe, *Social Sciences*, 51.

Dolton, P., Makepeace, G. and Treble, J. (1994) Measuring the effects of training in the Youth Cohort Study, in McNabb R. and Whitfield K. (eds.) *The Market for Training*, Aldershot: Avebury, 195–211.

Dyson, A. and Desforges, C. (2002) *Building Research Capacity: Some Possible Lines of Action*, Report to National Educational Research Forum.

Education and Training Statistics (1997) *Welsh Training and Education Survey 1995/96*, Cardiff: Welsh Office.

Edwards, A. (1972) *Experimental Design in Psychological Research*, New York: Holt, Rinehart and Winston.

Ellmore, P. and Woehilke, P. (1998) *Twenty years of research methods employed in American Educational Research Journal, Education Researcher, and Review of Educational Research from 1978 to 1997*, (mimeo) ERIC ED 420701.

ETAG (1999) *An Education and Training Action Plan for Wales*, Cardiff: National Assembly for Wales.

Eurostat (1995) *Education Across the European Union: Statistics and Indicators*, Brussels: Statistical Office of the European Communities.

Eurostat (1998) *Social Portrait of Europe September 1998*, Brussels: Statistical Office of the European Communities.

Evans, J. and Benefield, P. (2001) Systematic reviews of educational research: does the medical model fit?, *British Educational Research Journal*, 27, 5, 527–542.

Evans, L. (2002) *Reflective Practice in Educational Research*, London: Continuum.

Everitt, B. (1980) *Cluster Analysis*, London: Heinemann.

Everitt, B. and Hay, D. (1992) *Talking About Statistics: A Psychologist's Guide to Design and Analysis*, London: Edward Arnold.

Fairbairn, G. and Winch, C. (1996) *Reading, Writing and Reasoning: A Guide for Students*, Buckingham: Open University Press.

Farrall, S., Bannister, J., Ditton, J. and Gilchrist, E. (1997) Open and closed questions, *Social Research Update*, 17, 1–4.

Field, A. and Wilkinson, L. (2001) Getting your numbers wrong, *The Psychologist*, 14, 6, 316.

Fielding, A. (2000) 'Explanatory Modelling of Complex Social Structures with Case Studies in Educational Research', presentation at ESRC/BERA Advanced Training Workshop, Birmingham, July 2000.

Fielding, J. and Gilbert, N. (2000) *Understanding Social Statistics*, London: Sage.

Firestone, W. (1987) Meaning in method: the rhetoric of quantitative and qualitative research, *Educational Researcher*, 16, 7, 16–23.

Fisher, R. (1935) *The Design of Experiments*, Edinburgh: Oliver and Boyd.

Fitz-Gibbon, C. (1985) The implications of meta-analysis for educational research, *British Educational Research Journal*, 11, 1, 45–49.

Fitz-Gibbon, C. (1996) *Monitoring Education: Indicators, Quality and Effectiveness*, London: Cassell.

Fitz-Gibbon, C. (2000) Education: realising the potential, in Davies, H., Nutley, S. and Smith, P. (eds) *What Works? Evidence-based Policy and Practice in Public Services*, Bristol: Policy Press.

Fitz-Gibbon, C. (2001) *Value-added for those in despair: research methods matter*, pamphlet, British Psychological Society.

Flather, P. (1987) Pulling through: conspiracies, counterplots and how the SSRC escaped the axe in 1982, in Bulmer, M. (ed.) *Social Science Research and Government*, Cambridge: Cambridge University Press.

Fleiss, J. (1973) *Statistical Methods for Rates and Proportions*, New York: John Wiley and Sons.

Frankfort-Nachmias, C. and Nachmias, D. (1996) *Research Methods in the Social Sciences*, London: Edward Arnold.

Frazer, E. (1995) What's new in the philosophy of science?, *Oxford Review of Education*, 21, 3, 267–285.

French, S. and Smith, J. (1997) Bayesian analysis, in French, S. and Smith, J. (eds.) *The Practice of Bayesian Analysis*, London: Edward Arnold, 1–25.

Future Skills Wales (1998) *Technical Report*, London: MORI.

Gambetta, D. (1987) *Were They Pushed or Did They Jump? Individual Decision Mechanisms in Education*, London: Cambridge University Press.

Garrison, R. (1993) Mises and his methods, in Herbener, J. (ed.) *The meaning of Ludwig von Mises: Contributions in Economics, Sociology, Epistemology, and Political Philosophy*, Boston: Kluwer Academic Publishers, 102–117.

Gephart, R. (1988) *Ethnostatistics: Qualitative Foundations for Quantitative Research*, London: Sage.

Gershuny, J. and Marsh, C. (1994) Unemployment in Work Histories, in Gallie, D., Marsh, C. and Vogler, C. (eds.) *Social Change and the Experience of Unemployment*, Oxford: Oxford University Press.

Ghouri, N. (1999) Football approach risks an own goal, *Times Educational Supplement*, 4/6/99, 9.

Giacquinta, J. and Shaw, F. (2000) 'Judging Non-returner Induced Sample Bias from the Study of Early and Late Returners: A Useful Approach?', presentation at AERA Conference, New Orleans, April 2000.

Gigerenzer, G. (2002) *Reckoning with Risk*, Harmondsworth: Penguin.

Gilbert, N. (1993) *Analysing Tabular Data: Loglinear and Logistic Models for Social Researchers*, London: UCL Press.

Gilbert, N. (1997) *Researching Social Life*, London: Sage.

Gilbert, N. and Troitzsch, K. (1999) *Simulation for the Social Scientist*, Buckingham: Open University Press.

Gillborn, D. and Youdell, D. (2000) *Rationing Education: Policy, Practice, Reform and Equality*, Buckingham: Open University Press.

Gillham, B. (2000a) *The Research Interview*, London: Continuum.

Gillham, B. (2000b) *Developing a Questionnaire*, London: Continuum.

Glass, G., McGraw, B. and Smith, M. (1981) *Meta-analysis in Social Research*, London: Sage.

Gleick, J. (1988) *Chaos*, London: Heinemann.

Glenn, N. (1977) *Cohort Analysis*, London: Sage.

Glymour, C., Scheines, R., Spirtes, P. and Kelly, K. (1987) *Discovering Causal Structure*, Orlando: Academic Press.

Goldstein, H. (1987) *Multilevel Models in Educational and Social Research*, London: Griffin.

Goldstein, H., Huiqi, P., Rath, T. and Hill, N. (2000) *The Use of Value-added Information in Judging School Performance*, London: Institute of Education.

Goldthorpe, J. (2001) Causation, statistics, and sociology, *European Sociological Review*, 17, 1, 1–20.

Gorard, S. (1996) Three steps to 'heaven': the family and school choice, *Educational Review*, 48, 3, 237–252.

Gorard, S. (1997a) A choice of methods: the methodology of choice, *Research in Education*, 57, 45–56.

Gorard, S. (1997b) *School Choice in an Established Market*, Aldershot: Ashgate.

Gorard, S. (1997c) *The Region of Study: Patterns of Participation in Adult Education and Training. Working paper 1*, Cardiff: School of Education.

Gorard, S. (1998a) *The Call for a Middle-way in Educational Research*, BERA Internet Conference, March 1998, www.bera.ac.uk/debate/reply/g1.html.

Gorard, S. (1998b) Four errors... and a conspiracy? The effectiveness of schools in Wales, *Oxford Review of Education*, 24, 4, 459–472.

Gorard, S. (1998c) In defence of local comprehensive schools in south Wales, *Forum*, 40, 2, 58–59.

Gorard, S. (1999a) Keeping a sense of proportion: the 'politicians error' in analysing school outcomes, *British Journal of Educational Studies*, 47, 3, 235–246.

Gorard, S. (1999b) Examining the paradox of achievement gaps, *Social Research Update*, 26, 1–4.

Gorard, S. (2000a) One of us cannot be wrong: the paradox of achievement gaps, *British Journal of Sociology of Education*, 21, 3, 391–400.

Gorard, S. (2000b) *Education and Social Justice*, Cardiff: University of Wales Press.

Gorard, S. (2000c) A re-examination of the effectiveness of school in Wales, in Daugherty R., Phillips R. and Rees, G. (eds.) *Education Policy in Wales: Explorations in Devolved Governance*, Cardiff: University of Wales Press.

Gorard, S. (2000d) 'Under-achievement' is still an ugly word: reconsidering the relative effectiveness of schools in England and Wales, *Journal of Education Policy*, 15, 5, 559–573.

Gorard, S. (2001a) An alternative account of 'boys under-achievement at school', *Welsh Journal of Education* , 10, 2, 4–14.

Gorard, S. (2001b) International comparisons of school effectiveness: a second component of the 'crisis account'?, *Comparative Education*, 37, 3, 279–296.

Gorard, S. (2001c) *A Changing Climate for Educational Research? The Role of Research Capability-building*, Working Paper 45, Cardiff: University School of Social Sciences.

Gorard, S. (2002a) The role of secondary data in combining methodological approaches, *Educational Review*, 54, 3, 231–237.

Gorard, S. (2002b) The role of causal models in education as a social science, *Evaluation and Research in Education*, 16, 1, 51–65.

Gorard, S. (2002c) Can we overcome the methodological schism?: combining qualitative and quantitative methods, *Research Papers in Education*, 17, 4 (forthcoming).

Gorard, S. (2002d) *What is Multi-level Modelling for?*, Occasional Paper 46, Cardiff: University School of Social Sciences.

Gorard, S. (2002e) Political control: A way forward for educational research?, *British Journal of Educational Studies*, 50, 3, 378–389.

Gorard, S. and Fitz, J. (1998) The more things change... the missing impact of marketisation, *British Journal of Sociology of Education*, 19, 3, 365–376.

Gorard, S. and Fitz, J. (2000) Investigating the determinants of segregation between schools, *Research Papers in Education*, 15, 2, 115–132.

Gorard, S. and Rees, G. (2002) *Creating a Learning Society*, Bristol: Policy Press.

Gorard, S. and Selwyn, N. (1999) Switching on the Learning Society? Questioning the role of technology in widening participation in lifelong learning, *Journal of Education Policy*, 14, 5, 523–534.

Gorard, S. and Selwyn, N. (2001) *Information Technology*, London: Hodder and Stoughton.

Gorard, S. and Taylor, C. (2002a) What is segregation? A comparison of measures in terms of strong and weak compositional invariance, *Sociology*, 36, 4, 875–895.

Gorard, S. and Taylor, C. (2002b) Market forces and standards in education: a preliminary consideration, *British Journal of Sociology of Education*, 23, 1, 5–18.

Gorard, S., Rees, G., Furlong, J. and Fevre, R. (1997) *Outline Methodology of the Study: Patterns of Participation in Adult Education and Training*. Working Paper 2, Cardiff: School of Education.

Gorard, S., Salisbury, J. and Rees, G. (1999a) Reappraising the apparent under-achievement of boys at school, *Gender and Education*, 11, 4, 441–454.

Gorard, S., Rees, G. and Fevre, R. (1999b) Two dimensions of time: the changing social context of lifelong learning, *Studies in the Education of Adults*, 31, 1, 35–48.

Gorard, S., Rees, G. and Fevre, R. (1999c) Patterns of participation in lifelong learning: do families make a difference?, *British Educational Research Journal*, 25, 4, 517–532.

Gorard, S., Rees, G. and Selwyn, N. (2000a) Meeting targets?, *Adults Learning*, April 2000, 18–20.

Gorard, S., Selwyn, N. and Williams, S. (2000b) Could try harder!: problems facing technological solutions to non-participation in adult learning, *British Educational Research Journal* , 26, 4.

Gorard, S., Rees, G. and Salisbury, J. (2001a) The differential attainment of boys and girls at school: investigating the patterns and their determinants, *British Educational Research Journal*, 27, 2, 125–40.

Gorard, S., Rees, G., Fevre, R. and Welland, T. (2001b) Lifelong learning trajectories: some voices of those in transit, *International Journal of Lifelong Education*, 20, 3, 169–187.

Gorard, S., Rees, G. and Selwyn, N. (2002a) The 'conveyor belt effect': a re-assessment of the impact of National Targets for Lifelong Learning, *Oxford Review of Education*, 28, 1, 75–89.

Gorard, S., Selwyn, N. and Rees, G. (2002b) Privileging the visible: examining the National Targets for Education and Training, *British Educational Research Journal*, 28, 3, 309–325.

Greenhalgh, C. and Stewart, M. (1987) The effects and determinants of training, *Oxford Bulletin of Economics and Statistics*, 49, 2, 171–190.

Grinyer, A. (2002) The anonymity of research participants: assumptions, ethics and practicalities, *Social Research Update*, 36, 1–4.

Guidry, J. (2002) 'Misinterpretation of Multiple Regression Results', presentation at AERA, New Orleans, April 2002.

Hagenaars, J. (1990) *Categorical Longitudinal Data: Log-linear, Panel, Trend and Cohort Analysis*, London: Sage.

Hakim, C. (1982) *Secondary Analysis in Social Research: A Guide to Data Sources and Methods with Examples*, London: Allen and Unwin.

Hakim, C. (1992) *Research Design: Strategies and Choices in the Design of Social Research*, London: Routledge.

Hakuta, K. (2000) 'Perspectives on the State of Education Research in the US', presentation at AERA, New Orleans, April 2000.

Hammersley, M. (1995) *The Politics of Social Research*, London: Sage.

Hammersley, M. (1997) Educational research and teaching: a response to David Hargreaves' TTA lecture, *British Educational Research Journal*, 23, 2, 141–162.

Hammersley, M. (2001) On Michael Bassey's concept of the fuzzy generalisation, *Oxford Review of Education*, 27, 2, 219–225

Hargreaves, D. (1997) In defence of research for evidence-based teaching: a rejoinder to Martyn Hammersley, *British Educational Research Journal*, 23, 4, 405–419.

Harlow, L., Mulaik, S. and Steiger, J. (1997) *What if There Were no Significance Tests?*, Marwah, NJ: Lawrence Erlbaum.

Hartigan, J. (1983) *Bayes Theory*, New York: Springer-Verlag.

Harwell, M. and Gatti, G. (2001) *Review of Educational Research*, 71, 1, 105–131.

Hayes, E. (1992) The impact of feminism on adult education publications: an analysis of British and American journals, *International Journal of Lifelong Education*, 11, 2, 125–138.

Heath, A. (2000) The political arithmetic tradition in the sociology of education, *Oxford Review of Education*, 26, 3 & 4, 313–331.

Heise, D. (1975) *Causal Analysis*, New York: John Wiley.

Hendry, D. and Mizon, G. (1999) *The Pervasiveness of Granger Causality in Econometrics*, Nuffield College Oxford, (mimeo).

Henry, G. (1990) *Practical Sampling*, London: Sage.

Hillage, J., Pearson, R., Anderson, A. and Tamkin, P. (1998) *Excellence on Research in Schools*, Sudbury: DfEE.

Hinton, P. (1995) *Statistics Explained: A Guide for Social Science Students*, London: Routledge.

Howard, G., Maxwell, S. and Fleming, K. (2000) The proof of the pudding: an illustration of the relative strengths of null hypothesis, meta-analysis, and Bayesian analysis, *Psychological Methods*, 5, 3, 315–332.

Howell, D. (1989) *Fundamental Statistics for the Behavioural Sciences*, Boston: PWS-Kent.

Huberty, C. and Olejnik, S. (2002) 'Improving the Reporting of Empirical Research', presentation at AERA, New Orleans, April 2002.

Huck, S. and Sandler, H., (1979) *Rival hypotheses: Alternative Interpretations of Data Based Conclusions*, New York: Harper and Row.

Huff, D. (1991) *How to Lie with Statistics*, Harmondsworth: Penguin.

Hume, D. (1962) *On Human Nature and the Understanding*, New York: Collier.

Johnson, B. (2001) Towards a new classification of nonexperimental quantitative research, *Educational Researcher*, 30, 2, 3–14.

Kalton, G. (1966) *Introduction to Statistical Ideas for Social Scientists*, London: Chapman and Hall.

Kanji, G. (1999) *100 Statistical Tests*, London: Sage.

Kim, J. and Mueller, C. (1978) *Introduction to Factor Analysis. What it Is and How to Do it*, London: Sage.

King, J. (2002) 'Logistic Regression: Going Beyond Point and Click', presentation at AERA, New Orleans, April 2002.

Kline, P. (1994) *An Easy Guide to Factor Analysis*, London: Routledge.

Kline, R. (1998) *Principles and Practice of Structural Equation Modeling*, New York: Guilford Press.

Kreft, I. (1996) *Are Multi-level Techniques Necessary? An Overview, Including Simulation Studies*, http://www.calstatela.edu/faculty/ikreft/quarterly/, accessed 19/6/02.

Kruskal, J. and Wish, M. (1978) *Multidimensional Scaling*, London: Sage.

Kuhn, T. (1970) *The Structure of Scientific Revolutions*, Chicago: University of Chicago Press.

Lauder, H., Hughes, D., Watson, S., Waslander, S., Thrupp, M., Strathdee, R., Simiyu, I., Dupuis, A., McGlinn, J. and Hamlin, J. (1999) *Trading in Futures: Why Markets in Education Don't Work*, Buckingham: Open University Press.

Lee, E., Forthofer, R. and Lorimor, R. (1989), *Analyzing Complex Survey Data*, London: Sage.

Lehtonen, R. and Pahkinen, E. (1995) *Practical Methods for Design and Analysis of Complex Surveys*, Chichester: John Wiley and Sons.

Levacic, R. and Glatter, R. (2001) Really good ideas? Developing evidence-informed policy and practice in educational leadership and management, *Educational Management and Administration*, 29, 1, 5–25.

Lewis, J. (2001) *The Fluctuating Fortunes of the Social Sciences Since 1945*, mimeo (jane.lewis@applied-social-studies.oxford.ac.uk).

Lynn, J. and Jay, A. (1986) *Yes, Prime Minister*, London: BBC Publications.

MacKenzie, D. (1999) The science wars and the past's quiet voices, *Social Studies of Science*, 29, 2, 199–213.

Maddala, G. (1992) *Introduction to Econometrics*, New York: Macmillan.

Main B. and Shelly M. (1990) The effectiveness of the Youth Training Scheme as a manpower policy, *Economica*, 57, 495–514.

Mare, R. and Winship, C. (1985) School enrollment, military enlistment, and the transition to work: implications for the age pattern of employment, in Heckman, J. and Singer, B. (eds) *Longitudinal Analysis of Labor Market Data*, Cambridge: Cambridge University Press.

Marradi, A. (1981) Factor analysis as an aid in the formation and refinement of empirically useful concepts, in Jackson, D. and Borgatta, E. (eds) *Factor Analysis and Measurement*, London: Sage.

Marshall, G. (1990) *In Praise of Sociology*, London: Routledge.

Martin, J. and Roberts, C. (1984) *The Women and Employment Survey: A Lifetime Perspective*, London: HMSO.

Maruyama, G. (1998) *Basics of Structural Equation Modelling*, London: Sage.

Massey, D. and Denton, N. (1988) The dimensions of residential segregation, *Social Forces*, 67, 373–393.

Matthews, R. (2000) How to spot an Olympic cheat with a calculator, *The Sunday Telegraph*, 24/9/00, 13.

Matthews, R. (2002) The cold reality of probability theory, *The Sunday Telegraph*, 5/5/02, 31.

Maxwell, A. (1958) *Experimental Design in Psychology and the Medical Sciences*, London: Methuen.

Maxwell, A. (1977) *Multivariate Analysis in Behavioural Research*, New York: Chapman and Hall.

May, T. (1997) *Social Research: Issues, Methods and Process*, Buckingham: Open University Press.

McIlveen, R., Higgins, L., Wadeley, A. and Humphreys, P. (1992) *BPS Manual of Psychology Practicals: Experiment, Observation and Correlation*, Leicester: British Psychological Society.

McIntyre, D. and McIntyre, A. (2000) *Capacity for Research Into Teaching and Learning*, Swindon: Report to to the ESRC Teaching and Learning Research Programme.

McKim, V. and Turner, S. (1997) *Causality in Crisis? Statistical Methods and the Search for Causal Knowledge in the Social Sciences*, Indiana: University of Notre Dame Press.

McNabb, R. and Whitfield, K. (1994) *The Market for Training*, Aldershot: Avebury.

Medical Research Council (2000) *A Framework for Development and Evaluation of RCTs for Complex Interventions to Improve Health*, London: Medical Research Council.

Menard, S. (1995) *Applied Logistic Regression Analysis*, London: Sage.

Miles, J. and Shevlin, M. (2001) *Applying Regression and Correlation*, London: Sage.

Millett, A. (1997) speech to TTA Research Conference, 5.12.97. London: Teacher Training Agency.

Mitchell, P. (1994) The impact of educational technology: a radical reappraisal of research methods, *Alt-J*, 5, 1, 48–54.

Morgan, C. L. (1903) *Introduction to Comparative Psychology*, London: Walter Scott.

Morrison, K. (2001) Randomised controlled trials for evidence-based education: some problems in judging 'what works', *Evaluation and Research in Education*, 15, 2, 69–83.

Mortimore, P. and Sammons, P. (1997) Endpiece: a welcome and a riposte to the critics, in White, J. and Barber, M. (eds) *Perspectives on School Effectiveness and School Improvement*, London: Institute of Education, 175–187.

Moses, L. (2001) 'A Larger Role for Randomized Experiments in Educational Policy Research', presentation at AERA annual conference, Seattle, April 2001.

Murray, S. (2000) Relation between private health insurance and high rates of caesarean section in Chile: qualitative and quantitative study, *British Medical Journal*, 321, 1,501–1,505.

NACETT (1995) *Report on Progress Towards the National Targets*, London: National Advisory Council for Education and Training.

Nash, R. (2002) Numbers and narratives: further reflections in the sociology of education, *British Journal of Sociology of Education*, 23, 2, 397–412.

National Educational Research Policy and Priorities Board (2000) *Second Policy Statement with Recommendations on Research in Education*, Washington DC: NERPP.

National Institute of Health (1999) *Qualitative Methods In Health Research: Opportunities and Considerations in Application and Review*, www.nih.gov/icd (12/2/02).

National Research Council (1999) *Improving Student Learning: a Strategic Plan for Educational Research and its Utilization*, Washington DC: National Academy Press.

National Research Council (2002) *Scientific Research in Education*, Washington DC: National Academy Press.

Noden, P. (2000) Rediscovering the impact of marketisation: dimensions of social segregation in England's secondary schools, *British Journal of Sociology of Education*, 21, 3, 371–390.

Norusis, M. (2000) *SPSS 10.0 Guide to Data Analysis*, London: Prentice Hall.

Nuttall, D. (1987) The validity of assessments, *European Journal of Psychology of Education*, 11, 2, 109–118.

OECD (1993) *OECD Education Statistics 1985–1992*, Paris: OECD.

OECD (2000) *Education at a Glance: OECD Indicators: Education and Skills*, Paris: Organisation for Economic Cooperation and Development.

Oppenheim, A. (1992) *Questionnaire Design, Interviewing and Attitude Measurement*, London: Continuum.

Pallant, J. (2001) *SPSS Survival Manual*, Milton Keynes: Open University Press.

Paterson, L. and Goldstein, H. (1991) New statistical models for analysing social structures: an introduction to multilevel models, *British Educational Research Journal*, 17, 4, 387–393.

Payne, S. (1951) *The Art of Asking Questions*, New Jersey: Princeton University.

Pedhazur, E. (1982) *Multiple Regression in Behavioural Research*, London: Holt, Rinehart and Winston.

Peers, I. (1996) *Statistical Analysis for Education and Psychology Researchers*, London: Falmer.

Peters, S. (1998) Finding information on the World Wide Web, *Social Research Update*, 20.

Phillips, J. (2000) *How to Think About Statistics*, New York: W. H. Freeman.

Pifer, L. and Miller, J. (1995) 'The Accuracy of Student and Parent Reports About Each Other', presentation at AERA Conference, San Francisco, 1995.

Pike, C. and Forrester, M. (1997) The influence of number-sense on children's ability to estimate measures, *Educational Psychology*, 17, 4, 483–499.

Pirrie, A. (2001) Evidence-based practice in education: the best medicine?, *British Journal of Educational Studies*, 49, 2, 124–136.

Plewis, I. (1997) *Statistics in Education*, London: Edward Arnold.

Popkewitz, T. (1984) *Paradigm and Ideology in Educational Research*, London: Falmer.

Porter, T. (1986) *The Rise of Statistical Thinking*, Princeton: Princeton University Press.

Pötter, U. and Blossfeld, H. (2001) Causal inference from series of events, *European Sociological Review*, 17, 1, 21–32.

Prandy, K. (2002) Measuring quantities: the qualitative foundation of quantity, *Building Research Capacity*, 2, 2–3.

Preece, R. (1994) *Starting Research: an Introduction to Academic Research and Dissertation Writing*, London: Continuum.

Pring, R. (2000) *Philosophy of Educational Research*, London: Continuum.

Raedenbush, S. and Bryk, A. (1986) A hierarchical model for studying school effects, *Sociology of Education*, 59, 1–17.

Raudenbush, S. (2002) 'New Directions in the Evaluation of Title I', presentation at AERA, New Orleans, April 2002.

Reay, D. and Lucey, H. (2000) Children, school choice and social differences, *Educational Studies*, 26, 1, 83–100.

Reichmann, W. (1961) *Use and Abuse of Statistics*, Harmondsworth: Penguin.

Resnick, L. (2000) 'Strengthening the Capacity of the Research System: a Report of the National Academy of Education', presentation at AERA, New Orleans, April 2000.

Reynolds, D. (1990) The great Welsh education debate, *History of Education*, 19, 3, 251–257.

Reynolds, H. (1977) *Analysis of Nominal Data*, London: Sage.

Roberts, I. (2000) Randomised trials or the test of time?: the story of human albumin administration, *Evaluation and Research in Education*, 14, 3 & 4, 231–236.

Roberts, K. (2002) An introduction to Bayesian approaches, *Building Research Capacity*, 3, 2–3.

Roberts, K., Dixon-Woods, M., Abrams, K., Fitzpatrick, R. and Jones, D. (2002) Factors affecting uptake of childhood immunisation: an example of Bayesian synthesis of qualitative and quantitative evidence, *The Lancet*, (forthcoming).

Rogers, A. and Nicolaas, G. (1998) Understanding the patterns and processes of primary care use: a combined quantitative and qualitative approach, *Sociological Research Online*, 3, 4.

Rose, D. (1996) Official social classifications in the UK, *Social Research Update*, 9, 1–6.

Rosenthal, R. (1991) *Meta-analytic Procedures for Social Science Research*, London: Sage.

Rothschild, Lord (1982) *An Enquiry into the Social Science Research Council*, London: HMSO.

Rowntree, D. (1981) *Statistics Without Tears*, Harmondsworth: Penguin.

Salmon, W. (1998) *Causality and Explanation*, New York: Oxford University Press.

Saunders, L. (200) Understanding schools' use of 'value-added' data: the psychology and sociology of numbers, *Research Papers in Education*, 15, 3, 241–258.

SCELI (1991) *Social Change and Economic Life Initiative Surveys 1986–1987*, Colchester: ESRC Data Archive.

Scott, D. and Usher, R. (1999) *Researching Education: Data, Methods and Theory in Educational Enquiry*, London: Cassell.

Selwyn, N. (2002) Using computer-mediated communication in educational research, *Building Research Capacity*, 2, 8–10.

Selwyn, N. and Gorard, S. (2002) *The Information Age: Technology, Learning and Social Exclusion in Wales*, Cardiff: University of Wales Press.

Selwyn, N. and Robson, K. (1998) Using e-mail as a research tool, *Social Research Update*, 21, 1–4.

Shaughnessy, J. and Zechmeister, E. (1994) *Research Methods in Psychology*, New York: McGraw-Hill.

Shipman, M. (1981) *The Limitations of Social Research*, London: Longman.

Siegel, S. (1956) *Nonparametric Statistics*, Tokyo: McGraw-Hill.

Simpson, E. (1951) The interpretation of interaction in contingency tables, *Journal of the Royal Statistical Society*, Series B, 13, 238–251.

Snow, C. (2001) Knowing what we know: children, teachers, researchers, *Educational Researcher*, 30, 7, 3–9.

Solomon, R. and Winch, C. (1994) *Calculating and Computing for Social Science and Arts Students*, Buckingham: Open University Press.

Sooben, P. (2002) Developing quantitative capacity in UK social science, *Social Sciences*, 50, 8.

Speller, V., Learmonth, A. and Harrison, D. (1997) The search for evidence of effective health promotion, *British Medical Journal*, 315, 361–363.

Steele, T. (2002) The role of scientific positivism in European popular educational movements, *International Journal of Lifelong Education*, 21, 5, 399–413.

Stevens, J. (1992) *Applied Multivariate Statistics for the Social Sciences*, London: Lawrence Erlbaum.

Stuart, A. (1968) *Basic Ideas of Scientific Sampling*, London: Charles Griffin.

Sudman, S. and Bradburn, N. (1982) *Asking Questions*, San Francisco: Jossey-Bass.

Swadener, M. and Hannafin, M. (1987) Gender similarities and differences in sixth graders' attitudes toward computers, *Educational Technology*, January 1987, 37–42.

Taylor, E. (2001) From 1989 to 1999: a content analysis of all submissions, *Adult Education Quarterly*, 51, 4, 322–340.

TES (1998) Man's class helps boys, *Times Educational Supplement*, 6/2/98, 21.

Thomas, S. (1999) *Designing Surveys That Work*, London: Sage.

Thompson, B. (2002) What future quantitative social science could look like: confidence intervals for effect sizes, *Educational Researcher*, 31, 3, 25–32.

Thompson, S. and Seber, G. (1996) *Adaptive sampling*, New York: John Wiley and Sons.

Thouless, R. (1974) *Straight and Crooked Thinking*, London: Pan.

Tierney, P. (2000) The fierce anthropolgist, *The New Yorker*, 9/10/00, 50–61.

Tooley, J. and Darby, D. (1998) *Educational Research: A Critique*, London: OFSTED.

Torgerson, C. and Torgerson, D. (2001) The need for randomised controlled trials in educational research, *British Journal of Educational Studies*, 49, 3, 316–328.

Walford, G. (2001) *Doing Qualitative Educational Research*, London: Continuum.

Waslander, S. and Thrupp, M. (1997) Choice, competition and segregation: an empirical analysis of a New Zealand secondary school market, 1990-93, in Halsey, A., Lauder, H., Brown, P. and Wells, A. (eds) *Education: Culture, Economy, and Society*, Oxford: Oxford University Press.

Welsh Office (1994) *1992 Welsh Social Survey: Report on Education and Training*, Cardiff: Welsh Office.

Welsh Office (1995a) *Statistics of Education and Training in Wales: Schools No. 3*, Cardiff: HMSO.

Welsh Office (1995b) *1994/95 Welsh Training and Education Survey*, Cardiff: Welsh Office.

Welsh Office (1996) *1996 Welsh Employers Survey*, Cardiff: Welsh Office.

Welsh Office (1999) *Progress Towards Meeting the Targets in the 'BEST' White Paper*, Cardiff: Welsh Office, Statistical Brief SDB 76/99.

West, A., David, M., Hailes, J. and Ribbens, J. (1995) Parents and the process of choosing secondary schools: implications for schools, *Educational Management and Administration*, 23, 1, 28–38.

West, M. and Harrison, J. (1997) *Bayesian Forecasting and Dynamic Models*, New York: Springer.

Western Mail (1998) Boys need more male teachers, *The Western Mail*, 5/2/98, 1.

Whitfield, K. and Bourlakis, C. (1991) An empirical analysis of YTS, employment and earnings, *Journal of Economic Studies*, 18, 1, 42–56.

Woodhead, C. (1998) Academia gone to seed, *New Statesman*, 26/3/98, 51–52.

Woolford, H. and McDougall, S. (1998) 'The Teacher as Role Model', presentation to British Psychological Society (mimeo, Department of Psychology, Swansea).

Index